LOST ILLUSIONS

PAUL LEAUTAUD
AND HIS WORLD

Léautaud at home in a corner of his garden at Fontenay-aux-Roses

LOST ILLUSIONS

PAUL LÉAUTAUD
AND HIS WORLD

JAMES HARDING

*I have seen nothing great in life
except cruelty and stupidity*
Paul Léautaud

London
GEORGE ALLEN & UNWIN LTD
Ruskin House Museum Street

First published in 1974

© George Allen & Unwin Ltd 1974

ISBN 0 04 928031 7

Printed in Great Britain
in 12 point Barbou type
by W & J Mackay Limited
Chatham

ACKNOWLEDGEMENTS

No one can write about Léautaud without owing a very heavy debt to Mademoiselle Marie Dormoy. I am delighted to pay this tribute to a dear friend and remarkable woman who has spent years of selfless devotion in making Léautaud's work available and in furthering his literary reputation. I am also grateful to my friends the late André Billy, Marcel Jouhandeau and the omniscient Pascal Pia for many conversations and useful detail about Léautaud. For reasons of space alone I list alphabetically others of his compatriots who have kindly helped me in my researches: Madame Gabrielle Fort, the daughter of Alfred Vallette; M. Jacques Guignard, curator of the Bibliothèque de l'Arsenal; M. Claude Jouglet de Pontavert of New York; Dr Raymond Mahieu, author of an important thesis on Léautaud's early years; M. Daniel Morcrette of Luzarches; M. Jean-Paul Sartre; the lady who writes under the name of Véronique Valcault; the late Georges Van Parys, composer of delightful music and collector of manuscripts; and M. Lucien Vogt, the only man I have been able to trace who knew at all well Madame Cayssac, Léautaud's consort.

In England I acknowledge with pleasure the friendly co-operation of Professor Garnet Rees, who, while preparing his masterly study of Remy de Gourmont, had the privilege of frequenting Léautaud often. I am indebted as well to: Mr James Hepburn, who communicated information about Arnold Bennett; Sir Peter Hoare; Sir Samuel Hoare; the late Sir Gerald Kelly, who showed me the portrait of Léautaud he painted in 1903; Mr John Margetts, lately of The Taylorian Institution, Oxford; Mr Geoffrey Palmer of the National Trust; and Mr Roland Thorne, a friend who gave valuable advice.

Once again I must thank Mrs D. L. Mackay, who translates le gribouillage into impeccable typescript, and Mrs Stella Mayes Reed for her skill with the camera.

The dedication of this book commemorates an association

which, for me at least, has been unique and fruitful. I should also mention Professor John Weightman, who appraised the thesis of which the present volume is a distillation.

INTRODUCTION

Except for occasional truancies in the fields of music, theatre and soldiering, I have lived for the past eleven years in the company of Paul Léautaud. I came across him while preparing my book on Sacha Guitry. His drama criticism was as fresh and readable as it must have been when he wrote it, though much of it dates back sixty years or more.

At first his eccentricity and caustic wit amused me. An English equivalent to him would be that crabbed and testy gossip Anthony à Wood. Add a dash of John Aubrey's quiddity and Boswell's interest in human nature, and you have a rough idea of his personality. 'He's a clown', said Jean Cocteau, 'but a witty one. . . .' Then I read his essays, the autobiographical works and the *Journal littéraire*. It emerged from these that he was not just an entertainer. He was, on the contrary, a writer of the highest integrity. All those principles which everyone agrees to respect but which few practise – independence, honesty of expression, disinterestedness – were combined within his quaint person. How many writers can say that they have never written for the sake of money, applause, fame or vanity? Léautaud could. 'I write for myself,' he once said. 'I don't write for readers.'

It is difficult to situate Léautaud. He was not a literary journalist, nor was he, except in his writings on the drama, a critic. I suppose he could best be described as an autobiographer. His greatest ambition was to be a man of letters. Since he was unable to write novels or plays, he decided that he would write about the subject he knew best: himself. He could say, in the words of Pascal: 'Ce n'est pas dans Montaigne, mais dans moi, que je trouve ce que j'y vois.'

His childhood was wretched. The illegitimate son of a prompter at the Comédie-Française and a third-rate actress, he was deserted by his mother a few days after his birth. His father, a heartless womaniser, grudgingly allowed him house-room.

The infant often had to share a bed with Firmin Léautaud and his bedraggled mistresses. Brutality and indifference were all he knew. Then, as a young man, he met his mother again. She was still attractive and desirable. As a result he conceived an ambiguous passion for her that tortured him as long as he lived.

He had much in common with Jules Renard. *Poil de Carotte* was the product of an unhappy childhood. So were *Le Petit Ami*, which recounts Léautaud's early years and the relationship with his mother, and *In Memoriam*, which tells of his father. Both writers had incestuous yearnings for an unworthy mother. They both had acute powers of observation and a fine ear for conversation which abundantly qualified them as keepers of journals. They observed themselves with the same ruthless clarity they brought to observing those around them. It is this quality that gives their writing its peculiar astringency.

Léautaud's output was small because he wrote only when he had something to say. He never wrote to order and, except when writing drama criticism, he never worked to a deadline. Most of his life was spent in a humble clerical post on the literary magazine the *Mercure de France*. This 'second métier' gave him the independence he cherished. A small but regular wage enabled him to write as he pleased. When an editor tried to censor his copy because he had said something particularly outrageous about religion or family life or marriage, Léautaud simply withdrew his article and awaited an opportunity to publish it elsewhere. Freedom of speech was more important than money or currying favour.

Neither did he allow friendship to deflect him. When Paul Valéry, a friend he had known from youth, brought out *La Jeune Parque*, he attacked it vigorously. André Gide was another intimate who suffered from his ridicule. Yet both men continued to admire him, to respect him and even to help him in times of need.

Léautaud never married. His experience with his mother led him to distrust all womanhood. He always expected the worst and it always happened. He had a number of liaisons, the most permanent being with a shrewish mistress whose character he detested but whose amorous skill enslaved him with fleshly delights. Women, he early decided, were base, deceitful and of limited physical use. In any case, they interfered with the main purpose of life, which was writing.

He poured out his repressed tenderness on animals. At his ramshackle house in the unlovely suburb of Fontenay-aux-Roses he kept scores of cats and dogs, a monkey, a goose and on one occasion a donkey. Often he scoured the streets of Paris and rescued the strays he found there, many of them half wild, diseased and suffering from hideous sores. It was a point of honour with him to fuss most over the ugliest and least attractive. They repaid him with affection. They were all the family he ever wanted.

This atheistic figure led the life of a monk. Solitude was his natural state. His existence was one of poverty and self-denial for the sake of the animals which he tended with the love, as somebody once said, of a Saint Vincent de Paul. The thought of death and its mystery absorbed him, as it absorbs the inhabitant of the cloister. He was, perhaps, a monk without religion – though one might say that his religion was the noble and exalted conception of authorship which he often and defiantly proclaimed.

'Il n'y a que moi qui m'intéresse,' he observed. His enormous *Journal littéraire*, which incidentally is an invaluable document on Parisian literary life from 1893 up to 1956, gives a self-portrait of unique frankness, more devastating in its truth than Rousseau's and more natural than Renard's. He wrote it up every night, performing this 'travail de hibou' by candle-light with a quill pen whose squeak and splutter as it travelled over the paper were music to his ears. Each event of the day was charted in minute detail. His reactions, his remarks and those of other people were analysed with obsessive care. There are digressions and repetitions. This is inevitable when a man is speaking about himself with absolute truth. The *Journal littéraire*, which so vividly brings to life its author and the circle in which he lived, is a monumental work.

Léautaud belongs among the eighteenth-century French moralists he admired. He is to be placed with Chamfort and the Prince de Ligne. During his lifetime his readership was estimated, half humorously, half truthfully, at no more than four hundred. I hope, for his sake and that of my admirable publisher Malcolm Barnes, that this biography will arouse a wider interest. He will never have mass appeal. Those whom he gathers round him will sometimes consider themselves as 'the happy few' who Stendhal once fancied would appreciate his work, though it is improbable that a lottery of the Stendhalian sort will find Léautaud being widely enjoyed in AD 2035. Amateurs of Léautaud will continue to honour his memory because he was that rarest of phenomena, in literature or life: a truly free man.

J.H.

CONTENTS

ILLUSTRATIONS
Prepared by Stella Mayes Reed

I

THE CHILD IN THE RUE DES MARTYRS

'Good Heavens, what a horrid child he is!'
Léautaud's mother

'When was he born, this father among fathers?' Léautaud once wrote. 'I don't know for certain. Two dates were put on his gravestone. I can never remember the first one. He was sixty-nine years old, it seems. I do a sum: 1903 less sixty-nine makes 1834. Let's say 1834.'

Usually so vague about dates, Léautaud here was correct for once. His father, Firmin Isidor Léautaud, a rakish and indifferent parent, was born on 10 July 1834. The place of his birth was Fours, a hamlet in the lower Alps. It is a remote spot encircled by steep mountains and plunging valleys, as difficult to reach as it is to get out of. A rough mule-track links it with Barcelonnette, the nearest big town. Sheep rearing was, and is, the main local activity, which has led in turn to the establishment of spinning mills. There is a local tradition of emigration to Mexico, where, early last century, two brothers from the area set up a cloth business. It often happens that those who have gone to make their fortunes in Mexico return at the end of their lives to the Alpine village in which, if they have not wanted to live there, they at least are keen to die.

The origins of the Léautaud family are unknown. Victor Hugo, in *Choses vues*, remarks that the first man to suffer death by guillotining was a forger called, by a coincidence which may or may not be phonetic, 'Léotaud'. Firmin's parents were doubtless of peasant stock. There may also have been an Italian strain – Paul Léautaud sometimes spoke of this when referring to his mobile features and theatrical manner – since the frontier is close at hand. Firmin learned reading, writing and arithmetic at the little school. For a time he was a shepherd boy. At the age of twenty he emigrated not to Mexico but to Paris, which, so far as the villagers of Fours were concerned, was just as foreign and distant a place.

In Paris he lodged with an uncle, Jean-Baptiste Léautaud, who ran a jeweller's shop in the Faubourg-Montmartre. 'A la Maison Rouge' said the legend over the window. Outside also there hung a large clock of painted wood embellished in gilt. The name *Léautaud* ran across the dial.

Jewellery and clock-making did not interest Firmin. More attractive were the boulevard theatres where his aunt probably took him for evening treats. By 1857 he had decided to try his luck on the stage. At the age of twenty-three he was accepted as a pupil at the Conservatoire and a year later gained an honourable mention for his playing of comedy. In 1859 he won a second prize for tragedy. A group photograph of his class shows him with dark, almost frizzy hair, thick lips and expressive eyes. He wears a stock-pin in his cravat, a watch chain and an elegant waistcoat with high revers. He already has the air of a complacent womaniser.

The young Firmin was a sociable personality. He made a number of useful acquaintances at the Conservatoire, among them Sarah Bernhardt. When she appeared for her audition it was Firmin who had the duty of presenting her. 'He was a tall, very dark man,' she remembered, 'who rolled his enormous eyes under thick bristling eyebrows.' She heard his voice, heavily accented, booming through the room: 'Mademoiselle Chara Bernhardt . . . Mademoiselle Chara Bernhardt.' Despite all his efforts he had never been able to get rid of the native brogue that thickened his speech and, as a result, severely limited his scope as an actor.

That 'accent fouchtra', which, as Sarah recalled, 'turned the most dramatic situations into light relief', was to hamper him when he left the Conservatoire. Producers acknowledged his talent and stage presence, but his speaking voice doomed him to minor roles and character parts. In 1874, after he had made a series of not very impressive appearances in boulevard theatres, a friend obtained for him the job of prompter at the Comédie-Française. He had found his niche. There he was to stay for over twenty years until his retirement in 1897.

If he had not proved to be a very successful actor, as a prompter Firmin was ideal. He knew by heart all the roles in the Comédie-Française productions of Racine, Corneille and Molière. There was no need for him to consult the prompt-book as he sat hidden in the little cabin at the front of the proscenium, his face raised just above the level of the stage to note the movements of the actors and actresses before him. Not only did he know the lines but he also knew the tone of voice in which they were to be said, and he could indicate precisely the manner in which they should be delivered. Dust continually floated off the stage and into his lungs. The heat of the footlights made his eyes ache. He felt cramped and uncomfortable in his narrow little box. Yet he loved the old plays and savoured every word of the great tirades in Corneille, the quicksilver dialogue in Molière.

Many famous actors came to rely on him and were grateful for his expert help. Aimée Tessandier, later to become the star of the Comédie-Française, was one of those who appreciated him. When he was rehearsing her for her debut, she, nervous and confused, sometimes by error imitated his unfortunate accent. 'He was the first to laugh about this little mistake,' she wrote affectionately in her memories of 'the excellent man', as she called him. In 1898 his old friends at the Comédie-Française organised a benefit performance for him. Among the great names on the bill were those of Mounet-Sully and Sarah Bernhardt. In an odd way, it seemed, and despite the disadvantages he suffered, he had given the lie to the hamlet of Fours, his birthplace – for in theatrical slang the word 'four' means a flop.

There were other passions in his life besides the theatre. The former shepherd boy had a fondness for animals. At one time his household contained as many as fourteen dogs. He also loved women, though that is not quite the exact phrase to define the obsessive lust that drove him to conquer every presentable female who crossed his path. By the age of nineteen he was reputed already to have had forty women. At gatherings of colleagues he was introduced as the man who had enjoyed the prettiest girls in Paris. His exploits as a seducer surprised even his acquaintances in the free and easy world of the theatre. 'You'll end up in the courts one day, Léautaud,' he was told by an actress who warned him against his taste for girls under the age of consent.

Each morning he would go out for a drink before breakfast. Surrounded by his pack of frisking dogs he swaggered down the street, eyes alert for women. In his hand he carried a dog whip. If he saw a woman he fancied the whip-lash would flick out and circle her waist from behind. Then he would pull her towards him. The ploy was usually effective. For every woman who resisted angrily there were always two or three ready to acquiesce. By the simple law of averages he was bound to win most of the time.

'Ah, you know, he was a handsome fellow,' Paul Léautaud's mother said later with a certain huskiness in her voice at the memory. 'Above all else he had wonderful eyes. It was enough for him just to look at you. . . .'

Among the hundreds of women who shared his bed for a night, a day, a morning, an afternoon or a few minutes, was a young actress called Fanny Forestier. He made her acquaintance round about 1864 in a suburban theatre or on a provincial tour, some years before he entered the Comédie-Française. Her father was a musician who, winner of a first prize at the Conservatoire for flute playing, ended an honourable career as conductor of the Orchestre de la Garde Impériale. Her maternal uncle, Émile Pessonnaux, a scholar, translated into French many Greek and Latin classics. That the girl should have become an actress was a cause of regret to her middle-class mother.

Madame Forestier was justified in her anxiety when Fanny gave birth to a daughter by Léautaud. Using as her excuse the reason that Fanny would be unable to look after the baby properly as she was too busy with theatrical tours, Madame Forestier promptly took her granddaughter into custody. She kept the child, who was christened Hélène, under close and jealous supervision. Firmin argued, threatened, cursed, swore. He was only allowed to see his daughter at rare intervals when Madame Forestier was there to keep an eye on him. She feared he would corrupt the girl. As Fanny put it more crudely, he would probably have ended up in bed with Hélène if he'd had his own way. The little girl died of typhus at the age of twelve. Later events were to give her the pathetic distinction of being at the same time a half-sister and a cousin of Paul Léautaud, who was born six years after her.

Fanny, who acted in the 'straight' theatre, had a sister called Jeanne. She also was an actress, but, worse still in her mother's opinion, sang in operetta and was noted for her roles *en travesti*, her slim body looking more attractive than ever when she wore men's clothes on stage. One evening in about 1868 she stayed late to dinner with Fanny and Léautaud. His flat, in the Rue Lamartine, was a long way from Montparnasse where Jeanne lived with her mother and Hélène. Fanny did not like the idea of her 16-year-old sister walking alone on the streets at such an hour. She innocently suggested that Jeanne spend the night with them. It was obvious that even after living for two years with Firmin she still did not know him well.

The flat contained only one bed, though it was large enough to take the three of them. Firmin lay in the middle with the sisters on each side of him. It was a convenient arrangement. If there was anything Firmin enjoyed more than sleeping with a woman, it was sleeping with two of them at once. And sleep was the last thing he wanted. First he paid his respects to Fanny, as was only right and proper. Then he turned round and prepared to do the same with her sister. Fanny protested. She shouted her indignation at the top of her voice. Firmin ignored her. Jeanne was less obstructive. 'After an hour,' she later told Paul Léautaud, 'I knew everything that a man and a woman could do together.'

At dawn Fanny hastily packed her belongings and rushed from the house in disgust. Jeanne remained with her new lover. The incident encouraged Madame Forestier's hatred of Firmin.

Not content with seducing one daughter, he had now violated the other. Jeanne lived a tolerably congenial existence with him for the next two or three years. They even had a son who died at an early age. Their next child, also a boy, was born at one o'clock in the morning on 18 January 1872. They were living then at 37 Rue Molière, a street since demolished to make way for the Avenue de l'Opéra. It was a pleasant chance that the baby, who was christened Paul Firmin Valentin, should have first seen the light of day in a street named after the author whom he was to adore all his life.

His godfather, Paul Beauvallet, was an actor at the Comédie-Française, and his godmother, Blanche Boissart, also a member of the troupe, already counted Réjane's offspring among her godchildren. His mother's signature does not appear on the baptismal certificate. 'She left me in the lurch three days after I was born,' Paul Léautaud used to say bitterly. Although he exaggerated, it is true that she had no interest in him. A baby was a tiresome inconvenience to an ambitious actress. Nobody, in fact, cared much about him. He arrived at a time when his parents were on the point of breaking up. Jeanne had no desire for a child who would be a cumbersome reminder of a man she had ceased to like. Firmin did not wish his private life to be cluttered up with the tedious consequence of his pleasures. So Paul was bundled off to a nurse at Étampes, just outside Paris.

There he nearly died. Irritated by his whimperings, the ignorant country nurse used to soak a bit of rag in milk and stuff it into his mouth. The child quickly sucked at the milk and chewed at the rag. His stomach filled with air as he went on munching the rag, and soon he was afflicted by digestive upsets. A doctor was called in and gave his opinion that Paul would soon die. Firmin brought him back to Paris and entrusted him to a better nurse who soon restored him to health. When Paul was two years old Firmin took charge of him again. It may be that paternal feelings had stirred, ever so faintly, in his cold, sensual heart. On the other hand, his subsequent treatment of the boy was to show, if not positive dislike, at the best a frigid indifference.

Firmin was now living at 13 Rue des Martyrs, a long, narrow thoroughfare that starts down below at the church of Notre-Dame-de-Lorette and concludes its sinuous wanderings appropriately up by the Place des Abbesses. He engaged an elderly female called Marie Pezé to look after his son during the day. She lived round the corner in the Rue Clauzel. The house is still there. Her fellow tenants were all women. She herself had been a prostitute like her companions. When age came upon her she arrived at a respectability and a sense of moral rectitude which surpassed that of the most upright matron. There is no one stricter in ideals than the reformed rake. (Did not Anatole France, in *Thaïs*, show that a prostitute is more likely to become a saint than is a monk?) Marie Pezé had never married or had children. Little Paul basked in the warmth of the maternal feeling she lavished upon him, which until then had never found an outlet. She was the only human being in his whole life to give him pure, disinterested love. He responded with intense affection. There was the promise of security, of protection against the terrors of childhood, in this comforting person with the old-fashioned clothes. She never let him down. Though Jeanne Forestier had given birth to him, it was Marie Pezé who, in every other respect, was his true mother.

The years between 1874 and 1882, when Léautaud grew from a baby into a boy of ten, represent the most important period in his life. He could never afterwards see or write those dates without a pang of emotion. Paris of the eighteen-seventies and early eighteen-eighties was something more than the background of his childhood. It became a part of him. The double-decker buses with open stairs at the back, the men in the street all wearing top hats or caps (it was rare to see anyone bareheaded), and the traffic, lurching, creaking and groaning over uneven cobbles, were for ever engraved on his memory. Seventy years later he could remember it all with poignant clarity.

Everybody cherishes 'his' own Paris. Léautaud's is clearly defined. It is the region that, roughly speaking, comprises the middle slice of the ninth *arrondissement*. On one side it is bordered by the Rue de Clichy and the Rue de la Chaussée d'Antin, and on the other by the Rue de Rochechouart and the Rue du Faubourg-Montmartre. He sometimes ventured outside this magic circle to the Champs-Élysées or the Tuileries or the Comédie-Française, but his closest affections were attached to the heart of it.

If today you follow in his footsteps you can, despite the alterations made by a century of change, find occasional corners where it is possible to evoke the atmosphere he knew as a boy. The Rue Lamartine, where his father's barber plied his trade, remains as narrow and crowded as in Léautaud's day. Though delivery vans and motor-cycles have taken the place of the drays and carts that once rumbled and jostled within its narrow limits, the basic features cannot have changed much: the hilly pavement seemingly designed for a race of dwarfs, the peeling walls, the irregularly placed shop windows, the spacious music dealer's reeking with acrid smells from the grocer's next door, and the dark and decrepit bookshop. The Rue des Martyrs, where Léautaud's home was, still challenges traffic with its steeply cobbled incline. The market in the Rue Cadet continues to fill the air with the smell of bruised oranges, and the scanty trees in the Square Montholon are gaunt as ever.

In those days the Butte Montmartre was open ground dotted with windmills and orchards. Marie Pezé, on occasion, would take the boy there for a walk. Sometimes he would stroll with her to the Square Montholon where he played in the sandpit – the sand of a dark and earthy nature, turned over by generations of Parisian children – or he would saunter through the arcades of the Passage Jouffroy and the Passage de l'Opéra. At other times he wandered on his own, a grown-up little man, observing the busy life of the district – here a Punch-and-Judy show, there a toyshop full of strange and wonderful things. By night the place was quite different. Gas jets hissed and flickered, lights flamed over the surging crowds in the Faubourg-Montmartre, and the windows in the Passage Verdeau glittered mysteriously.

One day his aunt Fanny Forestier came to see him. Unlike

his mother, she took a kindly interest in him. She accompanied Marie Pezé and the boy on their way back home. At the corner of the Rue des Martyrs and the Rue Clauzel, in front of a coal merchant's (the shop is still there), Paul caught sight of a lady who lived in the same house as 'chère maman' Pezé. She was fond of him and he had an affection for her.

'Ah, there's Loulou!' he cried, calling out his pet name for her as he made to greet her.

'No, stay here,' whispered Marie Pezé.

Fanny was puzzled. 'Why don't you want him to go and say good evening to the lady? It shows he's polite.'

'Madame,' replied Marie Pezé with discreet professionalism, 'She mustn't be disturbed. She's on her beat.'

At this period Firmin Léautaud was a dim figure in his son's life. Most evenings he came home late, usually with a new woman, and rose late in the morning. After a hasty breakfast he went off to the theatre or to give lessons. When Paul was four or five years old he was sent to a school in the Rue Milton. Firmin chose it not because it was a Protestant establishment but because it was conveniently near. The frowning bulk of the place, fortress-like with its heavy stonework and iron railings, doubtless strikes as much of a chill into the hearts of today's new entrants as it did in the eighteen-seventies.

The journeys back and forth to school each day were too much for Marie Pezé's elderly legs, so one of Firmin's dogs was given the task of escorting Paul. The dark golden colour of his fur earned him the name of 'Tabac', since his coat resembled the tint of cigar-leaf. He was strict in fulfilling his duties. The boy was not allowed to play or loiter on the way. Tabac trotted close beside him, nudging him when his pace flagged or if he showed signs of wanting to look into a shop window – the money-changer's, for example, where the display of old notes and coins ever fascinated him. At the end of the day Tabac was always waiting patiently in the Rue Milton to take him home. He growled at anyone who spoke to the child, and, the moment he appeared, jealously urged him on the way. At home Paul would slip under the dining-room table. The cloth hung down at the sides and formed a little tent where he sat for hours with Tabac beside him. Here he reflected on his world and lost himself in reveries. Odd thoughts trailed through his brain. What if his father should die and leave him utterly alone? In his mind's eye he saw himself driving in the funeral procession to the cemetery. Tears poured down his face, and Tabac, wagging his tail, licked the salty drops as they fell.

At half-past nine each evening 'Maman' Pezé came to collect him. Firmin Léautaud's home was not, she felt, the right place for a small boy to spend his nights, and she took Paul to the attic where she lived in the Rue Clauzel. They toiled up five storeys and arrived in a dark narrow passage. This led to a curving staircase which brought them up ten steps to her door. Inside, on the sixth floor, was the tiny room where Paul spent some of the happier times of his childhood. He was alone, of course, but it was a different sort of loneliness from what he experienced in the Rue des Martyrs. Here he was unlikely to get in his father's way. He had a little table to himself and an armchair. There was an old chest of drawers with brass handles that fell back into place with a rather special sort of tinkle he never forgot. When it was time for sleep he snuggled up in the big bed against the warm friendly mass of 'Maman' Pezé.

Three or four years passed before Paul saw his mother. Then, for the first time since his birth, she reappeared. Firmin gave her some tickets for the Comédie-Française and she took the boy and Marie Pezé to the play. There was a scene where a beautiful actress sat on a sofa and put her arm round a little girl, perhaps her daughter. The boy always remembered this first visit to the theatre. It was not only the excitement of the occasion that moved him. There was also something about the woman's gesture, something maternal that he had not known, except indirectly from Marie Pezé.

A little later, when he was five or six years old, he met Jeanne Forestier again. He had measles, and his grandmother and her two daughters called to see him. The patient was in bed, his face to the wall.

'Turn round,' said Marie Pezé, 'here's your grandmother. Say good morning to her.'

The boy half-turned. 'Good morning, Madame'. He resumed his earlier position.

'Turn round,' repeated Marie Pezé, 'here's your Aunt Fanny.'

The same performance occurred and a reluctant 'Good morning, Madame' was squeezed out.

'Turn round again,' said Marie Pezé, 'here's your real Mummy.'

'Are there *still* people here?' muttered Paul without bothering to move.

The three women were indignant. 'Good Heavens, what a horrid child he is!' exclaimed his mother. Without realising it, she had uttered a perfect alexandrine: 'Mon Dieu, que cet enfant est donc désagréable!' The line, so easily remembered for its rhythm and its motherly feeling, was not to be forgotten by her son.

They met again on several occasions. Marie Pezé would dress him up in his best clothes and tell him that his 'real mother' was coming to see him. The expression puzzled him. Other children he knew only had one mother, and she was always with them. Was there something freakish about him that he should have two? Who was this strange woman who figured sporadically in his life? Why did she take him into restaurants and stuff him with expensive food? Who were the women she giggled with in the promenade at the Folies Bergère? Why did they wear the heavy scent that stifled him when they hugged him and gave him sickly bonbons? These and many other questions tormented him through the long lonely hours after she had gone.

Once his mother and Firmin took him with them to the fair at Saint-Cloud. Suddenly, in the middle of the crowd, they vanished. He looked everywhere for them. A fairground attendant saw his distress, comforted him and soothed his anxiety. A long time afterwards his parents turned up. Firmin teased the child: there was no cause for drama, people never got lost

at fairs! His rough badinage reduced Paul to tears again. Jeanne
Forestier grinned.

Paul was six or seven years old when his father decided to
move from 13 Rue des Martyrs to No. 21, higher up the street.
The house was self-contained and stood in a small courtyard
whose main door gave onto the busy pavement. There was an
ornamental fountain against the rear wall and a garden beyond.
Though a little altered in the course of the century that has
passed since then, the layout remains much the same. In the
spacious dining-room on the ground floor Paul's father had a
small stage built. There he rehearsed pupils or troupes of actors
about to go on tour. Above it was a room with a ceiling so low
that an adult could not have stood up straight. This was Paul's
room and he was enchanted with it. Here was his kingdom, a
place of his own, where he could sit undisturbed and dream as
long as he liked. Firmin gave him a key to the house and said:
'You can go out when you like, provided you come back again.
That's all that's asked of you.'

He revelled in the freedom of the streets. There were the
building sites and the wooden hoardings in the Rue Milton to
be explored. In the Place Saint-Georges he sailed his little boat
across the ornamental fountain. The striped shop front of the
colourman in the Rue des Martyrs dazzled his eye. His ears
caught the chirp of birds from cages in the pet shop at the corner
of the Rue Milton. Not far away was the old-clothes woman
with her jumble of rusty coats and faded dresses. In the Rue
Rodier stood a house where rouged women sang all day –
cabaret songs like the *Valse des roses* and *L'Amant d'Amanda*,
cheap and catchy but, once heard, imprinted on the memory
and always associated with childhood. He remembered the
tang of early morning mists in his throat. One winter – it was
1879 – the slope of the Rue des Martyrs was covered in thick
snow that muffled the clang of iron-shod cartwheels.

At home Paul would sit expressionless, on a chair, his mind
filled with passing fancies. Long evenings went by like this. A
rocking-horse and a few picture books were toys enough. The
silent companionship of Tabac sealed his pleasure. His father,

disturbed by the child's silence, would sometimes drive him out of the house to play with other boys. He did not like them, found their manner too rough and noisy. The little girls who played in the Rue Milton were gentler. They had a charm and a grace that pleased him. Firmin Léautaud was amused by what he called his son's 'mistresses'. In his rare moments of good humour he would give him some small change and say: 'Here's ten sous. Go and sleep with your women.'

With the money Paul would buy them skipping-ropes. They skipped gaily in front of their benefactor as, leaning against a wall or sitting on the edge of a pavement, he watched them admiringly. Sometimes they rewarded him with kisses.

The older Firmin grew the more insatiable became his taste for youth. At the age of forty-eight he was still attractive with his broad shoulders, his swagger and his hair that was as yet untouched by grey. On one of his morning walks down the Rue des Martyrs he had, with the invaluable dog whip, picked up a 15-year-old girl called Louise Viale. She was soon a permanent member of the household. Once again Marie Pezé rebuked him, emphasising the bad example he set Paul and up-braiding him for his conduct. He flew into a passion. She answered him back. His voice quivered with anger. He sacked her in a flurry of oaths and harsh words. Paul sat trembling in a corner, terrified by the violent scene.

He never again saw 'Maman' Pezé. She had sung him to sleep at night, quavering tunes from old operettas or from lullabies of her own childhood. When he needed clothes that Firmin refused to buy she had paid for them out of her own tiny wage. Their excursions to the circus and to conjuring shows had been financed from her own pocket. Soon after-wards Firmin gave away the dog Tabac to a friend. So now Paul was more alone than he had ever been. A few years later Marie Pezé died. 'It's a pity we didn't know,' remarked Firmin in-sincerely. 'We might have been able to help her.'

From Marie Pezé the boy received nothing but tenderness and sympathy. From his father he had little more than cuffs and blows. Once he played truant from school. When Firmin

heard of it he beat him roundly, kicked him and trampled him
on the floor. The louder Paul screamed for mercy the harder
Firmin beat him. So charming, so gay, so attentive to the ladies
in company, Firmin in his own home was morose and brutal.

Two or three times a week he would take his son with him
to the Comédie-Française. They walked through the passage
that led from the main entrance to the area backstage. It was
hung with mediocre portraits to which age had given charm,
and at intervals alongside the wall there stood benches covered
in red velvet and busts of famous playwrights yellowed with
the patina of the years. On the way they passed the property
store and its intriguing glimpse of chandeliers heaped pell-mell,
cardboard armour and fake period furniture.

Before the curtain rose Paul and his father mounted the stairs
to the prompt box. Though he understood little of what passed,
the boy stared in wonderment at the spectacle. Afterwards,
during the interval when he accompanied Firmin to the green-
room, there were more surprises. Racine's 'Britannicus', a
figure both noble and exalted on stage, swore foully behind
the scenes. 'Esther', who had been so pure in her winning
ways, flirted like the vulgar women Paul had seen at the
Folies Bergère. And Molière's 'Sganarelle', who had made
everyone laugh so much, turned out to be a bad-tempered
curmudgeon.

Once backstage Victor Hugo met Paul, and, entertained by
some artless comment about *Hernani*, patted him on the cheek.
Everyone in the building knew the child. He was free to wander
everywhere. The actresses were amused to see him come into
their dressing-rooms and watch, innocent-eyed, as they changed
costumes and adjusted their make-up. The heady atmosphere
of grease-paint, size and perfume lent magic to the scene.
The women took pity on him because they knew he had no
mother. They gave him little presents and dandled him on
their laps.

There was a scene in the current production of Molière's
Monsieur de Pourceaugnac which called for children to run on
stage shouting out, 'Ah! papa! Ah! papa!' The play is one of

1. Léautaud's father, Firmin Léautaud (1834–1903). 'I knew nothing about his early mistresses, but I did know some of the others, from my Aunt Fanny and my mother onwards'

. Jeanne Forestier (c. 1852–1916). 'The delightful creature who gave birth to me... scarcely knew her'

3. Léautaud as a small boy with his nurse, the former prostitute Marie Pezé, the only adult to show him kindness

4. Léautaud at the age of 29 in 1901, just after seeing his mother in Calais for the first time since childhood

5. The actress Marguerite Moreno (1871–1948), alias Madame Marcel Schwob. He was too shy to respond

Molière's hastier improvisations, a romp cobbled up by royal command, which ends with an entirely suitable couplet:

> 'Ne songeons qu'à nous réjouir!
> La grande affaire est le plaisir.'

What disturbed Paul was his father's insistence that he should take part as one of the children. For days the shy and retiring boy pleaded with Firmin to spare him. Firmin remained obdurate. His son's pleas only served to make him lose his temper. So the reluctant actor, awkward and tearful, shambled onto the stage as he was told and groaned in chorus, 'Ah! papa! Ah! papa!'

Every New Year's Day, knowing the affection the members of the troupe had for Paul, Firmin made him visit each one in turn to wish them seasonal greetings. When Paul objected he was threatened with a beating. The reason, of course, was that they usually gave him a tip. Urged on by the menace of his father's boot, he made the rounds and came back with three or four hundred francs in his pocket. These were immediately seized by Firmin. Ah! papa! Ah! papa!

All this time Paul's mother, Jeanne Forestier, had been following her theatrical career. Her existence was one of second-rate touring companies, easy love affairs and drab provincial theatres. In 1881 she happened to be in Paris and had a sudden whim to meet her 10-year-old son again. To avoid the embarrassment of finding herself in the presence of Firmin's new mistress, she suggested that Paul come to see her at the place where she was staying. This was a shady establishment – the sort that let furnished rooms for whatever period a transient clientèle required – in the Passage Laferrière.

Paul knocked hesitantly at a door. 'Entrez,' replied a voice. He turned the handle and stood speechless at what he saw. His mother lay in bed. She wore a low-cut chemise that had slipped revealingly. A vast mirror showed those other aspects of her body which her exiguous dress concealed. 'Come in,' she said, 'come on in quick and shut the door. You're making me freeze.'

He approached the bed. She drew him down, his face on her

bosom, and kissed him. As she did so he felt the softness of her breasts. They quivered slightly in time to her kisses. He eyed the elegant underwear thrown on chairs throughout the room. The air was hot and dizzy with scent. It reeked of flirtation and love and woman's flesh. She jumped out of bed and cleared a chair for him to sit down while she dressed and washed, showing off her slim waist, her long legs, her beautiful arms. 'Oh, what a pretty mother she was, I can tell you,' he wrote later, 'so lithe, vivacious and graceful. It was the first time I'd seen a woman in such intimacy. . . .'

She treated him to the zoo and dinner at a restaurant. After seeing a performance of Jules Verne's *Michel Strogoff* they ended the evening at the Folies Bergère. On the promenade – in a corner opposite the sixth pillar, he remembered with precision – he stood while she chatted with the many people who came up to greet her. He could not take his eyes off her. She laughed frequently. Her voice was clear and lively. Her look held at once a challenge and an invitation. Among the brilliant lights, the fluster of silk skirts and the rhythmic blare from the orchestra in the hall, she was a centre of attraction. At closing time they had a late supper and she took him back to his father in the Rue des Martyrs. She kissed him goodbye. He was not to see her again for another twenty years.

A few months later Firmin Léautaud decided to move house yet again. Some theatre friends of his had settled in Courbevoie, then as now an unexciting suburb but one that Firmin and his colleagues believed to be delightfully rural and a change from the bustle of Paris. His belongings were loaded into a large furniture van. He took up his place next to Louise Viale and the driver. Then he remembered Paul and the fourteen dogs he didn't want to leave behind. There was no room for them in the van, so they were stuffed into a huge larder that hung from the axles. When the van came to a hill Firmin and Louise jumped off to ease the horses' task. It would have taken too much time if Paul and the dogs had been let out as well, so they were left inside. After a journey of seven miles lasting some three hours they arrived in Courbevoie. The dogs, released at last, bounded out joyfully and inspected their new home. Paul was so weary, so bruised and dazed, that he had to be lifted out.

On 1 May 1882, he entered the *école communale* at Courbevoie. Here he made one of the few friends in his life. Adolphe van Bever was a bright and lively boy who, like Paul, had an unhappy life at home. His father, the owner of a local factory, made him carry out menial tasks there. When the Factory Inspector called on one of his visits all the apprentices under age who should not have been employed were hidden in the cellar. In the corner of a workshop he caught sight of a pale little fellow, resigned, sad and pensive.

'Who's that?' the Inspector asked.

'That?' replied van Bever senior. 'It's my son.'

The Inspector could do nothing about it. Although the law forbade an employer to take on child labour, it did not prevent him from exploiting his own son.

Adolphe van Bever had a precocious love of literature. Although his parents would snatch up the books he enjoyed and throw them on the fire, nothing could stifle his passion for the written word. At night, when the household slept, he would creep down to the kitchen and scribble by candle-light plays inspired by Schiller and other German dramatists who had captured his imagination. He was only sixteen when he hired Neuilly town hall and gave lectures on the drama. His persuasion encouraged Léautaud to recite poems and extracts from plays at these lectures. Van Bever was full of enthusiasm, running about everywhere in a tightly belted overcoat, a top hat jammed on his head and hair spilling over his collar at the back. When he left school he became a shop assistant, then took a job as foreman in a workshop. Inevitably he was sacked. After which there was no alternative for him but a literary career.

His friendship with Paul sprang partly from their similar backgrounds and also from the fact, doubtless impressive to him, that Paul's father was connected with the theatre. It is clear that he was responsible for awakening Paul's interest in literature. Probably, too, he inspired him to enter a poetry recital competition which was held for Neuilly schoolchildren in 1884. Paul won first prize and rushed to the café where he knew he would find his father. He proudly announced the news.

Firmin looked up angrily from his glass. 'Clear off, will you? I don't like being disturbed when I'm drinking.'

II

FIRST LOVE

'I've never had any luck with women. I was scarcely born before my own mother left me in the lurch.'

Paul Léautaud

Courbevoie pleased Firmin Léautaud so much that in 1884, two years after his arrival, he bought, or had built, a house there. It was a solid, square, one-storey building at No. 44 Rue de l'Ouest, since renamed the Rue Eugène Caron. The man who gave his name to the street was, by coincidence, also an actor who lived a few houses away. Like Firmin, Eugène Caron was to die at his home in the Rue de l'Ouest. The citizens of Courbevoie wished to honour these two local celebrities but could not resolve the problem of which to choose. They drew lots and the name of Eugène Caron emerged.

Firmin raised money for the house by his customary method, the exercise of a wheedling charm which, though he thriftily avoided wasting it on his son, when used on persons outside the family was nearly always effective. If a creditor lost patience at a long overdue account, Firmin would honour him with a personal visit. Such was his persuasiveness that not only would he soothe the angry tradesman but would, more often than not, come away with a fresh loan on top of what he already owed.

Soon after arriving in Courbevoie Paul went to his First Communion. It meant nothing to him and he took part in the ceremony only because most of his classmates did. Afterwards one of them invited him to lunch with the family. They took pity on him since he had no mother. He was surprised by this first and only experience of family life: a father, a mother, children who laughed and played. At the same time an odd feeling – was it sorrow? regret? – pinched at his heart.

He returned to a home where his father ignored him and his

'stepmother', Louise Viale, detested him. Often she would lock him up alone in the house. He spent whole days with only the dogs for company, lying under the table, his head nestling on some shaggy flank. With a key that had been overlooked he opened his father's cupboard. His puzzled eye fell on obscene prints that evoked a momentary interest because of the extravagant positions they illustrated. There were albums crammed with photographs of women. Each carried an intimate dedication. Many were of his mother, Jeanne Forestier, and he also found letters from her. 'I know only too well how you can chat up women,' she had written to Firmin, 'and how you enjoy letting yourself be led if one of them looks like making a pass at you.'

Paul did not mind his solitary days in the empty house because when Louise Viale was there they clashed endlessly with each other. She took a delight in crushing him, in raining punishments on his head. Although he was usually a quiet, timid child, her maltreatment drove him one day to throw a bottle of ink at her. Firmin, in a great rage, selected a favourite toy and slowly smashed it to pieces before his eyes.

Not content with inflicting physical pain on him, the lubricious creature would tell Paul that his mother was a prostitute, that she let herself be seduced by men in cabs. While making the bed in the morning she told him of the caresses she had given Firmin the night before and mimicked their pleasures with lustful relish. Anxious to further the boy's education, she sometimes crept into his bed at night when Firmin was away. Or she would tell him to take off his trousers so that she could mend them. Her dislike for him increased when he ignored her attempts to seduce him.

It is strange that through it all he retained his innocence. Though he lived in a home that was more like a brothel than a family household, and heard every day conversations that were blunt and worldly, he was not at all curious about what went on. In 1884 Louise Viale gave birth to a son, Maurice, Paul's half-brother, and a maid was engaged to help with the extra work. Since there was no spare room she slept in Paul's bed.

One of Firmin's dogs had produced a litter and sometimes Paul and the maid took a few of the puppies into bed with them. As the girl lay beside him he felt something furry and warm. 'So you've brought one of the puppies with you?' he inquired, stroking it mechanically. She said nothing but squirmed pleasurably and gave a little groan. He went on stroking the object as it seemed to lend itself to his caresses. Then he turned over and went to sleep. 'I've had several missed opportunities like that in my life,' he commented later, 'two or three from ignorance, the others through shyness. This one was the first – among many firsts.'

After her child was born Louise Viale suddenly conceived theatrical ambitions. She took lessons and went on tour as a member of the chorus in operettas. The house echoed with her off-key bellowing of melodies from *Les Cloches de Corneville* and *Le Petit Duc*. The dogs, alarmed by the weird noise, howled nervously. While she was away on tour Firmin consoled himself with new friends. A procession of women passed through the front door in the Rue de l'Ouest. At three o'clock one morning a cab stopped outside and a voice shouted: 'Léautaud!' (All his women addressed him by his surname.) It was Louise, returning unexpectedly. She stormed into his room and found him in bed with his latest companion. A noisy scene followed: tears, insults, shouts. Firmin knew women. He simply locked up all the drugs in the house and put away his gun in a safe place. Then, smiling impassively, he waited for the emotion to die down. When it did, all three clambered into bed and the night was still again. For the next few weeks there were two mistresses of the house. Paul enjoyed the new arrangement since it meant peace for him. He no longer had to run on tiresome errands, and the ladies even took care to be nice to him. The interlude did not last long. Soon Louise Viale was in sole possession again. Ten years later Paul recognised the other woman in the street. She told him that when she had left the house she was pregnant. A girl was born to her and had died soon afterwards.

In 1887, when he was fifteen years old, Paul left school. His

time at the *école communale* had not been unpleasant. True, he
had made no friends there except for Adolphe van Bever. Most
of his schoolmates were boisterous children who had little in
common with the dreamy, secretive boy. Yet he had done
reasonably well and gained his school-leaving certificate. What
he had most enjoyed was writing the essays for which he nearly
always gained a good mark. Even at this stage, without his
being really aware of it, the handling of words gave him pleasure.

Firmin was only too keen to put him out to work instead of
sending him for further education or to a university where he
would only eat his head off in idleness. Paul was quickly found
a job sweeping floors and carrying heavy bales of goods. One
day of this was enough. Firmin agreed he was not suited for the
life of a labourer and placed him elsewhere. For a year or so he
worked in the Rue de l'Echiquier, just off the Rue du Faubourg-
Saint-Denis, at an office where, if the routine proved dull, the
duties were not exhausting. The pay was twenty-five francs a
month. This he handed over to Firmin, who, each day, doled
out fifty centimes for his lunch in Paris. He was able to treat
himself to cheese for twenty centimes, bread at fifteen and
coffee at ten, with five centimes left over for the tip. For years
this was his daily menu.

A spell with an insurance company followed. The office was
in the Rue d'Amboise near the Opéra-Comique. From his window he could see the busy street outside and, across the way,
the reflections in the windows of the bank that stood on the
corner. The office manager was a genial ex-cavalryman who
liked, for the benefit of his young staff, to recall his early
adventures both military and amorous. If there was not much
work to be done he would send one of them out for a walk. He
took a liking to Paul. When he saw him gazing thoughtfully out
of the window he would tell him to go for a turn in the Latin
Quarter and come back after lunch. The atmosphere was so
relaxed that sometimes Paul failed to arrive for work until
eleven in the morning – or did not put in an appearance at all.
He was never rebuked.

His strolls through Paris made up a little for the tedium of uncongenial work. He disliked being tied down by regular hours. The slightest restriction on his freedom was an annoyance. The company of dull-minded clerks and workmen bored him. They mocked his shabby clothes and the odd garments he was obliged to wear. Firmin had given him some cast-offs from the wardrobe at the Comédie-Française, and when he turned up at the office wearing, among other things, a pair of silver buckled shoes with red heels, last seen on the feet of Tartuffe in some production years ago, he became a laughing-stock.

He was old enough now to question his father's decisions. A trifling disagreement over food at home led to Firmin's declaring: 'If you're not satisfied you can eat somewhere else and hop it.' Paul took him at his word. That evening he left Courbevoie and rented a room at a dirty, run-down hotel in the Latin Quarter. When he had laid out his few belongings he went to a café off the Boulevard Saint-Michel. Overwhelmed by the memory of his childhood, of all the wrongs he had suffered, he burst into tears. Next morning, at the office, his sympathetic employer lent him money. Firmin wrote in haughty tones that if Paul did not return he would send the police to collect him. A few discreet words from Paul's employer persuaded the righteous father to calm down. The runaway went home and things continued as before. He had, however, seen that Firmin was no longer the all-powerful god of his childhood. His final departure was only postponed.

In an attempt to escape from the round of mediocre jobs to which he was condemned, Paul obtained an interview with the famous actor Mounet-Sully. This 'monstre sacré' was the embodiment of flamboyant theatricality. He crossed the pavement and climbed into his cab with the same grandeur as he showed when mounting the palace steps in the fifth act of *Oedipus Rex*. All his gestures and actions were performed as if before an audience of fifteen hundred people. Even when he was alone, or believed himself to be, the index finger was raised to his forehead, the hair drooped in a tragic curl, the eye flashed with the haggard gleam of Hamlet. One of the plays to which he lent his majestic presence called for the nine Muses to appear on stage with him. 'Nine?' said Mounet. 'That doesn't make much of a show. Suppose we had twelve?' A drama set in the time of Luther included among its props an ancient Bible which had been secured after a great deal of rummaging through anti-quarian bookshops. 'No, no,' observed Mounet, fingering the object disdainfully, 'it won't do. In those days it was a *new* book.'

For his audition with Mounet Paul had chosen a tirade from *Ruy Blas*. It was not the best of choices. Neither his physique nor his presence entirely suited it. Mounet himself always refused to act in the play – it only offered, he declared grandly, 'a lackey's role'.

When Paul had finished the great man delivered his opinion. He made a curious remark – curious because he, who was laughed at behind his back for his lack of intelligence, on this occasion at least showed intuition. 'The actor's profession is a tough one,' he said. 'You'd do better to become a writer.'

So Paul went back to the life of a petty clerk and the daily journeys between Courbevoie and his office in Paris. One morn-ing on the train he renewed acquaintance with a former school-fellow called Léon Marié, a student of sculpture, eighteen years old, handsome, dashing, filled with noble ideas about art. He had, Paul remembered, 'the most delicate sensibility and was the perfect friend, always ready to make use of you and also, from time to time, to do you a favour if only for the pleasure of reminding you incessantly about it afterwards.'

Léon had a sister, a tall, voluptuous girl called Jeanne. Her hair was auburn, her complexion fresh and clear. When Léon introduced her to Paul she fell in love with him straightaway. 'His skin is soft, like a peach,' she said. 'I'd pay for the privilege of kissing him.'

Jeanne was then twenty-two and five years older than Paul. The situation, though pleasurable, confused him. He had never known spontaneous affection before, except from Marie Pezé, and even so this sort of feeling was rather different. As on similar occasions in later life, he regarded it with suspicion. Nothing in his childhood had prepared him for such an eventuality. Still, he accepted what was given – experience had taught him not to rebel – and he was ready to go with the tide. Jeanne being his senior, it was she who took the lead and initiated him. She treated him with a maternal care.

On Sundays – and, as time passed, on as many evenings as he could manage – he would call at her home in Courbevoie. While the family sat drinking tea and playing lotto, the two lovers held hands under the table. Once, after daring manoeuvres, they found themselves alone in her bedroom. Having taken such pains to stage-manage the incident, Jeanne doubtless thought that the crucial moment had arrived. All she received from her bashful lover were a few hugs and kisses. After an hour he quietly departed. Had shyness or fear of interruption hampered him? 'When I think of it,' he later observed, 'it was another failure more or less.'

The sympathetic girl was not annoyed by his lack of resolution. Perhaps, with feminine perversity, she saw it as a proof of delicate feeling. She gave him her photograph, and on it she wrote, spelling her name the English way: 'Souvenir de sa bien-aimée à son Paul chéri. Donné le 14 avril, 1889. Amour et Fidélité. Jane. 14 avril 1889.'

With tickets provided by Firmin, Paul took Jeanne and Léon to Paris for an evening at the Comédie-Française, a trip fully approved by the Marié family because it was 'cultural'. Once there, of course, Léon slipped off on his own shady business leaving the two lovers in a room Paul had booked for the occasion. Again the proceedings lacked excitement. The evening recalled for Jeanne's lover that incident several years earlier when he had shared his bed with Firmin's maid and the furry little dog. Jeanne, good-hearted as ever, bore him no ill will and thriftily pocketed the candle ends that were left over so that she might read in her bedroom at home. When they arrived at the railway station with Léon to take the train for Courbevoie, they found Paul's father on the platform. Firmin blossomed in company. All through the journey he chatted amiably with

Léon and encouraged him in his boastful talk. They had much
in common.

A few months later Jeanne's family moved from Courbevoie
to Paris – or at least, what was left of her family, since by then
her father had settled down elsewhere with his young mistress
and the child he had by her. (Léon was shortly to seduce his
father's pretty companion but remained none the less on excellent terms with Monsieur Marié.) Jeanne's mother took a flat
at 13 Rue du Faubourg-Saint-Jacques where her daughter
joined her. Soon their household was increased by the arrival
of Paul. His father was past caring where he went and his 'stepmother' could not hide her pleasure at seeing the back of him.
They even let him take away a little work-table and a Louis
XVI clock. As he walked through the streets one evening
carrying these modest items of furniture to his new home, the
clock chimed continuously in strident alarm.

For a time he lived happily with Jeanne under her mother's
complaisant eye. A routine established itself. When he came
home from work at the end of the day he would go out and
draw two buckets of water from the little drinking-fountain in
the Boulevard de Port Royal at the top of the street. Then they
would have dinner. Afterwards, in the cool of evening, the
three of them took a walk. Often they ended up in the Jardins
du Luxembourg, where Madame Marié sat on a bench and
chatted with the elderly strollers who haunted the place, while
Paul and Jeanne wandered lovingly up and down the paths.
Another favourite resort was the Place de l'Observatoire
which, in those days, still preserved the charming old café of
the Closerie des Lilas, with, near at hand, the picturesque Bal
Bullier. Since Paul remained on fairly good terms with his
father, he was sometimes able to get tickets for himself and
Jeanne at the Comédie-Française on Sundays. Firmin even
took Jeanne backstage and introduced her to members of the
company. He showed himself so agreeable to her that Paul,
waiting in the auditorium, experienced a twinge of anxiety.

Obscure ambitions had begun to stir in him. At the age of
eighteen he felt the urge to write. What he would write he did

not know. All he knew was a compulsion to put words together on paper. There was nothing in his background to encourage a love of literature except the atmosphere of the Comédie-Française and its emphasis on the fine language of the classic plays. Somehow he must have picked up an appreciation of the verse he used to hear his father reciting at home, or have found something to hold his attention in the yellowing prompt-copies Firmin kept about the house. The influence of van Bever also counted for something. There were evenings when he sat at his work-table and looked hopelessly at the paper spread out before him, waiting, waiting for inspiration. Jeanne fell ill. Her groans bored him. He had more important things to occupy his attention. He got up from his chair, deserted the blank paper and went out for a walk, leaving Jeanne to suffer on her own.

Madame Marié was getting on his nerves. Annoyed by her trivial chatter, he told her what he thought about her lack of intelligence. Despite the pleas of a tearful Jeanne, he decided to live on his own. She helped him find a room on the sixth floor at 14 Rue Monsieur-le-Prince. Here, in January 1891, he installed a few bits of furniture and a bed that Jeanne helped him to, as it were, inaugurate. A job in a newspaper office addressing labels gave him a small independence. The rest of the time he spent scribbling hundreds of lines of poetry in the Rue Monsieur-le-Prince.

One night, very late, he heard his name called in the street. He looked out and saw van Bever, who, having lost his job, was seeking a roof over his head. For several months they shared the room and contrived to live on two francs a week. Since there was only one chair, they made another one out of bricks taken from a building site nearby. Clothes provided another challenge to invention. Van Bever 'repaired' his worn check trousers by touching up the black and white squares with paint and brush. Paul wore the famous buckled shoes, a top hat green with age, and a coat held together by string. He carried an umbrella lettered with advertising slogans. Decked in this outfit he once promenaded ostentatiously at the doors of the Comédie-Française hoping to shame his father into giving him money. The idea was unsuccessful. It did, however, inspire one of the actors to create a grotesque make-up for an eccentric character in a current production. At the first night he went up to Firmin and said: 'Don't you recognise anyone? It's your son!' Firmin was not amused.

In their poverty the two young men were happy after a fashion. They argued late into the night about literature. Sometimes they slept for forty-eight hours at a stretch. Often they did not know what day it was. Although they could not agree on any literary topic they discussed, they remained on good terms. Even van Bever's unfortunate physical peculiarities failed to disturb their good humour. His feet sweated badly and gave the room an acrid tang. When Jeanne came to stay at weekends Paul sent van Bever off to lodge with relatives and spent Saturday changing the sheets and airing the place with desperate energy.

After six months in the Rue Monsieur-le-Prince the two friends had to separate. There was not enough money to keep their little establishment going. Van Bever found himself a post at the Théâtre de l'Œuvre with the pioneer Lugné-Poe, whose productions of Ibsen and Symbolist drama were bringing new influences into the French theatre. There the intense young man worked as an actor – he was of such small stature that Lugné-Poe cast him as one of the children in Ibsen's *An Enemy of the People* – as publicity man, as box-office manager and as printer of tickets and posters. He slept at night in the theatre, his bed an empty orange-box furnished with a straw mattress. Gradually he made the acquaintance of authors and publishers. In time he became that familiar type of literary figure who edits series, produces anthologies, initiates symposia, compiles bibliographies and brings out editions of neglected authors. One of his most popular series was *Les Maîtres du livre* which inaugurated the inter-war French vogue for luxury books. To celebrate the hundredth volume a banquet presided over by the then famous writer Maurice Barrès was held in his honour. Van Bever must have felt very happy.

The interlude with van Bever in the Rue Monsieur-le-Prince had done something to undermine Paul's relationship with Jeanne. Though not lacking intelligence, she was unable to talk literature with him as van Bever had done. His habit of writing intently by the hour, oblivious of all that went on around him, helped to cool her ardour. She found herself a more attentive lover, an actor called Paul Fugère, the brother of Lucien Fugère the opera singer who, in comic roles by Mozart and Rossini, enjoyed a large following at the Opéra-Comique. Lucien also played an important part in first performances of several operas by Massenet, who dedicated to him one of his loveliest works, the late-blooming *Don Quichotte*.

Yet Jeanne retained an affection for Paul. He often went to see her at the flat in the Rue des Feuillantines off the Boulevard Saint-Michel where her new lover had set her up. Since Fugère was frequently away on tour in the provinces there were many opportunities for Jeanne to see the young man who had been her first love, the man for whom, despite changing circumstances, she felt a lingering tenderness.

All this time Paul had had no job. His father, in desperation, suggested that he anticipate military service and volunteer for the army. The more Firmin thought about the idea the more he liked it. He was always keen on military parades. His patriot's heart beat ever more quickly when he heard *La Marseillaise* and he loved taking part in processions at Courbevoie on 14 July. The experience would make a man out of Paul, would put fire in his belly, declared Firmin – who, after the French defeat in 1870, had speedily left Paris to avoid fighting in the Commune.

For seven months Paul wore a rifleman's uniform at Courbevoie barracks. Since Firmin neglected to pay him the weekly allowance of twenty-five francs he had promised, there was not much opportunity for diversion from a routine of drilling on the square and clerical duties. In the middle of the barrack room, surrounded by noise and clatter, he went on writing poetry. His adjutant was a sympathetic man called Esterhazy, the officer who, a few years later, became a sensational figure in the Dreyfus affair. Esterhazy was one of the few men to show Paul kindness in his youth. The ungainly soldier, disappointed in his hopes of promotion by reason of myopia and weak health, protested to his adjutant. The charm and understanding with which Esterhazy interviewed him went to his heart.

Paul's weekly visits to Jeanne were all that relieved the bleakness of army life. At Christmas, for some reason, his leave was cancelled. The thought that he would not be seeing her was too painful. He picked up a loaded rifle and prepared to shoot himself. A friend snatched it away from him. For the next half-hour he enjoyed himself as the object of unaccustomed solicitude. His reward was longer leave at New Year's Day and reunion with Jeanne. In February 1892, short-sightedness and heart trouble earned him three restful months in the hospital of Val de Grâce, which, by a convenient chance, was only a few steps away from Jeanne's flat in the Rue des Feuillantines. She went to see him there. So did Firmin, who thoughtfully arranged his calls so that he arrived a few minutes before visiting time ended and did not have to spend too long with his son.

In May Paul was invalided out of the army. Jeanne was now pregnant by her lover and planning to marry him. She wrote a last letter to Paul signifying that their relationship had ended. He kept it, along with her signed photograph, a lock of hair and some bits of ribbon. She was the inspiration of his first published poem, 'Retraite', which appeared in a magazine called *Le Courrier français* on 16 July 1893. It is the first of a series mourning his lost love. One of the poems in this series is dedicated to Jeanne's brother Léon, another to van Bever, and yet another to Armand Silvestre, that outmoded Parnassian figure whom Paul must have admired at the time.

And Jeanne? Fourteen years after receiving her fatal letter he still could not repress the tears that caught him by the throat whenever he recalled their last evening. Sometimes he saw her out shopping in the street, a typical housewife, grave and pre-occupied with family cares. Her seductively rounded figure had plumped out into grossness. Her arms were fat and flabby, her face had thickened. She now had two, perhaps even three, double chins, and the auburn hair was dulled and straggling. Often he meant to step forward and speak to her, but each time shyness restrained him. When he glimpsed her the little shock of pain gripped him and he murmured to himself: 'Toi que j'ai tant aimée. . . .'

— III —

THE *MERCURE DE FRANCE*: VALLETTE, RACHILDE, GOURMONT AND SCHWOB

*'So long as I'm here Léautaud can write
anything he likes in the* Mercure.'
Alfred Vallette

In the early afternoon of Friday, 24 August 1894, Paul happened to be walking by the Café Mahieu. Among the people sitting at tables outside he glimpsed a face that was familiar: the Mongolian mask, piggy eyes and wispy beard of Verlaine, a syphilitic hulk slouched over his absinthe. At a florist's nearby he bought a bunch of violets and sent an errand boy over to give them to Verlaine. Then he stood on the other side of the street to see what happened. The poet raised the violets to his nose and smelt their scent. He looked in puzzlement to right and left, trying to discover who had paid him this unexpected tribute. Paul went on his way, delighted with his gesture.

He still wanted to be a poet. Probably through van Bever's help, he was given an introduction from Lugné-Poe to Alfred Vallette, editor of the newly born *Mercure de France*. Vallette received him affably. 'You don't need an introduction to come here,' he told him. What is more, he accepted the poem offered, a Mallarmian piece entitled 'Élégie', and printed it in the issue for September 1895.

Not long afterwards Vallette showed the perception that made him one of the shrewdest editors in the history of French literature. He saw instantly that verse was not the means of expression best suited to his new contributor. Why not, he suggested, try prose?

Sooner or later Paul would probably have reached this conclusion without prompting from outside. None the less, it was the perceptive Vallette who helped him clarify his ideas. This was the beginning of an association between editor and writer that was to last forty years. It also signalled an attachment to the *Mercure de France* that endured even longer. Paul regarded the *Mercure* as 'his' firm and was rarely to be disloyal. At Vallette's death in 1935, he wrote: 'I owe him everything as a writer. I wonder where else I could have published what I have written over the last twenty years at the *Mercure*. The answer is undeniable: nowhere.'

The inimitable Vallette, who was to make the *Mercure de France* one of the greatest French literary magazines and publishing houses, began life as a mechanic. Then he worked as a master typographer. He had always been strongly interested in literature but, with rueful self-knowledge, admitted that he lacked creative gifts. He also possessed an eye for practical detail and the ability to organise neatly which are essential for the typographer – and also for the editor.

No greater contrast with his character could have been imagined than that of the lady whom he married. She was Marguerite Eymery, who, under the name of Rachilde, gained notoriety as the author of sensational works. As a young woman she came to Paris determined to make a career in literature. She was fond of recounting how Victor Hugo once dandled her on his knee. Verlaine was her friend, and so were Barbey d'Aurevilly and Villiers de l'Isle Adam. Masculine dress was her favourite wear. She found it convenient for shooting and fencing. Upon her visiting cards she engraved the legend: 'Rachilde, man of letters.'

Her novel *Monsieur Vénus* was impounded by a Belgian court and a two-year prison sentence imposed on the author. Rachilde, safely in Paris, was delighted at the fame she had won with that improbable mixture of prostitution, androgyny, homosexuality and transvestism. Heartened by this success, she went on to write such extravagances as *La Marquise de Sade* and *L'Heure sexuelle*. These and many others are all distinguished by a propensity to sadism and various forms of perversion. They are also totally lacking in the slightest trace of humour. As late as the nineteen-thirties she was still manufacturing novels to the formula. In 1953 she died, irrepressible as ever, at the age of ninety-three.

Such was the flamboyant creature with whom the sober Vallette fell in love. The situation may be explained by the attraction of opposites. She certainly felt affection for the quiet, authoritative man who looked like a warrant-officer in civilian clothes. He wore a high-cut jacket. His hair was cut short. The military moustache had a permanent reddish tinge left by the cigarettes he chain-smoked. He made no pretence of rivalling her vivacity and was modest about his own literary status which relied on two rather dim novels, one of them written in collaboration. They were married in 1889. Their daughter Gabrielle was later to be the wife of the poet Paul Fort's nephew.

For some years the marriage remained idyllic. Soon after the *Mercure de France* was founded Rachilde began her famous Tuesday evening receptions where the star was her protégé Alfred Jarry. Her capriciousness, which in the young girl had seemed so amusing, had become, in the mature woman, a source of embarrassment. Many of the young writers who came to the *Mercure* saw her as a butt for mockery. They gave the nickname of 'Rachilde' to the proprietress of a nearby brothel. Her antics, which often led her into most undignified situations, were accepted by Vallette with silent resignation.

Vallette's main interest came to centre on the administration of the *Mercure*. 'Monsieur Vallette married me,' Rachilde is said to have remarked. 'Immediately afterwards he married books.' She, on the other hand, continued to lead a Bohemian existence, even as an elderly lady, and toured night clubs surrounded by a band of young admirers who paid for her patronage – introductions to publishers, literary collaboration – in kind. Vallette went on tranquilly with his work. He was a strict but affectionate father. His few leisure hours were spent tinkering with his motor-car and fishing the river by his country house at Corbeil. He prudently refused to be drawn into his wife's endless quarrels with her many publishers.

The magazine's office was at 26 Rue de Condé, near the

Théâtre de l'Odéon in the Latin Quarter. This lovely old house had once been the home of Beaumarchais. Under its roof he had written *Le Barbier de Séville*. The entrance hall opened onto a narrow stairway that led to a landing above. On the next floor was Vallette's office, a large square room decorated with fine old wood panelling. Ledgers and account books peeped out of half-open cupboards. Vallette sat behind a desk littered with papers that overflowed onto a table beside him.

Since he lived upstairs in a self-contained flat with Rachilde and his daughter, he had only to step next door to be in his office. He was there at six o'clock every morning, writing letters and planning the business of the day. By the time the employees arrived he had already prepared their work for them and was able to devote himself to matters of editorial policy. To the end of his days he refused to allow a telephone or typewriter in the building. If people wanted to talk to him, he declared, they could come and see him in his office. He would not budge for anyone. They knew where they could find him.

Vallette never read the articles the *Mercure* printed. He was content to rely implicitly on the opinion of an editorial committee which included his second-in-command Louis Dumur. (Dumur, like Vallette, actually lived at the *Mercure*, where he had a bachelor flat at the top of the building.) His literary ambitions were overlooked in the flood of administrative work that engulfed him. The books he published were put away unread in his cupboard.

'I'll read them when I retire,' he would remark. He never did, of course, and when he died at the age of seventy-seven he was still chained to his office. His only reading apart from business correspondence and contracts was the *Almanach Vermot*, a sort of *Tit-Bits* compilation of funny stories and odd facts that was popular with concierges. He liked the jokes and found that a glance through its undemanding pages helped him get to sleep at night.

Although he had long since given up literary hope for himself, he retained a natural sympathy for authors. They were like children, he said, and were liars, cheats and traitors into the bargain. They would sign contracts without the slightest intention of honouring them. Yet he did not bear a grudge against them. They carried, he declared, a 'flame', a 'spark', without which life would lose its interest.

That, in the end, is the justification of Vallette and the reason why he will have an honoured place in literary history. Thanks to him, many a 'flame' was able to spread its light. He was inspired by a respect for the creative faculty which lifted him above the everyday annoyances inseparable from dealing with such unreliable creatures as authors.

Vallette gave complete freedom to his contributors. If X wished to criticise the work of Y, the *Mercure* was open to him. If Y wished to answer, Vallette was just as ready to offer him the magazine's columns in turn. Besides fulfilling his belief in liberty of expression the custom ensured healthy controversy and interesting reading. He was even ready to publish articles that might cause annoyance to his personal friends.

As a publisher of books he put his imprint on works he did not care for at all. Even though Claudel was quite foreign to the liberal atmosphere of the *Mercure*, Vallette willingly published three of his important early pieces. Claudel was grateful to him. Gide, too, appreciated Vallette. Writing to a friend in search of a publisher, he observed: 'I don't think you'll find better terms anywhere else than those offered by Vallette. He treats writers as friends and really *honestly*.'

Though in later years Vallette's judgement sometimes faltered and the freedom he gave his writers might on occasion have sprung from sheer inertia, at his best he was a model publisher. He actually practised all those principles that are often invoked but not always followed. 'A publisher's craft is like no other,' he said. 'When a publisher accepts a manuscript he isn't thinking of the present moment; his gaze must be fixed ten years ahead.'

He looked on the *Mercure* not as a commercial enterprise but as 'a society of authors who publish themselves'. Advertising had little part in his philosophy: 'I never advertise the works I publish. If they're bad there's no point whatever in doing anything to save them. If they're good they end up by making their way on their own.'

The proof that he practised what he preached is obvious from a perusal of the back-list, the truest test of good publishing. After the passage of some fifty years, the *Mercure* titles, while they inevitably include names that changes of fashion have obscured, are seen to contain works of solid value. There is nothing there that is merely ephemeral or dictated by the urge to capitalise on a passing novelty. When one of the *Mercure* authors obtained a Prix Goncourt and all that it implies in big sales, Vallette's reaction was wry amusement.

To Paul Léautaud, his most junior and inexperienced contributor, Vallette extended the same courtesy and respect as he gave to established writers. His suggestion that Paul write prose and not poetry was a suggestion and nothing else. He was too conscious of other people's freedom to wish to impose his own ideas. From 1896 onwards Paul developed the habit of spending every Sunday afternoon with Vallette and his friends. The most important of these was Remy de Gourmont.

One day Paul happened to be present when Gourmont was signing presentation copies of his latest book. Gourmont made a remark calculated to appeal to Paul's cynical temper. 'One sends one's books,' he observed benignly, 'to people one profoundly despises.'

Gourmont lived in the Rue des Saints-Pères, that charming old street much haunted by antique dealers which is bounded at one end by the Seine and at the other by the church of Saint-Germain-des-Prés. His apartment, low-ceilinged and poky, was high up in one of those houses with typically peeling walls and dark winding passages. Except for a small area where he sat and wrote, every piece of furniture was buried under piles of manuscripts, books and magazines. At home he always wore a monk's robe and pointed cowl. The room where he worked was stuffy and reeked of the stale smoke from his continual cigarette. An odour of rancid butter was curiously predominant. The principal ornament consisted of a chamber pot, usually full. There were some, among them the poet Apollinaire, who could never bring themselves to set foot in the place. Paul, who was well accustomed to squalor, had no such qualms.

The flat was shared by Gourmont's brother Jean, a critic and novelist. Above them lived the formidable Madame de Courrière. She had been a model for the sculptor Clésinger and the associate of Huysmans, from whom she inherited a taste for Satanism and the Black Mass. Like a Cerberus she watched over Gourmont with jealous attention. Whoever came to knock at his door was instantly confronted on the landing by this ancient, shapeless blonde in a faded pink dressing-gown. She seemed to spend all her time spying on visitors through a little window, her ear alert for the sound of footsteps. Odd though it seemed to Gourmont's young disciples, she was passionately in love with him. At the time Paul made acquaintance with this peculiar ménage Gourmont was beginning to tire of this constant surveillance. It was said that she then, resignedly, sought consolation with his brother Jean. Paul got on well with her and even ran little errands for her.

Gourmont was difficult and reclusive. The reason for this lay in the hideous disfigurement from which he suffered. As a young man he had been handsome and enjoyed a reputation for gallantry. At the age of thirty-three he was suddenly afflicted with an attack of tubercular lupus which spread from the edge of his eye and covered the right side of his face down to the corner of his mouth. The scars of burns resulting from cauterisation in the attempt to stop the lupus spreading remained with him all his life. His own father did not at first recognise him. For several weeks he stayed at home. Then he began to go out at night under the friendly cover of darkness. Before his illness he had been in the habit of calling on Vallette and talking with his friends. One evening he reappeared at the usual hour, sat in the chair that had become through long custom his own, and, as if nothing had happened, remarked simply: 'Well, here I am again.'

Gourmont never spoke of the affliction which cut him off from the human race, nor of the anguish it must have caused him, a man of warm and sensual feeling, in being deprived of relations with women. His *Lettres à l'Amazone* are the literary expression of a passion he cherished over many years for Nathalie Barney, the American lady who had settled in Paris and there established one of its most famous literary salons. From 1910 onwards her sixteenth-century villa in the Rue Jacob, just round the corner from Gourmont, was a 'temple de l'amitié' where many leading authors and politicians gathered each Friday. (If Nathalie had her 'Fridays', Rachilde was bound to have her 'Tuesdays'.) Men were very impressed by her formidable combination of beauty and intelligence. Some went so far as to propose to her, among them, it is said, Lord Alfred Douglas. None was accepted, for she was not interested in the male sex. She died in 1972 at the age of ninety-five. Gourmont's love for her would never anyway have been consummated.

He loved, too, the music hall entertainer Jane Avril and wrote her letters of pathetic desperation. This highly intelligent and subtle man became enslaved by her trivial charms and was doomed again to see his feelings unrequited. Her attitude was perhaps understandable. When Gourmont entered a restaurant it was not uncommon for people to move hastily and choose a table as far from him as possible. In the street passers-by turned away their heads on seeing him. He put up a facade of Norman hardness. He was rough and surly of approach. The shock of disfigurement drove him into a premature retirement from the world. The only pleasures left to him were those of the intellect and the friendship of a small group that included Paul Léautaud. Despite his gruff exterior he remained deeply sensitive. Alone in his room he would weep, his face in his hands, at some snub from a woman.

Day after day he sat writing at his table. His output was enormous and included nearly a hundred volumes of fiction, drama, poetry, criticism and philosophy. He wrote because there was nothing else for him to do, and also because he had no other way of earning a living.

If Vallette provided the administrative genius that launched and kept the *Mercure de France* running, it was Gourmont who supplied the intellectual stimulus. His wide interests were reflected in its pages, and so too was his intellectual curiosity. The magazine carried the impress of his independent personality and his detestation of cant. The *Mercure* was 'his' paper in a way that annoyed André Gide, then a rising young author. Gide could never master the distaste he felt for Gourmont. The older man's ugliness repelled him. 'Just reading what he wrote was enough to make me sense his ugliness,' said Gide. He was jealous of Gourmont's dominance at the *Mercure* and reluctant to concede second place to him. This was one reason why he played such a leading part in founding the rival *Nouvelle Revue Française* where he could assume the leadership denied him elsewhere. More than thirty years after Gourmont's death Gide still harboured a dislike for him that had lost none of its potency.

Where so many other people were rebuffed by Gourmont's brusqueness, Paul was welcomed into his intimacy. Gourmont doubtless took to him on account of his youth, his obvious passion for literature, and his shyness which masked an inner sensitivity. It may be, too, that Gourmont saw in him the makings of a writer such as he was himself, withdrawn, independent and appealing to a small elite. Their relationship was easy and informal. Gourmont did not mind being contradicted by a youth twenty years his junior. He accepted in the best of humour opinions that disagreed with his own.

The isolation imposed on Gourmont by his disfigurement emphasised certain of his characteristics and coloured his ideas. Withdrawal from the social round increased his distaste for the shallowness and insincerity of society. Self-pity was not, however, a feature of his writing or of his conversation. He was led, rather, to proclaim the importance for a writer of being 'different' from his colleagues. Schopenhauer, who was then much read by French intellectuals, gave him the starting-point for his concept. According to Schopenhauer, Gourmont explained, the world and everything outside the self only exists according to the idea formed of it. The world is one's own representation. One can only reason from appearances. One does not see what is – what is, is what one sees.

Gourmont argued that the worst crimes a writer can commit are, therefore, conformity, imitation, observance of rules and of formal teaching. His work is valid only in so far as it expresses his own true personality. He must say things hitherto unsaid and in a way that is fresh and novel. The aesthetic he creates must be his own and no one else's. He must also have complete freedom. This was what Gourmont enjoyed in the columns of the *Mercure de France*. Without freedom to express his opinions, said Gourmont, he would never have been able to develop his personality.

As for style, Gourmont aimed at short sentences and clarity. Each idea was to have its sentence. Good style, he said, came from experiencing life and from trying to interpret what had been seen and felt through one's own sensibilities. Imitation is involved, of course – one does not learn anything otherwise – but the interpretation must add something that could only come from the writer himself. Matter, therefore, is more important than manner. Style changes with fashion, and a style that is not supported by worthwhile thought soon dies.

From Gourmont and their discussions together Paul learned many valuable things. He saw that Gourmont would never be a popular writer because his audience would always be restricted to the cultured readers who appreciated his intricate reasoning and wide allusions. This was part of the price he paid for his liberty. It meant that he was free to express opinions that would have shocked narrower minds, and that he did not have to flatter the prejudices of the majority. As a writer his position was that of an aristocrat.

After Vallette and Gourmont, the third member of the *Mercure* circle to influence Paul was Marcel Schwob. He looked, Paul thought, rather like Napoleon. Though he was immensely erudite his conversation never degenerated into pedantry. His life for years had been that of a semi-invalid. In his mid-thirties he had an elderly stoop. His complexion was pallid. His eyes shone with a brilliance caused perhaps by the morphine and the ether to which he was believed to be addicted. He lived on the Île Saint-Louis among a cluster of old and exquisite houses which make that island in the middle of the Seine one of the loveliest areas of Paris. A Chinese servant showed visitors into the light and high-ceilinged rooms of the flat where Claudel, Gide, Gourmont and Maeterlinck often gathered. In another room a monkey gambolled.

Paul was soon almost a part of the Schwob household. Madame Schwob was none other than the actress Marguerite Moreno. At the turn of the century her strange Spanish beauty and her alluring voice made her an irresistible queen of the Paris stage. More than forty years later, when her looks had decayed into oddity and her voice become a rusty squawk, she achieved the greatest success of her career in the title role of Giraudoux's *La Folle de Chaillot*.

Since Moreno was often away from home acting at nights, Paul kept Schwob company in the little room where he worked. The sickly author lay in bed under a large mirror that reflected the stools and chairs loaded with books and papers. A La Tour reproduction hung on the wall. On a carpet in front of the fireplace two dogs, Flossie and Flip, played or dozed. As the room gradually darkened the Chinese servant lit the lamps and served dinner. Schwob talked into the night.

In that lamp-lit bookish atmosphere Schwob drew on his wide and curious stock of knowledge to entertain the disciple whose education had ended when he left the *école communale*. He spoke of Plato and Aristotle and Rabelais and Daniel Defoe. The evenings spent with him were a form of continuation school for Paul. Schwob was a great admirer of John Aubrey and Boswell. In his *Vies imaginaires* he in fact quotes Aubrey as a model for biographical method. Men of distinction, he believed, stood out because of their peculiarities. It was important to know that Socrates had a snub nose, that Johnson preserved dried orange peel in his pockets, that Milton had a distinctive way of pronouncing the letter R, that Bacon loathed the smell of calf's leather and so dressed his servants in Spanish leather, that Erasmus didn't like fish, and that Pepys's great concern at the outbreak of the fire of London was to bury his Parmesan cheese in the garden.

Schwob also wrote on François Villon in a way that aroused the admiration of the medieval scholar Gaston Paris. His volume *Spicilèges* includes delightful studies of Robert Louis Stevenson and George Meredith. One of the most far-reaching effects of his association with Paul Léautaud was the interest he stimulated in English literature. Defoe's *Moll Flanders* set an example for Paul of a vigour and freedom of writing that were much to his taste. Inspired by Schwob he even started to teach himself English. The attempt was short-lived, but the seed had been sown, and a lifelong affection for England persisted.

Schwob made a remark one evening that Paul never forgot. Discussing the survival of literary reputations, he pointed out that an author did not need to have written in quantity to be read long after his death. 'I only write when I feel I have something to say,' Schwob said, 'when I feel an overpowering need to.'

This apparently commonplace observation was to become a central part of Paul's doctrine. Schwob also influenced him by his example. Like Gourmont, he did not complain about the smallness of his audience. To be a writer *en marge* was no dishonour. He encouraged Paul's interest in the anecdotal, the eccentric, as revelatory of human nature and therefore worth seeking out. His integrity, his refusal to write if he did not feel a genuine urge to expression, remained an inspiration for his young protégé.

After Schwob's premature death his wife Moreno married a horse-dealer. 'Oh, I've had enough of brains!' she exclaimed. Like her close friend Colette, she was not an intellectual, though very attractive and full of intelligence. During her married life with Schwob she was mistress of the poet Catulle Mendès. Another of her lovers was the Comte de Dion, a partner in the de Dion-Bouton car firm, whose subsidies helped the Schwob household to meet their bills. The complaisant Schwob delighted in going out for drives in the handsome car that the Comte de Dion gave as a present to his wife.

Paul admired her as an actress – her recitation of Baudelaire moved him to tears – and was captivated by her disturbing sexuality. Her wit, amusing and often unkind, enchanted him. He would visit her dressing-room at the theatre and eye the charms which she unconcernedly displayed before him as she changed costumes. She was frank about her life with Schwob, whose invalidism and perversity – which probably involved the Chinese servant – prevented him from playing to the full his conjugal role. Her conversation was flirtatious and tempting.

Bemused by this charming intimacy, puzzled by the tantalising innuendoes of the sophisticated actress, Paul still hesitated. There was the fear that he might have mistaken her meaning, that embarrassment, even ridicule, would follow if he took action. His inborn diffidence and a scruple about deceiving Schwob, who after all was a good friend, prevented him from doing what a more confident man would have done. The episode followed a pattern that recurred with disappointing monotony throughout his life and helped to increase his gloom about women. Much later, a long time later, he realised that she had never forgiven him for his reluctance.

In 1947, at the age of sixty-six, the insatiable Moreno married a lusty young man recently demobilised from the Foreign Legion. Royalties were still coming in from Schwob's books and she needed every penny. She explained, with engaging frankness: 'A mon âge, et avec ma gueule, mon cul me coûte cher!'

—IV—

DIDEROT'S NEPHEW

'La Rochefoucauld, Molière, Voltaire,
Chamfort, Diderot, Courier, Stendhal –
the man and the work.'
                                    Paul Léautaud

One morning in 1897 Léautaud met an acquaintance whom he already knew by sight. The man's name was Paul Valéry. He had a black moustache waxed at the tips and handsome dark eyes. His manner of speech was exuberant and he rarely finished his sentences. The two men found that they were both on the way to Rachilde's Tuesday salon in the Rue de Condé, and they walked on there together.

Valéry was one year older than Léautaud. At the age of twenty-six he had already completed *La Soirée avec Monsieur Teste*. It was his habit, one that continued until the end of his life, to rise at dawn and note his ideas in the still hours of early morning before the bustle of the day made reflection impossible. After which he reluctantly deserted his studies of philosophy and mathematics for the War Ministry, where, on the advice of Huysmans, he had embarked on a career as civil servant. For the rest of the day he occupied himself punctiliously with the affairs of the French artillery.

As they walked to Rachilde's, Valéry and Léautaud discussed poetry. Valéry mentioned the name of Baudelaire. Léautaud countered with Mallarmé. Their friendship dated from that moment.

Valéry had the prestige of being a guest at Mallarmé's famous evenings at his flat in the Rue de Rome. His talk was a perpetual entertainment. On the spur of the moment he would throw out epigrams such as: 'The more you write, the less you think.' Upon a piece of paper he scribbled:

'Story.

For Paul Léautaud.

Once upon a time there was a writer – who wrote.

Valéry.'

Though they disagreed in politics – Léautaud sympathised
with Dreyfus and Valéry bitterly opposed him – they had much
to talk about. Most evenings found them wandering through
Paris together. They took a bus, went from terminus to terminus and found themselves in the remotest neighbourhoods,
lost in argument and discussion. On Sundays they walked the
quais behind Notre-Dame. It was Valéry who did most of the
talking. Léautaud was intimidated, almost embarrassed, by
the intricacy and brilliance of his exposition. Valéry needed
an audience. Léautaud provided it.

At Rachilde's 'Tuesdays' Valéry shone brilliantly. All the
other guests crowded round to hear him analyse, with algebraic
precision, artistic and literary problems. His set-piece was a
discussion of Poe's *The Raven*. He carried his listeners from
deduction to deduction over bridges built out of crystalline
reasoning and ornamented with endless refinements of logic.
So complicated was his argument, so involved were his conceits,
that in the end even he lost his footing and was compelled to
murmur vaguely, flapping his hands: 'Enfin, vous voyez. . . .'
Vallette nicknamed him 'the man who never finishes'.

In those days when few people used the telephone, least of
all impecunious literary men, Léautaud and Valéry kept in touch
with frequent letters. Valéry wrote to him in affectionate and
humorous tones, sometimes addressing him with the jocular
phonetic spelling: 'Mon chair Léoto.' He invited him to dinner
with the family, unwittingly embarrassing his shy friend who
had little knowledge of social conventions. After everyone else
had gone into dinner Léautaud was confronted by a terrible
dilemma: should he take the arm of Madame Valéry, or of her
sister, to enter the dining-room? Madame Valéry solved the
problem graciously by taking his arm herself. Under the influence of Valéry's family circle he gradually came to feel more

at home, and the gauche young man no longer feared to spend an evening there.

Valéry sympathised with Léautaud's money problems. He himself knew only too well the degrading shifts imposed by lack of means. In 1900 he left his post in the War Ministry and worked part-time for Édouard Lebey, the head of the Agence Havas. The arrangement continued some twenty years and gave Valéry the necessary leisure for writing. Lebey was an invalid who needed someone to do secretarial work for him and to read to him during the tedious hours he was condemned to spend in his room. The work was not unpleasant and enabled Valéry to make interesting contacts with public figures and important men in high finance. When he became liable for military service he did both himself and Léautaud a good turn by arranging for the latter to deputise for him in his absence.

Although Léautaud was still at the height of an enthusiasm for Mallarmé when he met Valéry, new idols were gradually to usurp, over the next year or two, the place of honour he once reserved for the author of 'L'Aprés-midi d'un faune'. He came across Diderot and acquired a passion for his *Neveu de Rameau* and for Voltaire. The memorialists and letter writers of the period charmed him. He spent what he called his 'soirées de grand lecture' meditating on the disillusioned epigrams of Rivarol, Chamfort and the Prince de Ligne. Next to them he placed Molière, who seemed to him a supreme master of the comedy of character. Coming nearer modern times he found the slashing irony of the pamphleteer Paul-Louis Courier much to his taste and a model for the sharp little vendettas he was himself to carry on in the columns of the *Mercure de France*. As for the nineteenth century, there were only two writers who mattered: Balzac and Stendhal. ('Ce pauvre Flaubert' was dismissed as nothing more than 'a literary cabinet-maker polishing away until everything shone nicely'.) 'Stendhal!' he wrote in a rare moment of lyricism, 'the delight of my youth, the delight of my maturity.'

Léautaud was deeply, if not widely, read in the handful of authors he had chosen. He did not come upon them through education or upbringing, nor were they imposed on him from outside. He discovered them through his own explorations. The choice he made was personal but genuine. He accepted only those authors whose work and mode of expression tallied with life as he knew it. The criterion was his own pleasure.

Literature, he decided, was his vocation. He had found his models. His ambition was to live up to them. The urge to write was imperious, overwhelming. But the awful question remained: what was he to write about?

MOTHER AND SON

'A very pleasant dream last night . . . I found myself with my mother, looking just as she did when I discovered her again at Calais. Lunch together. After lunch we made love very passionately, on her part and mine, with the same ardour. She was completely naked, her face shining with pleasure. I've always had her – in my dreams!'

Paul Léautaud, at the age of sixty-five

Léautaud knew that the poetry he had written was worthless and that his mannered little 'prose poems' were without value. Perhaps believing that the daily life around him would be a source of inspiration, he had begun to keep a diary. This dated back some years. The first entry was made on 3 November 1893 and recorded a dream he had about the man who eventually married Jeanne Marié, his first mistress. As yet, though, the diary was a haphazard affair with long gaps between entries.

He had also started to write what he described as a novel, though it was really a chain of autobiographical reminiscences. In it he told the story of his childhood. On paper he evoked images that were vivid in his mind. The events were set against a background that included the Rue des Martyrs, Montmartre, the Folies Bergère and the Comédie-Française. Among the characters were Firmin Léautaud and his troupe of women, Jeanne Forestier, Marie Pezé and the dog Tabac. He remembered with gratitude the kindly prostitutes who, amused and touched by his awkward innocence, mothered him and sometimes, when they could not find a customer for the night, shared their bed with him. Since a novel must have some sort of story, he invented a romance with one of them, a girl called La Perruche. Since, also, a novel must have an ending, he gave her a mortal illness and killed her off. It is possible that he could think of no other way of bringing his story to a close. For the novelist who does not know what to do with a character, death is a convenient solution of his problems and an excuse to conclude his labours. So La Perruche had to die.

This left Paul with a very short book indeed. There were only five chapters. Having put into it everything he could he was at his wit's end to find the extra material needed to make it into a respectable length. Then a wonderful piece of luck came his way: he met his mother again for the first time during the twenty years that had passed since their ambiguous encounter in her Paris hotel room. Then he had been a child of ten. Now he was a grown man nearly thirty years old. Their meeting gave him the profoundest emotional experience he was ever to know. It also provided him with the material he needed to complete the book that eventually became *Le Petit Ami*.

In October 1901, an urgent message arrived from Calais where his grandmother, Madame Forestier, had settled. His Aunt Fanny lay dangerously ill and was not expected to survive. It was his mother's sister Fanny, the only member of the family to show him kindness, who had fussed over him as a youth, told him to be careful when crossing the street, worried about his smoking, warned him against working too much at night, and taken him out for dinner on her occasional trips to Paris. Now she lay helpless in bed, looking like an overgrown girl, her face puffy and yellow.

He made the long train journey to Calais – it meant overspending his fragile budget, but a death in the family naturally involved expense – and arrived at his grandmother's house. Madame Forestier told him that his mother was also expected. He learned that Jeanne Forestier was married and had two children. She lived in Geneva where her husband was a well-known professional man. Her disreputable past lay buried under a thick rind of bourgeois respectability.

On Thursday, 24 October, she entered the front door. Léautaud peeped over the banister and saw a woman dressed in black mounting the stairs. Her profile was clear-cut and her voice warm and musical. Her movements were quick and lithe.

He went back into the room, hastily, and looked at himself in the mirror. His face had turned pale.

His grandmother came up with Jeanne and introduced her.

'How do you do, Monsieur,' said Jeanne after a slight pause.

'How do you do, Madame,' he replied with grave formality.

Later he overheard them talking next door. 'Who is he?'

'It's Paul,' said his grandmother.

'Who's Paul?'

'Why, your son, of course!'

Because the place was so small Léautaud had to move out and put up at a hotel nearby. After dinner he went and sat with his mother in Fanny's room. The sick woman groaned continuously. Her breathing was laboured. When she opened her eyes they stared without recognition at the people by her bedside. Round about eight o'clock she fell asleep. At one end of the room sat the night nurse and a maid. Paul and Jeanne took chairs at the other.

How desirable she looked, thought Léautaud, and how young she'd remained. The light emphasised the contrast between her brown hair and pale complexion. Her eyes were gentle and bright. She told him to pull his chair closer. He did so and their knees touched. He felt at once happy and embarrassed.

'Listen, Paul, I know who you are . . . ,' she said.

Then, as if a tap had been turned, she spoke intently of her past life and loves, of her childhood, of the existence she now led as the mother of a family in Geneva. She protested that she had always tried without success to discover what had become of him. If only she'd been able to keep in touch!

It was time for bed. He went with her to her bedroom. As soon as the door was shut they embraced.

'My darling!'

'Maman!'

He kissed her neck, her eyes, her throat. 'What a long time it's been!' he whispered.

'I hope you don't mind,' he went on.

'Mind what?'

'I'm not quite sure, but I don't feel I'm kissing you as a mother.'

'What do you mean?'

'I can't quite put it into words. It's just that I feel I'm not kissing you as I should a mother.'

She smiled, and there was uneasiness in her smile. He asked if he might sit beside her when she was in bed. She gently refused. They parted. As he made his way to the hotel he wondered why she did not want him to kiss her as he had done twenty years ago, at that delightful, unforgettable reunion in the Passage Laferrière. Was it because she feared he would see the wrinkles that had aged the once-fresh skin of her throat?

Next morning he came back at eight o'clock to find that his aunt had died an hour previously. It was a busy day and there were many errands to be run. After lunch he sat again with his mother and they talked freely.

'Do you like women?' she asked suddenly.

Embarrassed, he murmured: 'Well, I think I'm very fond of them indeed. But the pleasure they give me is perhaps a rather special one. . . .'

'What a funny boy you are!'

'You can't imagine the sort of way I've often thought of you. It's very difficult for me to explain.'

'Go on. Tell me.'

'No, I wouldn't dare.'

'Why? What does it matter?'

'Oh, it's very wrong – at least, you'd think so. In any case, it can't be done.'

Still, he went ahead and talked to her of their last meeting. Since then, he said, he'd always thought of her in bed, with a very low-cut nightdress. 'How odd!' she said.

From time to time when she was out he would steal into her room and look through her belongings. He found that she wore a size 4 in shoes and that she used crimson face powder. Her toilet water came from Houbigant. These discoveries thrilled him. He hugged the knowledge to himself like a miser cherishing his treasure.

When they were alone together they stole furtive kisses. While his aunt lay dead in the nearby room, a crucifix between her cold hands, Jeanne Forestier would take him by the neck, mischievous, like a child: 'Kiss me quick, we're alone!'

She called him 'mon enfant', 'mon chéri'. But all the same: 'What would people think if they saw us kissing secretly like this?' she said. 'You know, we look like two lovers even now. What would things have been like ten years ago?'

He wished he was a child again that he might snuggle up in her arms. 'My darling Jeanne!' he whispered to himself. He thought of her body and longed to possess it. But they were never alone for long. Somebody always interrupted them: his grandmother, the maid, the undertaker. In the evening he took his leave of her. She kissed him as they stood on the dark threshold. 'No,' he said quietly, 'in spite of everything I said, you'd never know how much I love you!'

Back in his hotel room he scribbled on paper everything he could remember. His habit of taking notes had become so ingrained that he often started writing before the incident he wished to record had ended. Jeanne Forestier commented on it. 'What are you up to, continually taking papers out of your pocket and going off to write in corners?' He told her he was keeping an account of his expenses. It was ironic: he had found his mother again after twenty years, and yet his overwhelming desire was to get it all down in writing. Already he had five or six pages of notes. They would give him almost another chapter. Grandeur of the man of letters! he thought ironically. The moment you have a book on the stocks it takes precedence over everything else.

The last day in Calais was a full one. There were the funeral to be supervised, rooms to be tidied, the coffin to be taken to the railway station for transport to Paris and eventual burial. All this time he thought of nothing but Jeanne. When it was over they went for a stroll together. His heart leaped as he watched her primp along in her high-heeled boots. They returned to the

house and did their packing. She gave him some little presents
and a few keepsakes: an old card-case she'd had when young,
a sweet-box, a photograph of her son, a piece of soap. . . .

He was to travel overnight to Paris with the coffin. She
would be returning next day to Geneva and they agreed to
meet when she came through Paris. 'Tomorrow, at the Gare
du Nord, at six o'clock?' he said. She nodded, took him in her
arms and kissed him. He was near to tears.

The train left at six in the evening. It was a slow one, not
due in Paris until five next morning. Stations flickered past in
the night. He caught glimmers of the sea, plains flecked with
marshes, clumps of trees. Boulogne, Étaples, Abbeville, came
and went. Alone in his compartment he sat and repeated to himself the sweet word 'maman'. At last the grey outlines of Sacré-
Coeur appeared.

The coffin was soon disposed of and his aunt laid in the
cemetery. The rest of the day passed with agonising slowness.
At five o'clock he was already at the Gare du Nord, a little
bouquet of violets in his hand. They would go nicely with her
mourning clothes, he thought. He walked up and down the
platform reading the public notices automatically: 'Travellers
are requested. . . . Official notice. . . . It is forbidden to. . . .'
Six o'clock struck. No Calais train with his mother arrived.
Panic-stricken, he assailed the porters and inspectors with
questions. They knew nothing. By eight o'clock the violets had
faded and the paper wrapping was creased. He stuffed them
into his pocket.

Perhaps there was a telegram waiting him at home? He went
to the enormous expense of taking a cab. No – there was no
telegram. He rushed to the Gare de Lyon, for he knew the
Geneva train left there at eight-fifty. It was eight-thirty-five
when he arrived.

There she was, looking calmly out of her carriage window.
'Eh bien, mon garçon, what's the matter?' He climbed in. Face
to face with the woman he loved more than anything in the
world, he burst into tears. She retained her composure. It was
only a missed appointment after all!

'Poor boy, everything will be all right. We'll meet again. We'll make up for it.' She kissed him. Once. There were quite a lot of people on the train, she remarked nervously, who came from Geneva and knew her.

Porters began to slam doors. He put the violets on the seat beside her and said goodbye. How he wished, he thought as he walked home through the squalid surroundings of the Gare de Lyon, how he wished he'd been an orphan from birth.

Next day he wrote to her a passionate letter six pages in length. Why had she been so cold towards him at the Gare de Lyon? He had wanted so long to be able to love her. During their affectionate meeting in Calais he had glimpsed, for a moment, the happiness he had sought for years. His letter crossed with one from Jeanne Forestier. 'Cher fils tant aimé,' she began, and then apologised for the disappointment of last night, asked him to write to her often, promised they would meet again, and told him how touched she had been by his flowers. 'Goodbye, my dear, and receive the tender kisses of your mother who has never forgotten you. Your presence has been like a ray of sunlight in my heart,' she concluded. Despite his emotion, when he came to this last sentence he could not repress the cynical thought: 'She must read some pretty awful books.'

Over the next few months they exchanged many letters. In their joy at having found each other again they often wrote every day. Once she sent him half the bunch of violets he had given her at the railway station. 'I've kept it as a token of remembrance,' she said. 'And I'm sharing it with you, my darling, to prove to you once and for all that you are very close to my heart.' Knowing how little money her son possessed and what a modest life was his, she would enclose small gifts with her letters, tea, chocolate, handkerchiefs and towels.

Their correspondence began on 28 October 1901. By 9 November the tone of his letters had become so intimate that she warned him never to send her postcards: she was afraid her children might see them in the letter-box. He went on pouring out his feelings for her in page upon page of urgent declaration.

All the repressed emotions of his bleak childhood, all the natural springs of love within him that had been dammed up by the harshness of life, seemed at last to have found an outlet. He was transported with an almost unbearable sense of happiness. The man of thirty spoke with the innocent faith of a 10-year-old boy.

Gradually, however, a discordant note could be detected in his mother's letters. She was afraid outsiders might get to know about their correspondence. What if her family, her respectable family in Geneva, should hear of the odd situation in which she had let herself become involved? The strain was giving her repeated bad headaches.

Her mother, Madame Forestier, had now come into the picture. Jeanne never got on well with her, and she was furious when she learned that Paul had shown Madame Forestier one of her letters. On 7 January she asked him to send back to her everything she had written. She rebuked him for the over-sensitiveness, the sentimentality, that made him construe her remarks into things that she never intended. His habit of reading between the lines exasperated her.

Again and again she asked for her letters back. Still he ignored her requests. At last she wrote coldly:

'I only regret one thing, and that is having given you in my letters, and through a sense of duty, the illusion of an affection I was unable to feel since I did not know you. It might, however, have come if you'd shown yourself worthy of it. I can only congratulate myself on not having brought you up, because I'd have been deeply humiliated otherwise!'

He replied with bitter accusations of neglect. She had deserted him the day he was born, she had let self-interest come between her and her maternal duties, she had caused him to quarrel with his grandmother, Madame Forestier. She was, he charged, a liar and a trouble-maker. On 4 April 1902, she replied in a long letter. Her message was simple. She wished to forget him. He meant nothing to her. It would have been better had she remained unaware of his existence. As it was, he had passed through her life as if in a bad dream which she intended to wipe out promptly from her memory.

He went on writing to Geneva without ever receiving a reply. On her birthday and at the New Year he regularly sent her an affectionate little note. Sometimes he did not even bother to post his letters since he knew they would bring no result. The violets she had sent him were put into a box and labelled: 'Flowers sent by my mother on the 13 November 1901.' They were found in a drawer after he died more than fifty years later. The stalks had withered, the petals were crumbled into dust.

He preserved every scrap of what she had written to him except for three letters towards the end. The envelopes were kept but the contents are unknown. Her final letter he did not open. Fearful of what it might contain, he asked a friend to read it on his behalf. She did so and advised him to remain in ignorance of what his mother had said.

Jeanne Forestier was never forgotten by her son. At certain times of the year he thought of her with a specially poignant feeling. The tang of autumn air and mist always reminded him of their climactic meeting at Calais. Often in the street he saw women whose appearance brought her back sharply to him. He would read her letters over and over again until he wept. His ardent longing for her retained all the anguish he had felt at their meeting. Hoping against hope, he wondered if he would ever see her again.

Her presence coloured his everyday thoughts and was liable to be conjured up by the most trifling incident. Once he overheard a mother say: 'Is that you, son?' There, he thought, was something that had never been said to him.

At night he had dreams in which he possessed her. Every erotic detail was clear in his mind. Next morning he would be troubled by strange emotions. In his sixties he still dreamed of making love with her. He was to take to the grave that unbearable mixture of love and hatred, of affection and rancour, which Jeanne Forestier inspired in him. His moods alternated between yearning and reproach. The cruel dilemma in which he found himself was incapable of solution. There was no way out.

Only much later did he realise that other people, even her closest relations, had nothing good to say of Jeanne Forestier. When her Genevan husband became a widower – a state to which, one suspects, he had for long aspired – he described her as possessing a 'detestable' character. She was, he said, incapable of running a household, and her touchiness made family life a trial. How, one wonders, did they come to meet, and at what point did his world of sober professionalism make contact with hers, one of flashy theatrical troupes? Perhaps during a tour of the provinces he had admired the sexual charm she adroitly displayed on stage. And she, weary of the tiring existence, conscious that her beauty could not last much longer (she must have been in her late thirties), was ready to sacrifice her hopes of fame for a less glamorous but comfortable marriage. After they settled in Geneva her husband realised, too late, the mistake he had made.

Her own children shared the father's view. When her son learned, after Léautaud's death, the circumstances of his relationship with Jeanne Forestier, he remarked that it was just as well for him that he had been abandoned as a baby. 'She had a hellish character,' he went on. 'When I was little she used to beat me all the time. When I was fifteen or sixteen years old she was jealous of me. It was an equivocal sort of jealousy that deeply estranged me from her.'

Of course she was a monster. Yet at the same time she represented for Léautaud all that was beautiful and desirable, all that he knew he could never have. The knowledge of her viciousness did not prevent him from wanting her. He saw now that he had been the dupe of his emotions. As a clumsy, stumbling male he had shown himself unable to cope with feminine perversity. He believed that all women were like his mother. They were tarred with the same brush, egotistical, ruthless, treacherous. Her brutal rejection of him made him swear never to be caught out again. From now on a mask of cynicism would conceal his lacerated feelings. When somebody once asked him: 'What is your favourite quality in women?' his answer was ready. 'I didn't know they had any,' he snapped.

~VI~

FATHER AND SON

'How he made me suffer! If anyone had told him so he'd have burst out laughing. What a father he was, I ask you! And now. . . . Well, now he's at the bottom of a regulation hole in that delightful cemetery at Courbevoie, and I'm afraid we're in danger of becoming sentimental.'

Paul Léautaud

However much Jeanne Forestier's treatment of Léautaud was to scar his soul, as a writer he had cause to be grateful to her. The meeting at Calais gave him all he needed to round off his book, enough, in fact, for three chapters. He wrote them very quickly, swept on by the excitement of reliving his unique experience. Surely Providence might favour him again later on and give him a sequel? 'Ah! What pages I shall write when she dies,' he noted. 'I'm so good on funerals.'

He offered the manuscript to the editorial committee at the *Mercure de France* and it was accepted immediately. Vallette, however, did not like the original title of *Souvenirs légers*.

'What's your book about? What happens in it?' he asked.

'It's the story of a boy who's the *petit ami* of a few prostitutes,' replied Léautaud.

'That's it! There's the title: *Le Petit Ami*! We don't need to look any further!'

Le Petit Ami began serialisation in the *Mercure* in the autumn of 1902. Early next year it was published in book form. Some who read it praised the realism of the treatment and the intensity of feeling. Others were shocked by its implied attack on the sacred concept of mother-love and found it distasteful. Either way it made little stir. *Le Petit Ami* had the extra misfortune of appearing on the same day as Zola's new novel *Vérité*, which, already selling 41,000 copies, overwhelmed Léautaud's modest volume. On his strolls around the bookshops Léautaud saw only one customer pick up his book. He leafed through it and read passages here and there. Then he put it down.

Just over a thousand copies of *Le Petit Ami* were printed. By 1905 298 had been sold. It was twenty years before the small quantity was exhausted. During that time Vallette steadfastly refused to remainder it. An ordinary publisher would have waited no more than three years, if that, before cutting his losses by selling off the copies cheaply. Whenever somebody ordered *Le Petit Ami* at the *Mercure* it was regarded as an occasion. 'Un *Petit Ami*!' shouted an assistant. 'Un *Petit Ami*!' chorused surprised voices in the stock-room as a copy was lifted with mock reverence from the dusty pile. Today this first edition is an extremely valuable collector's item.

Léautaud's next piece of writing was not, as he had hoped, to complete the story of his mother with an account of her funeral. By a shapely but macabre stroke of chance it was to be a chronicle instead of his father's death. Since 1897 Firmin had been living in retirement at Courbevoie with his wife, the former Louise Viale. With them lived their son, Maurice, Léautaud's half-brother. Firmin spent most of the time drinking in cafés. His black hair turned grey and sparse. His eyes glazed into dullness. The handsome features became coarse and thick. He no longer troubled about the appearance of his clothes.

He had been ailing for the past six years. A malady of some description, perhaps venereal in character, paralysed his legs and gradually deprived him of the ability to move any of his limbs. In the early days he had still managed to drag himself to his beloved café. Then he found himself unable to travel farther than the garden. In the end he was confined to his room. Léautaud had been going to see him, with reluctance, every fortnight or so. At these meetings they sat in silence, the father morose, the son bored beyond measure.

On 19 February 1903, one day after the publication of *Le Petit Ami*, Firmin's illness took a turn for the worse. Urgently summoned to Courbevoie, Léautaud arrived and found his father dying. He was met by his half-brother Maurice, who, having planned to go out bicycling that day, was annoyed at having to stay at home.

Firmin was still conscious of what went on around him. His

face was red and puffy. As Léautaud bent over him he opened his eyes and tears came from them. All that day there was company round his bed – Louise Viale uttering the usual commonplaces, Maurice sulking over his wasted trip, and Léautaud watching expectantly. Before Léautaud returned to Paris they opened his eyes. The look was veiled and sightless.

Two days later a telegram came asking Léautaud to return at once. It was just his luck that this should happen when he was caught up in all the excitement caused by the publication of his first book.

'Mon Dieu, why can't he die and leave us in peace!' Léautaud thought to himself as he trudged through Paris on his way to the station. It was Shrove Tuesday and the streets were already full of holidaymakers, some wearing gay masks and carnival clothes. He remembered he had an appointment with Vallette and wrote him a note to cancel it. 'What an odd idea to be dressed in a shroud on Shrove Tuesday!' he added.

Firmin now breathed with difficulty. The sound of his heartbeat was loud. His jaw had fallen and the mouth was contorted. As Léautaud watched at the bedside his irritation vanished. He had always been interested in death, and here was an absorbing opportunity to study it at close quarters. He gazed, enthralled, as the face visibly changed with the onset of death. Sometimes he knelt at the bed-head for a better view of the curious grimace that distorted the profile. And while his father lay dying, the Shrove Tuesday merrymakers in Paris, where he returned for dinner, were spraying confetti over each other, were singing and dancing among the winking electric signs of the music halls and cabarets.

The vigil went on. Firmin was still alive on Wednesday morning. His brain, his reflexes, were dead. Only the heart continued to beat furiously. 'How long do you think he'll last?' inquired one of the people who called. Another, an old friend, observed: 'Oh well. He's had his share! He's had a lot of fun!'

That night Firmin's breathing lost its natural rhythm and turned into a dry, monotonous noise, like the click of tongue on palate. The room felt bitterly cold because the window had been kept open to relieve the stench. Trains whistled past at the bottom of the garden and shook the house with their leaden rumble. Candles flickered in the draught and threw grotesque shadows. It was so cold that Léautaud and Maurice huddled by a fire in the kitchen, their ears on the alert for the silence that would follow the death rattle. Every now and then Léautaud took a candle and, holding it close to Firmin's face, watched him die a little more.

Suddenly he felt a mild stirring of pity. It was such a long time since they had talked to each other or shaken hands with genuine feeling. How little Firmin had loved him! Except for the very early years, he could remember no affectionate gesture, no kindly remark. And at the thought of how Firmin had sometimes dandled him as a small child and pinched his cheek, he nearly broke down. Firmin, he thought, had really loved Jeanne Forestier once. But when her memory in time was overlaid by other mistresses, the son had become a nuisance.

Just after two o'clock in the morning Léautaud realised that the sound of his father's breathing had ceased. He hurried into the room. Firmin raised his head and groaned a strangled 'Ah!' His face miraculously changed to its former appearance. He raised his head again, made as if to sneeze, and fell back. A third time he lifted his head and, on this occasion, actually did sneeze. His breathing stopped. Maurice and Louise Viale came in to help lay him out. Léautaud felt the weight of his head as he raised the body so that it could be wrapped in the winding-sheet. 'This is what gave me life,' he thought, turning away a little to avoid touching the face. 'How is the seducer fallen!'

The rest of the night Léautaud slept badly. He was haunted by the noise of the death rattle, the jerky breathing, the smell of the sickroom. The wind rattled the doors in their frames. Suddenly he heard sounds that made him think for a moment he was back again at his father's bedside listening to the dying man's gasp. Then he realised that the noise came from a prowling cat.

Next morning the dead man's face was yellow and cold as marble. A bandage looped round his head to keep the mouth shut was so tight that his nose was curved and the cheeks were

6. Jeanne Marié, 'a pretty girl with golden hair', who was Léautaud's first love

7. Blanche Blanc, a devoted and long-suffering mistress

8. Georgette Crozier as an old lady, forty years after her bitter-sweet affair with Léautaud

9. The tempestuous Madame Cayssac (1869-1950), 'Le Fléau', which was both the scourge . . . and the delight of Léautaud's life. A rare snapshot

10. Madame Cayssac poses with two of her beloved cats

hollowed. By the time he was in his coffin the features had changed still more and the smell was worse than ever.

The day of the funeral was cold and windy. Léautaud, walking behind the coffin, noted that a black liquid was oozing from it. No one spoke of the deceased's virtues at the graveside. Everything was over by midday. Jeanne Forestier, of course, had not been among the mourners. Léautaud wrote to her with the news of Firmin's death but she, as usual, did not reply.

The man who had treated Léautaud so harshly and made his childhood such a wretched experience was gone. Yet the work he did lived on. The son's character was living evidence of the effect he had had during those crucial early years. By a curious reversal of circumstances Léautaud now began to find resemblances between himself and Firmin. There were certain physical links that bound him to his father, certain attitudes that reminded him of the dead man and made him feel less alone, less free. Sometimes he would screw his features into the dying grimace he remembered so well. There was no doubt about it; father and son looked like each other.

From time to time he would visit the grave. Loitering dutifully beside the tomb he saw that the level of the earth had sunk a little further. How long ago was it that he died? He thought about all that must be going on a few feet below. Perhaps by now the coffin had burst open. The body that lived and laughed and made love must now be a black putrid mass.

Throughout the whole episode he had been taking copious notes. Even as Firmin struggled in his last throes his son was industriously making a record of every incident that occurred. The result was the slim volume called, not without sardonic undertones, *In Memoriam*. Léautaud gave the manuscript to Vallette, who, most uncharacteristically, read it from start to finish. This must have been one of the very rare occasions when the editor of the *Mercure* actually acquainted himself with the contents of what he intended to publish in the magazine. He shut himself up in his office with instructions that he was not to be disturbed. When he emerged he declared that *In Memoriam* was even better than *Le Petit Ami*.

Vallette realised that it contained material likely to shock and scandalise because of its frankness. None the less, during November 1905, he serialised it in the *Mercure*. He was not surprised when nearly twenty-five subscribers cancelled their subscription. 'We're losing readers?' he shrugged. 'We'll get new ones.' This was at a time in the magazine's fortunes when even the loss of such a small number of regular subscribers was a serious matter.

Vallette was right in his estimate of the superiority of *In Memoriam*. The style is at once tauter and more fluent than that of *Le Petit Ami*. Léautaud is completely self-assured in his handling of the material. No longer a timid beginner, he is confident enough to acknowledge that his book will not be to everyone's taste. The reader is free to take it or leave it.

Spontaneity gives a liveliness and veracity to Léautaud's style which a more formal mode of expression might have lacked. He is conversational and easy in manner, with all the digression and informality of a man who is telling us something face to face. What he has to tell is harrowing enough, and the unremitting detail he provides would be unbearably depressing if it were not for the occasional lightness of irony.

In Memoriam completes the diptych inspired by the mother and father to whom, through a paradox he was the first to relish, he owed so much as man and writer. Looking back on the ill treatment he suffered at his father's hands, he concluded:

'Today I realise that I was the one to benefit. My mother herself . . . doesn't lack grounds for my gratitude. In all conscience, would I be the fellow I am if I'd enjoyed a traditional happy family life? . . . I don't even need to complain as a writer, if you think about it. Can you see me with a married father and mother being unfaithful to each other, and me obliged to tell it all? It wouldn't have been possible. While with a father and a mother like mine! . . . I won't insist, it wouldn't be modest. The advantages are so striking! Dear benefactors – and I'm not joking!'

Given such luck, it must be admitted that Léautaud made

the best of it. Of the two books he had written to date, the second is his masterpiece. If *Le Petit Ami* deals with a situation that is not very common, *In Memoriam* treats of a subject that has universal application. Death hangs over the narrative like a pall of disintegration. By concentrating in detail on the physical aspects, by painting a picture of steady and inevitable destruction, Léautaud conveys the fear and horror of death that pursued him throughout his earthly existence. At the same time, he produces a Chekhovian mixture of grief and hilarity, of tragedy and comedy, which is all the more effective in that it is achieved without conventional literary artifice.

There is, in truth, nothing quite like *In Memoriam* throughout the whole of French literature. It answers perfectly to Léautaud's own definition of what he thought a good book should be: 'The merit of a book does not lie in its good or bad qualities. Its value depends entirely on the fact that no one but its author could have written it. Every book that anyone but its author could have written is good only for the waste-paper basket.'

In the matter of style, too, he had achieved his ideal. It was 'simple, dry, bare, *completely natural*'. He used to say afterwards that his career as a writer began with *In Memoriam*. Certainly he was never to surpass this unique piece of writing.

Although *In Memoriam* lost subscribers for the *Mercure*, in other quarters it awoke admiration. One day the office was invaded by an explosive personage with a bristling moustache and a barrack-room manner. This was the novelist Lucien Descaves, who, having read the first instalment, was anxious to find out if the complete work could be submitted for the Prix Goncourt. His colleagues at the Académie Goncourt had not made their choice, but several of them, including Huysmans, author of the supremely decadent novel *A rebours*, already favoured *In Memoriam*. Descaves was an expert at vigorous lobbying and he assured Vallette that Léautaud's work was almost certain to succeed. The only drawback was that it did not reach the required length. Would Léautaud be able to enlarge it?

Knowing the trouble he had had in finding material for his

writing, Léautaud was thrown into a state that varied between despair and elation at the thought of a possible success. Five thousand francs was a lot of money. There would be more coming in from sales, and the prize would also help *Le Petit Ami*. On the other hand he would be faced with the unattractive task of writing to order and providing the extra material within a month. At last he decided, after much heart-searching, not to do it. He felt he would be sacrificing his independence and self-respect, just to be patted on the back like a good schoolboy. A month later the Académie Goncourt announced its choice: a novel by the now largely forgotten Claude Farrère. Like most of the choices which, apart from the occasional flash of brilliance that lights on a Proust or a Simone de Beauvoir, make the list of awards a dull record of solid middle-brow taste over the years, it was not to be vindicated by history.

And yet . . . and yet Léautaud would have enjoyed the little bit of notoriety and the modest share of recognition the Prix Goncourt was able to confer. Writing is a solitary art. When an author strikes off a happy phrase or succeeds at last in moulding the stubborn words into the pattern he is after, there is no audience to applaud him. Unlike the actor, who enjoys the immediate stimulus of a crowded theatre, or the politician, who draws strength from the response of his supporters, the author is condemned to solitude. He is a shadowy figure in a back street. He will never know the excitement of an audience rising to cheer him. The Prix Goncourt provides one of those occasions when he is allowed to savour just a whiff of the public acclaim that is won so easily in other professions.

All of Léautaud's friends urged him to think again. Valéry told him what a pity it was that he had not been able to pad out *In Memoriam*. His colleagues at the *Mercure*, though respecting his independence, hinted that a prize-winning author would do the firm no harm. He began to think of new subjects to write about. Of course, they would have to relate to himself. As he said: 'I can only write well, with pleasure and without labour, about what I draw from within myself. If I have to write on subjects outside myself it becomes a chore.'

What was there left for him to do? He had covered his childhood in *Le Petit Ami*. With *In Memoriam* he added the details of his life under Firmin's tyranny. There was one area of experience he had not yet chronicled: that of his youth. He decided to take up the story where *Le Petit Ami* ended and to recount the events of that period, his early attempts to earn a living and his first adventures with women. All this he set down under the title of *Amours*. The main theme is his affair with Jeanne Marié. He treats it with a lightness and an irony which make for agreeable reading and little more.

Amours is the weakest part of the trilogy begun by *Le Petit Ami* and continued by *In Memoriam*. It has not the poignance of the one nor the anguish of the other. Léautaud realised this himself.

'It's a bit my fault,' he told Vallette. 'I didn't have enough talent to tell the story of my *Amours*. Do you know what I'd really need to get me going? My mother's death. What a fine sequel to *In Memoriam* that would be. And then, too, it's a bit my father's fault. If he hadn't stayed quite so dumb perhaps I'd have been able to write another fifty pages and carry off the Prix Goncourt last year, or even this year, with *In Memoriam* alone. That fellow went on doing nothing for me right to the end.'

His new piece appeared in the *Mercure* during the October and November of 1906. Once again Descaves arrived in the office anxious to know whether *Amours* could be expanded into a book of prize-winning length. The answer, again, was no. Why not, suggested Descaves, write some linking material and tack *Amours* onto *In Memoriam*? Half-heartedly, Léautaud thought of doing this and of calling the hybrid *Le Passé indéfini*. He tinkered. He fiddled. He took up his manuscript and put it down again. He found, as he was to find during the rest of his career, that once he had written something he was incapable of changing it. Any alterations he made were usually for the worse and hampered the spontaneity of his style. The Prix Goncourt for 1906 went to that faintly comic pair of literary brethren Jérôme and Jean Tharaud. Their novel, entitled *Dingley, l'illustre écrivain*, had as its central figure an Imperialist writer modelled on Rudyard Kipling. This little curiosity was dedicated to the memory of Cecil Rhodes.

Léautaud had learned the lesson that writing was to bring him neither fame nor money. The act of writing was in itself its own reward. He decided that the pleasure it gave took precedence over everything else. Even the physical aspect pleased him: the squeak of his quill pen scratching on the paper was a delight. Much of the spiritual enjoyment he derived came from spontaneity. This was only achieved when he wrote with passion about something that fully engaged both heart and mind. He concluded that 'anything worthwhile is written straight off, in the almost physical pleasure of writing, in the heat of a mind full of its subject. It seems undeniable to me that what is written with warmth and vivacity is more alive than what is written with hesitation, searching, arrangement, like a child putting together a jigsaw puzzle.'

The writer, in Léautaud's experience, should beware of straining after the boring perfection of such as the 'abominable' Flaubert. His aim should be to write sentences that were tough, dry, crude even. Adjectives should be kept to a minimum. This sort of style had its own harmony, its own beauty. It preserved the vividness of reality.

Yet the writer must be humble. Léautaud himself was only too well aware of his deficiencies. Very little that he wrote ever pleased him completely and he lived in a permanent state of dissatisfaction with his own work. Conscious of all his faults, however, Léautaud argues that the writer must plunge straight ahead into his task and do his best to record his ideas and impressions with the utmost brevity and simplicity. As Stendhal said to Mérimée when the latter expressed qualms about starting to write: 'You're on the field of battle. You must fire!'

There must be no attempt to impress by erudition or facility with words. The writer should try to tell the truth as he sees it. 'Writing,' said Léautaud, 'is telling lies. Perhaps "lies" is too strong a word. Writing means distortion. To hit the target is very rare. You're always either just above or just below it.'

The words the writer uses should be the first that spring to mind. Léautaud never owned a dictionary. Simplicity in writing, he believed, depended on the use of everyday words, and they could say everything. Instinct was the surest guide. Having once written his passage the author should leave it as it stands. The 'elegant variation' disliked by Fowler was just as repugnant to Léautaud. If it was necessary to repeat a word in a sentence, he repeated it and did not waste time looking for a synonym. When a sentence displeased him he crossed it out and wrote another. He took no special credit if a phrase delighted readers. He said that the words just happened to come like that without conscious effort. Indeed, he was not quite sure whether he didn't prefere sentences with obvious flaws, because they sometimes expressed a feeling better.

Revision, he argued, militates against spontaneity. The faults and irregularities must be left in for fear of damaging that quality he prized so much. By an amusing irony he himself gave a prime example of this. From time to time and for various reasons he would return to *Le Petit Ami* and try to 'improve' it. Apart from changing occasional slang phrases and adding new material he never did much except to dilute the flavour and slow down the pace. The same happened with *In Memoriam*. For purposes of re-publication he went over it again, altering, adding, deleting. At the age of seventy-seven, disgusted with the futility of the task, he threw the bulky manuscript into a bonfire.

— VII —

WOMEN . . . AND ANIMALS

'My love for animals grew out of my misanthropy.'
Paul Léautaud

In 1906, the year when *Amours* was published in the *Mercure de France*, Léautaud resolved to devote himself wholly to writing. For twelve years he had been working as a solicitor's clerk after being lucky enough to break away from the series of menial jobs that depressed his spirit and humiliated his independent character. Valéry had suggested a clerical post in some town hall. There were no exams to be taken and no age limit. There would be plenty of time for writing. In the event, Léautaud decided to apply for work in a lawyer's office on the Quai Voltaire. He described himself as a law student and, on the strength of this, was engaged. Eight years later he took a job with a *liquidateur judiciaire* who ran a flourishing practice in winding up estates and administering bankruptcies. Léautaud's own share in the liquidation of a big estate in 1906 was large enough for him to think of giving up regular employment for a time and concentrating on his literary projects.

His years in the legal world had not been wasted. Everything is useful 'copy' for the writer. This is notably so in an area where those two basic preoccupations of human nature, love and money, are heavily involved – Léautaud's first employer specialised in divorce and the second in financial disaster. Léautaud's vicarious experience of marriage, gained from the study of many divorce files, gave him, he commented drily, 'a tremendous admiration for the courage it demands'. His dealings with legatees and creditors brought him endless entertainment in the contemplation of human baseness.

Experience in the Balzacian atmosphere of lawyers' dusty offices gave him a certain tenderness for rogues. Two of them, a pretty young woman and her half-brother, were legatees of an

estate that he wound up. The girl, avid for money, raised huge
sums on her expectations. Her relative eagerly helped her to
spend them, and after five days in Monte Carlo both were
destitute. 'I have rarely met simpler, more cordial, more open-
hearted people than those two equivocal characters,' Léautaud
recalled. 'If I hadn't already known that rascals are often less
hard of heart and head than those we call honest folk, I would
have learned it from them. You'll soon size up an honest man,
as well as the stupidity that's often a part of his character. With
rogues there's more to satisfy your curiosity.'

Another agreeable business acquaintance was a well-known
money-lender who figured in several notorious cases. He knew
the law backwards, could distinguish to a nicety the point at
which prison threatened, and was withal 'a charming man,
distinguished, penetrating in look, cold in speech, prudent, a
true character out of Balzac, even in appearance'. Léautaud
often had dealings with him – had, in fact, to clear up his affairs
when he died – and their conversation went beyond the immediate business matters that occupied them. The money-lender
enjoyed the young man's cynicism and lack of illusion. He paid
him the supreme compliment: 'I like you. You're not like all
those other fools. . . .'

Once he had left his job, however, Léautaud found that
things were not so easy. The work may sometimes have been
boring, the people he had to associate with may not always have
been attractive, but at least at the end of every month there was
a regular salary awaiting him. His small resources began to
vanish rapidly. He was reduced to correcting articles for a
newspaper to help with expenses. The novelist Octave Mirbeau,
a member of the Académie Goncourt who admired his writing,
arranged an interview for him with the politician Aristide
Briand. This brought no result. An approach to Armand
Fallières, then President, through his son whom Léautaud had
worked with, was equally unproductive.

At this time he was living with a mistress called Blanche
Blanc. She was, to date, the twelfth woman whose favours he
was to enjoy, though in the matter of numbers he was never to

rival his insatiable father. Others included Jeanne Marié, his first love, a Thérèse, a Laure, a Denise, an Hélène, the vague figures of a washerwoman and a maid, and chance encounters in the street.

Perhaps the most sympathetic of them was Georgette Crozier, the illegitimate daughter of an actress. She had been brought up in a theatrical orphanage whose director, in all simplicity, entrusted her as a ward to Firmin Léautaud. If the father, uncharacteristically, was to keep his hands off her, the son was not. In 1894, at the age of eighteen, she spent a holiday in the Léautaud household. Very quickly she fell in love with Paul. As usual in such a situation, he treated her not very warmly, absent-mindedly rather. He was still recovering from his affair with Jeanne Marié and had little emotion to spare.

They saw each other off and on during the next few years. Then in 1903 she reappeared to announce that she was leaving to work in England. Was this a subtle attempt to persuade him to ask her to stay? If so, it did not succeed. The indecisiveness that marked his actions was no less evident in matters of the heart. She vanished from his existence, turning up again on rare occasions still hopeful that they might end their days together. Only in 1940, when they were both nearly seventy years old, did she realise that her hope was unfounded. She was a sympathetic and intelligent girl who grew into a dignified and handsome old lady. Her love for him was lifelong, though she was too gentle for bitterness.

By the time Georgette told Léautaud of her departure for England in 1903 he had already been living with Blanche Blanc for six years. Blanche's strong features betokened a force of character and an ability to organise. It was thanks to her management of domestic affairs that he had the time and the peace necessary to write *Le Petit Ami*. They lived at various addresses in Paris, chiefly around the Latin Quarter, and at each one she made a home where everything was arranged so that he could read and write in quiet. She encouraged his ambitions, strove for his comfort and did everything to relieve him of material worries likely to hinder his great purpose in life.

What did she get in return? Little more, it would seem, than the unselfish pleasure of caring for a man she loved. In later years he spoke of her with intense dislike. 'That silly cow Blanche!' he called her. The year before he died he was still fuming about 'that bitch of a creature' and erasing all mention of her from his diary. Such violent hatred suggests a hidden sense of retrospective guilt. He may have realised that this educated young woman who taught him a little English, who borrowed books for him on her subscription to a lending library, and who loved him for a time with all her heart, did not deserve to be treated as indifferently as he had treated her. When he discovered, in 1909, that she had deceived him with another man, he conveniently forgot that he himself had already betrayed her several times with other women.

The fact remains that for seventeen years the sad eyes and wide mouth of Blanche Blanc dominated Léautaud's private life until he parted from her for good in 1914. The third member of their household was a small, white, fluffy cat whom Léautaud called 'Boule'. In time he was to give Boule more love and attention than he could spare for Blanche, and their final break was precipitated by his growing interest in animals.

Meanwhile the practical Blanche decided to set up a boarding-house. She was tired of her lover's indifference and a little jealous of the care he gave to Boule and to the other pets who were beginning to take up more and more room in their home. She went out to Fontenay-aux-Roses, which, despite its attractive name, is a melancholy suburb about fifteen minutes' distance on the mysterious 'Ligne de Sceaux' from the Gare du Luxembourg. Here she found a dilapidated house at 24 Rue Guérard, up on the heights overlooking the railway station.

The house was self-contained and stood in a large garden covering nearly 2,000 square yards. Of its five rooms Blanche chose one for herself and another as the communal dining-room. The remaining three were to be reserved for lodgers. She furnished the place, quite tastefully, with old furniture Léautaud had inherited from his father. Then she prepared to welcome her lodgers.

Unfortunately no one seemed to want to live in Fontenay-aux-Roses, let alone become a paying guest at 24 Rue Guérard. In those days the rail connection went no further than Denfert-Rochereau, which is well within the city limits, and the bus to the centre of Paris only functioned every hour. Once in Fontenay, moreover, there were two very steep hills to climb. Blanche's three rooms stayed empty.

Although Léautaud and Blanche had been living apart for a time, she persuaded him to settle in Fontenay also. He rented an apartment in the Rue Ledru-Rollin, a street further up the hill. When he had to go into Paris he would bring his dogs to spend the day with her and would collect them on his return in the evening. It was a useful arrangement and, probably, the only reason why he agreed to join her in Fontenay.

In the late summer of 1911, not long after she had moved in, Blanche's creditors threatened to distrain since she could neither pay her rent nor meet the debts incurred in furnishing the house. Léautaud came to the rescue. He transferred the house into his name and took on responsibility for the money she owed. He also installed himself and his pets at the address. The garden was perfect for his ever-increasing menagerie. Here there was ample space for them to run about and play to their hearts' content.

Soon, however, Blanche could not help a sense of annoyance at the procession of animals that came regularly into their home. One, two, perhaps even three dogs were acceptable, but when the number of four-legged creatures running about reached double figures her patience was exhausted. He heard her reproaches in silence.

One day she said to him: 'If you bring back another one, I'm going.' That very evening he returned with yet one more stray dog. Next day, true to her word, she left.

Shortly afterwards she came back to collect some belongings she had overlooked.

'Have you brought in another dog since I left?' she inquired, looking around suspiciously.

'It's quite natural,' he replied equably, 'when one animal goes another comes to take its place.' Upon which gallant rejoinder she left for good.

His love of animals had been unexpectedly stimulated by a deed of kindness. Through Blanche he had met a young wife who, deserted by her husband, was struggling to keep herself and her three children. He gave her what little cash he could spare, asked all his friends for help, and provided her with food and clothes. Her plight moved him, for he knew from his own experience what poverty was like. Suddenly, to his great surprise, the unfortunate woman turned on him and attacked him with bitter rebukes. There were painful scenes when she criticised him for only giving her a few coins from time to time. What she really needed, she stormed, was large sums, banknotes. For Léautaud himself a banknote was not all that familiar an object, and his astonishment was intense.

This example of ingratitude confirmed a feeling he had nourished for some time. His dealings with humanity so far had not been such as to inspire in him any fond love of men and women. Animals, on the other hand, were not ungrateful. They did not seek to cheat you or do you down. They gave you their company unselfishly, rejoiced in your presence and were always glad to see you. They did not know that you were old and ugly, that you were considered an eccentric, that the rest of the world saw you as a failure. They, alone of all creatures, offered you disinterested companionship.

He had been especially sensitive to animals since childhood. It was one of the few traits he inherited from his father. Firmin Léautaud kept a pack of dogs in the house, all of them bred from the couple with which he started. In addition he had a pet monkey whose antics fascinated the boy Paul. Dogs, monkey, father, mistresses, son and maid all lived and slept together in malodorous confusion. So he early acquired the habit of sleeping with animals crowded into his bed. Now that he was alone in the house at Fontenay he could bring home as many strays as he liked and share his life with them. He wrote once:

'Last night, with six or eight of my cats sleeping on my bed, I woke up, and, feeling them there, began to stroke them hesitantly. At their purring and the way they fell into contented attitudes, I thought to myself that these dear little creatures, their company and their sweetness, interest me far more than adventures with women.'

As a grown man he adopted his first pet, the kitten Boule, in 1903. He wrote proudly to Valéry: 'For the past few days I've had a 4-week-old cat who takes up a tremendous amount of my time.' When Boule fell ill everything was sacrificed to his well-being. Boule's recovery even took precedence over the exciting possibility of *Le Petit Ami* being awarded the Prix Goncourt. 'If', Léautaud decided, 'fate drove me to choose between my cat Boule's health or the Prix Goncourt, I wouldn't hesitate at all. I'd choose Boule's health.'

Boule was the first of hundreds of cats and dogs Léautaud was to cherish. Once he was on his own at Fontenay the roomy house and spacious gardens quickly became overrun with animals – not only cats and dogs but also, at various periods, a donkey, a goat and a goose. 'Having just one pet alone isn't keeping animals,' he would remark. These inmates of the Rue Guérard were not pedigree beasts or salon darlings but starving strays he found in the streets of Paris. He went out of his way to rescue the ugliest and dirtiest he could find. It was almost a matter of principle with him. Though he approved of the novelist Colette for her sympathy with animals, he did so with the reservation that she limited herself to the pampered and well fed: she was wrong to ignore the hungry and miserable ones abandoned in the streets.

For the sake of his animals he spent without counting the cost. When there was no money left he sold his possessions. When there was nothing to sell he deprived himself of food and heating. He dressed in shabby cast-off garments to save money that could be spent on animals. Feeding, nursing and cajoling his charges took up most of the time he could spare from writing. Each animal was registered under its name and date of arrival. Its death was chronicled with sad punctiliousness, and a coloured map indicated the whereabouts of its grave in the garden. Those he loved best were given a place of honour in the middle. Others were buried farther out.

He had numerous acquaintances among the concierges, the street-sweepers and the small tradesmen in the area that lies around the *Mercure de France* office in the Rue de Condé. He was the familiar of many 'mères aux chats' who abounded there. United by the freemasonry that links animal lovers in spite of their differences on everything else, they hunted the streets and *quais* in search of suffering animals. Among those friends was the picturesque Madame Huot, an ageless female who always wore a dress like the one shown in portraits of Catherine de Médicis: a black corsage ending in a pointed shape over a voluminous skirt that covered her feet. Whenever she passed a herd of mules or horses on their way to the slaughterhouse she would make the sign of the cross. Another of these ladies, when 'placing' a lost dog with a new owner, would, as she expressed it, 'baptise' the animal. Taking its head in her hands and kissing it, she would say: 'There! May God preserve you from vivisectionists and motor-cars.'

Léautaud showed endless patience in soothing the half-wild creatures he found in the streets and on waste ground. Those he could not entice away he called his 'pensionnaires' and visited them regularly with gifts of food. At great expense, both of money and detective work, he tracked down the owners of stray dogs and restored their pets to them. Often he received little thanks for his kindly errand.

The brutalities of the dog pound and the horrors of vivisection distressed him acutely. Passing a Sorbonne laboratory one day he saw dogs being unloaded from a lorry. The sinister purpose for which they were intended was clear. Usually so timid and self-effacing, he found himself suddenly shouting indignant abuse at the attendants.

'Poor defenceless creatures,' he wrote, 'always ready to show their affection, after being taken from the cages in the dog pound they are dragged into dark cellars awaiting the time they're put into the hands of their executioners. I'll never go back on what I've always said: I consider "scientists", the majority of them so third-rate, so restricted, so stupid outside the bounds of their limited knowledge, to be lower than thugs.'

Dogs and cats were not alone in receiving Léautaud's affection. He felt for the whole of the brute creation. One of his greatest worries on moving out of a flat was the thought of the birds he had got into the custom of feeding and of their disappointment when they arrived to find a window-sill bare of food. Luckily the incoming tenant promised to keep up the custom.

Another of his 'adopted' animals was a donkey he used to see each morning on his way to work. Harnessed to a rag-picker's cart, it would be standing outside the Luxembourg railway station as he passed by at ten minutes to nine. On the first occasion of their meeting Léautaud offered some sugar which was very well received. The gesture became a custom. Scarcely was Léautaud out of the station than the donkey would be looking round expectantly towards him. Sugar was produced, a few words of encouragement were whispered in the shaggy ear ('There are so many who are unhappy: a life of work and blows!') and embraces bestowed.

'He's truly a new friend in my life. He certainly takes up more room in it than many other donkeys I know. Each morning, before leaving, I make sure I've the sugar he's expecting. When I miss my train, and on Sundays when I don't go to Paris, I'm upset at the thought of having broken our date and of the disappointment he must be feeling.'

Léautaud was assuredly not one of those animal lovers who give all their attention to the obviously lovable creatures and who ignore less attractive ones. He was ready to defend even the cause of rats. One morning he arrived in the Rue de Condé to find some typographers preparing to entertain themselves with a rat caught in a trap. They had sprinkled it with petrol and were about to set it alight. Léautaud intervened. They

11. Remy de Gourmont (1858–1915), his hideous disfigurement concealed by a kindly shadow

12. Marcel Schwob (1867–1905), like Gourmont an early patron of Léautaud

3. André Gide (1869–1951) as he looked hen he first knew Léautaud

14. Paul Valéry (1871–1945) as the young man Léautaud knew in his twenties

15. Alfred Vallette (1858–1935), a great editor

16. Vallette's wife Rachilde (1862–1953), still autographing her prolific output in old age

laughed at him. He asked a policeman for help. But the policeman, too, was amused by the fun. The rat agonised in flames
before a delighted audience. 'A rat is only a rat, agreed,' wrote
Léautaud. 'But it's no less of a being that lives, has its needs,
habits, anxieties, feeling, physical satisfactions, and, who
knows, a certain intellectual grasp. In short, a living creature.'

Time and again the frail figure of Léautaud was involved in
public scenes that were quite out of keeping with his shy and
peaceful character. Undeterred by the jeers and missiles thrown
down on him by labourers, he would clamber across a building
site to feed a stray cat sheltering under the scaffolding. Once he
saw two big men, typical bullies, harassing a frightened cat.
When their prey had escaped Léautaud caught up with them,
indignant to the verge of tears, and reproached them for their
cruelty. He followed them down the street, a tiny David rebuking two giant Goliaths. At any moment he could have been
punched in the face. Perhaps through a secret feeling of shame,
the two Herculean bullies contented themselves with abuse in
reply.

For the sake of his animals Léautaud was ready to expose
himself to any humiliation and to go against the deepest prompt-
ings of his character. As he looked around him at the creatures
who romped and played through his house and garden, he
thought to himself:

'Poor, poor beings, all of them, the dead and those who remain,
and the dead ones especially. How they've grieved me in their
wretchedness! What pleasure I've had in rescuing them! What
worries they've given me, and how they've delighted me. How
they've spoilt my life and how they've made it beautiful. How
they've driven me to the necessity of putting up with many
hard things and how, as a result, they've made me love them all
the more.'

Sometimes he would come home depressed by money problems, shamed by the straits to which he was reduced in order to
keep his household going. When he reached his gate and the
animals came rushing excitedly to greet him, his tenderness

towards them was all the greater: 'None of it matters because
it's all for your sake and because of you.'

Of course he had his favourites among them. Some of them
he remembered in essays. Dogs, he wrote, are the same as
human beings: they have their differences of character, moods
and ways of showing them. They are gay or reflective, noisy or
silent, reserved or demonstrative. His Alsatian 'Span', one of
those whom he celebrated in a moving little obituary, had been
rescued one winter in the Jardins du Luxembourg where it
shivered and starved in the snow for a fortnight. Span was a
serious and thoughtful creature:

'For Span I was the only person to exist. He was always the
first to follow me. When I arrived there was no question of playing with the other dogs. Wherever I went he was there at my
side, in my room if I was working, in the garden when I took
a stroll, his head always lifted towards me, his eyes never leaving me, and when I left for work each morning he watched me
go with a sort of resignation.'

'Mademoiselle Barbette' was another dog he wrote about.
As a mongrel she wouldn't have fetched more than twenty
francs in a pet shop . . . but she had 'the most beautiful eyes
in the world'. She would sit quietly beside him as he wrote and
reflected, watching him with a look full of things impossible to
express. He would quickly be called to order if he happened to
forget her for a moment. When he had to go away, at his return
she would jump almost a yard in the air for joy. In her youth
she had been very destructive. Often he would find his papers
torn to shreds on the floor. He solved the problem by giving her
the *Ballades* of the poet Paul Fort, twenty or so volumes that
kept Barbette happy for days on end. 'She was delighted. Not a
sheet has survived. Rarely has a work of literature been
appreciated to such an extent.'

Léautaud himself admitted that his love of animals grew at
the same time as his misanthropy. Yet his dislike of humanity
only extended to the members of it who were happy. For those
who were wretched and suffering he had immediate com-

passion. He often lamented the fate of the human wrecks he saw in the street – little old women who, he knew, existed on practically nothing in slum attics, and the men in rags who spent their nights in railway station waiting rooms sleeping on benches. It pained him that he could not afford to give them the money they needed.

He had no great love of policemen who, in those days, often acted as oppressors of the poor. One afternoon, on the Pont des Saints-Pères, he saw two inspectors seize a tramp and hustle him, limping on his wooden leg, into a taxi. 'What harm was the poor fellow doing where he could be seen every day in the same place?' Léautaud wondered. 'God knows what those bullies can have done to him in that taxi, alone with him and capable of everything as they are.'

A similar feeling overcame him when he saw a soldier weighted down with a heavy pack and chained to one of two gendarmes guarding him. What, Léautaud thought to himself, could the poor wretch have done? Despite the fine phrases of the politicians, the brutalities of military life continued.

So long as a person was afflicted by misfortune he could rely on Léautaud's pity. He saw a man and woman in the street, obviously reduced to the very depths of poverty. The man held the hand of a 3-year-old boy swaddled in rags and munching a piece of bread. Léautaud gave the boy two francs. 'I could scarcely speak I was so moved,' he commented. 'I should have given at least a 100-franc note.' This was the action of a man who lived almost on the poverty line himself.

For over forty years until the end of his life he kept open house at Fontenay, welcoming every diseased, undernourished, ill-treated animal he could find. In their company he experienced the solace and the affection he had been deprived of as a child. He arrived at a concept of Christian charity that owed nothing to formal teaching or example. 'A reflection struck me this morning while I was thinking how quickly one grows old,' he noted. 'It's not very pleasant to think that I shall die one day without having been able to change anything of the suffering I've seen around me.'

It is not surprising that even Léon Bloy, a notoriously harsh and loveless Catholic bigot (he was delighted when he heard of so many Protestant heretics being drowned in the *Titanic* disaster) should have been moved to describe Léautaud as 'the Saint Vincent de Paul of poor dogs'. Nor that the Abbé Mugnier, a witty cleric whom Léautaud was to know well, should have told him: 'God will forgive you, Monsieur Léautaud, because you have loved animals.'

━VIII━

A SEAT IN THE STALLS

'When Léautaud liked a play he talked about it. When he didn't, he talked about his cats. He was right.'

Jean Cocteau

In the August of 1907 the poet André-Ferdinand Hérold (he was the grandson of the composer of *Zampa*) gave up his temporary post as drama critic at the *Mercure de France*. Remy de Gourmont had a flash of inspiration. Knowing Léautaud's family connection with the theatre, and sensing that his talent was critical rather than creative, he offered him the vacancy. Léautaud accepted without enthusiasm.

It was agreed that he would contribute reviews for a year. At the end of his term he stood down. Then, in 1911, when Hérold's successor fell ill, he took over again. He remained drama critic on the *Mercure* until 1920, by which time he had succeeded in outraging both his long-suffering editor Vallette and many subscribers to the magazine.

The son of an actor and actress, bred up from his earliest years in a theatrical atmosphere, Léautaud was well qualified to be a drama critic. But if, generally speaking, he delighted in the theatre, he did so with reservations. As with everything else, he was not the man to accept pleasure wholeheartedly. There was always a worm in the bud. His familiarity with life back-stage had long ago destroyed all illusions. He had seen the dashing young hero as a middle-aged man anxious about his make-up. He had heard actors maliciously attacking one of their colleagues as they watched him from the wings, only to shower effusive compliments on him when he came off stage. He had known all the backbiting, all the vicious rivalry that went on behind the scenes. 'How on earth could I have kept my illusions? It would have called for a huge amount of idealism, and idealism has never been my strong point, any more than admiration or respect.'

For various reasons he chose to write under the pseudonym of 'Maurice Boissard'. An assumed personality may have helped him overcome the lack of confidence he felt at having to write to a deadline. A critic on a daily or even a weekly news-paper would have thought the conditions easy, since the *Mercure* was a fortnightly publication, and for a journalist a period of ten days or so in which to deliver copy is an eternity. For Léautaud, who disliked writing to order, it was still far too short. Another more practical reason for anonymity was pru-dence. Through his family background he knew many theatrical folk, and a pseudonym would give him a freedom of comment unhindered by reasons of friendship or acquaintance. Neither, perhaps, had he forgotten that his hero Stendhal was partial to such little deceptions and used no fewer than 171 pseudonyms during his career.

There was a flavour about the Boissard reviews that in-trigued the many readers of the *Mercure* who did not know the secret of the author's identity. A tone of mockery was set, and this, combined with unconstrained savagery and a pitiless refusal to acquiesce in what he considered mediocre, caused Boissard to be regarded with loathing by many and with delight by others. Vallette was too good an editor not to value the originality of his contributor and the way in which his articles helped to make the magazine still better known. He gave Bois-sard his head and stood by him when the inevitable protests began to stream in, even though he often disagreed with his opinions and his manner of expressing them.

In 1920 Vallette resolved that the time had come to pension off the mythical old gentleman. He was often late in delivering his copy, and this held up production of the magazine, a capital sin which deeply offended such a methodical administrator. When Boissard wrote some particularly acidulous comments on Rachilde's literary friends, Vallette made his decision. Hemmed in on one flank by the angry Rachilde and on the other by the nonchalant Léautaud, he decided to end Boissard's reign as tactfully as he was able. As proof, however, that he still valued his contributor despite the troubles he caused, Vallette suggested a new niche for him as the author of articles that would enable him to follow his own caprice rather than be tied down to a set task. What were the articles to be called? Léautaud suggested 'Gazette'. Somebody looked up the word in the dictionary. Among the definitions were: 'Gossip, slander, calumny.' Vallette burst out laughing. 'That's absolutely it. It's very good!' he chuckled. He knew his Léautaud.

Readers of the *Mercure de France* had never been sure of what they were going to find in Boissard's article from one issue to the next. Sometimes he would take them into his confidence and tell them all about the critic's hard lot. In one fortnight, for example, he had heard eleven plays – that is, 25 acts and 116 roles. But still, he assured the reader, 'so long as I'm not forced to listen to a play by M. Catulle Mendès I shan't complain'.

When a play bored him, a not infrequent happening, he would write about something else. One of his articles was entitled 'Ma pièce préférée' – a pun on the word *pièce* which can mean either 'room' or 'play'. The result was a delightful essay on his favourite room, the place where he did his writing surrounded by mementoes of his beloved eighteenth century, on his garden and on his tastes in women. The three plays he was supposed to be reviewing, which, he says, astonished him by the depths of stupidity they plumbed, are briefly mentioned at the end. Sacha Guitry's *Pasteur* outraged and saddened him. What a pity, he wrote, that Sacha, the author of so many charming plays, should dramatise the life of a brutal torturer who performed experiments on living animals. And off he went on his hobby-horse of vivisection.

In drama criticism, as in all other forms of writing, Léautaud demanded complete independence. Even when he reviewed plays written by people he knew well, he often spoke his mind with a painful freedom. Apart from independence he offered no cut-and-dried critical principles. 'I have never been – how shall I say? – a doctrinaire. A play should never bore an audience, that's all; in the same way as with books, the greatest of talents for whoever holds a pen is not to be boring. And the critic, too, has a duty, which is to talk about plays without boring.'

As for actors, his view of their place in the hierarchy of the theatre was not an exalted one. He put them a long way behind the authors who gave them the words to say. The parts they played were often only an excuse for them to deform the creator's purpose and to falsify his inspiration with their vain self-importance and lack of understanding. Léautaud had many stories to illustrate the vanity and obtuseness of actors.

Although he agreed in principle with the idea of a state establishment dedicated to the maintenance of an artistic tradition, he often criticised the Comédie-Française. It served the theatre badly, he argued, by encouraging actors to indulge in stereotyped mannerisms. Rigid training and stylised delivery perverted naturalness. He was ready to concede that the result was often graceful movement and charming gesture, but he pointed out that the overall effect was to produce a deadening monotony and a tendency to empty declamation. Of one production he wrote mockingly: 'You feel that the women could just as well play the men's roles and the men the women's, and except for the costumes it wouldn't make any difference. Such is perfection.'

What Léautaud expected of the actor was versatility. Just as in literature he assessed a book by its quality of uniqueness, so he judged an actor by his ability to make of each role a different creation. If the actor's aim is to imitate life he must logically imitate life's diversity also. No one person is exactly the same as another, and the actor should show this in his acting. Léautaud found what he was looking for, not at the Comédie-Française but in the boulevard theatre. He was able to praise Firmin Gémier, whose period of management at the Odéon during the nineteen twenties was one of the most brilliant that theatre has known. Other pioneers whom Léautaud supported were Lugné-Poe, Antoine and Copeau. He also saluted the debut of Louis Jouvet, to whom he accorded the rarest of tributes by linking his name with that of Molière. There is nothing more difficult than recapturing in print the magic of an actor's performance. Léautaud's description of Jouvet – a good example, incidentally, of his gift for detailed observation – goes a long way towards reconstructing his achievement for the reader.

It might be thought that Léautaud had no time for the comic affectations often associated with the craft of acting. This would be wrong. He himself had a strong vein of the 'cabotin'. Often he was so stirred that he wanted to jump up over the footlights and take a part himself – anything would have done, young suitor, middle-aged lover, disappointed wooer, cuckold, even Alceste, that character who was dearer to him than any other. Often he returned from a Molière play, the *Bourgeois Gentilhomme*, for example, in a haze of pleasure with the Lully tunes running through his mind. At home, standing in front of his mirror, he would hum the well-known melodies to himself, raising now one leg, now the other, as he traced for his own pleasure the movements of the famous dancing lesson he had known by heart since childhood: 'La la la – la la la – la la la . . . la la la la . . . la la. . . .'

He felt a bond with actors. His affection for the obscurer members of the profession and their endearing absurdities was great. The theatre was a domain rich in the 'originals' and eccentrics of every kind whom he collected. Provincial actors he found much more sympathetic than their exalted colleagues at the Comédie-Française. Those old hands who played every sort of part, who took farce and tragedy in their stride yet who never knew glory, were more genuine 'theatre' than the famous much decorated darlings of the Comédie-Française. The Mounet-Sullys and the Coquelins had about them something that didn't seem quite right: they were like writers who'd become millionaires.

He loved clowns as well. Sacha Guitry's play *Deburau* about the great nineteenth-century mime recalled to him a friend of his father. This old Pierrot had acted with Deburau's son. Léautaud remembered him coming to dinner and pausing on the threshold, his actor's face creased up into an air of expectant greed, his features pale, his little brown eyes twinkling with mischief, like something out of a picture by La Tour. 'Ah! Sweeties! More sweeties!' he croaked. Here was the true theatre, a world away from the pompous members of the Comédie-Française who could only play one role, that of them-selves, and who identified with the official honours and modish acclaim that are foreign to real art.

When Léautaud's views on acting are taken into account, it is obvious that his preference will be for plays that actors are able to perform with naturalness and sincerity. Corneille, as to be expected, receives very short shrift. He is, for Léautaud, the incarnation of all that is lifeless and tedious in the theatre. The concept of heroism, the grand manner, the cult of honour, the paraphernalia of Greek and Roman classicism, sent Léautaud into a trance of boredom. The spectacle of Horace rejoicing in the slaughter to come disgusted him, as did Corneille's apologia for cruelty and war. Corneille was a 'Déroulède supérieur', says Léautaud, comparing him with the late nineteenth-century fabricator of jingoistic verse and rodomontade. His 'tragédies civiques' were bombastic and ridiculous. For a long time one of Léautaud's favourite terms of abuse was 'stupid as a Corneille hero'.

Racine fared a little better. Léautaud knew whole passages by heart and often repeated them to himself for the joy of savouring the language. *Andromaque*, which he saw as a psycho-logical comedy, analytical and extremely penetrating in its simple eloquence, was his favourite Racine play. And *Phèdre*? It was a play about the change of life!

It was no coincidence that Shakespeare and Molière, the dramatists who satisfied Léautaud most completely, should both have been practical men of the theatre and fully experienced in every department of their craft. Certainly they had an insight into the realities of daily life that Léautaud prized.

'I often say so,' he wrote, 'in a linking of names for which I have sometimes been reproached: Molière and Shakespeare. There, in my opinion, are the two poles of the theatre. In ex-change for them I'll hand over all the Greeks and all the

Romans, all the Corneilles and all the Racines. When you have lived, and known how to live while observing, and while observing you've been able to remember what you have observed, you cannot not like Molière, who has painted men so truthfully.'

To define what he thinks the true theatre should be, Léautaud goes back to its origins. He sees it as an essentially popular activity quite different from the fashionable and stilted atmosphere of the Comédie-Française. Actors and audience in those far-off days knew each other well. There was a friendly connivance between them. The theatre should remember its humble origins in fairs and sideshows. It should remain, above all, a national theatre. Corneille and Racine, Léautaud argued, were foreign to the Gallic spirit: 'We are not a romantic, solemn, declamatory people. Quite the opposite; sceptical, mocking, balanced.'

Where, then, is the model of what the French national theatre should be? Léautaud finds it in Molière, and also in those examples of French wit and delicacy, Marivaux and Beaumarchais. They give him simplicity and naturalness, lightness and truth. Their plays are sensitive and free of declamation. The language paints men and manners as they really are, for the drama is made up of talk between people and not of extracts from learned or poetic books.

Truth was what Léautaud sought in the theatre. Whether a play was written in verse or prose, it should contain truths that were recognisable as belonging to life. There was, of course, room for fantasy – and Léautaud was quick to praise it when he saw it – but it must be original fantasy that came from within and did not spring from mere preciosity or the wish to appear 'literary'. The theatre is, above all, a place of illusion and reverie. We do not go there to hear sermons on social issues or to have our morals improved. We go in the hope of being amused, excited, stimulated. The test of time has proved Léautaud right. Who except a specialist would today want to see one of Brieux's 'pièces à thèse'? Who, except the connoisseur of 'star' acting, would wish to see Dumas *fils'* lumbering vehicles revived? Bernard Shaw's plays hold the stage not because of their social themes, which are now dead and irrelevant, but because of their immense theatrical vitality. For the same reason Ibsen is still revived while the plays of Voltaire, so fashionable and 'improving' in their time, remain confined to the library.

Of all theatrical forms, Léautaud believed that comedy – the comedy of Molière, that is – was the supreme expression of genius, and that *Le Misanthrope* offered the perfect example. He was profoundly moved by the melancholy truth that lay beneath Molière's outwardly comic manner. 'Comic,' he explained, 'doesn't mean entirely that which gladdens the heart. Comic means that which paints us as we are. Real comedy has its basis in melancholy. The portraits he [Molière] draws of us are rarely flattering. It's no laughing matter when we see ourselves.' And again, when he speaks of Molière's great comic roles: 'They are true, they are certainly ourselves, our own portraits, scarcely exaggerated by theatrical illusion. They make us laugh, of course, but how they touch us, too, with their humanity.'

It is strange that he nowhere mentions Molière's *La Critique de l'école des femmes*. He may neither have read it nor seen it performed. Given his habit of re-reading a very small number of favourite works, it is not unlikely that he knew little about it. This play happens, by chance, to express his own dramatic theories. When Dorante mentions the fashionable snobbery of patrons in expensive seats who think it beneath their dignity to join in the laughter of the pit, he tilts at the affectation that Léautaud himself attacked. How often had he been forced to sit through pretentious dramas which intellectual snobs, mistaking obscurity for profundity, afterwards praised to the skies! This, Molière implies, is not real theatre.

As the argument of *La Critique de l'école des femmes* develops it becomes clear that Molière is enunciating Léautaud's idea: the superiority of comedy to tragedy. It is much easier, says Molière, to talk grandly of lofty feelings, to brave destiny in verse, to insult the gods, than to show how ridiculous men are and to display amusingly on the stage their little faults. There is no difficulty in portraying a hero. You simply follow your imagination, you create from whim and are free to desert reality for the miraculous. But when you describe men you have to work from life. Your portraits must be likenesses, and you have failed if the people you have taken as your models cannot be recognised. It is enough, in a tragedy, to write with good sense and style. This will not do for other types of play, says Molière, and he ends with the famous words: '. . . . c'est une étrange entreprise que celle de faire rire les honnêtes gens.'

Elsewhere in the play he obligingly summarises Léautaud's view of the drama critic's function as well. Says the character Uranie: 'When I go to a play I'm only concerned if the things I see involve me personally; and when I have been well entertained I shan't start wondering whether I'm wrong or whether Aristotle's rules forbade me to laugh.' That, from an unimpeachable source, was Léautaud's opinion too.

FRIENDS: BILLY, APOLLINAIRE, ROUVEYRE, GIDE

'I have friends in the ordinary meaning of the word. But friendship of the sort that makes you happy with another person, that means you'd beggar yourself for him if need be, that you just can't bear the idea of a quarrel separating you from him? I've never known that.'

Paul Léautaud

A few weeks after the venerable figure of 'Maurice Boissard' introduced himself to readers of the *Mercure de France*, Remy de Gourmont invited Léautaud to join the magazine as a full-time employee. He and Vallette were obviously offering their contributor the job out of sympathy. They wanted him to have a living wage that would at the same time enable him to carry on with his writing.

Léautaud couldn't make up his mind. After a year or so of freedom from office routine he did not feel he could settle easily into it again. Independence was sweet to him. He adored strolling about Paris, collecting stray animals, gossiping with the concierges and shopkeepers, and writing a few pages whenever he felt like it. On the other hand there was the brutal fact that he had little or no money.

His old friend Adolphe van Bever added his arguments to those put forward by Gourmont and Vallette. At the *Mercure de France* he would be working at the centre of literary life and not in an ordinary office. There would be plenty of time for him to write what he wanted. Van Bever was himself then employed at the *Mercure* and spoke from experience of the sympathetic atmosphere Vallette created there. At last, after much discussion, Léautaud reluctantly allowed himself to be persuaded. On 2 January 1908, he joined the small *Mercure* staff at a monthly salary of 150 francs, a figure that had been decided on only after lengthy negotiation with Vallette, who drove a hard bargain in this as in all other business matters. There Léautaud was to remain for thirty-three years until 1941.

A little later van Bever left the *Mercure* to strike out as a free-lance. Léautaud moved into his office, a cramped little room on the first floor at 25 Rue de Condé, where gradually bound volumes of past issues began to take up the small space remaining. His duties were not onerous. They included receiving proofs from the printer, sending them on to authors, and checking the corrections made. Every fortnight or so he brought up to date the *Mercure* book catalogue and revised the card index system. Manuscripts sent to the office passed through his hands, and he was also responsible for handing out review copies to contributors as well as sending the *Mercure*'s own publications to other papers for review. Advertisements for the *Mercure* were another of his concerns. Perhaps one of his most important duties was to intercept visitors who wanted to see Vallette and to guard him from those who were likely to waste his time. In fact, Vallette used to acknowledge that this was Léautaud's chief value as an employee, since no ordinary clerk would have been familiar with the niceties of literary reputation or with the problem of how to handle according to their merit the authors who for various reasons wished to call on the editor of the *Mercure*.

On Léautaud's door hung a notice bearing the words: 'Manuscrits, Publicité.' His chair, Second Empire style, was so low that the desk was at a level with his chin. He wrote with his nose close to the paper, his quill pen tracing the small, crabbed handwriting with the shrill squeak that was music to his ear. Piles of books surrounded him, and proofs and invoices and lists of subscribers' addresses. On the shelves lay bundles of dusty manuscripts.

Visitors were confronted with a glower. Then, in an elaborate display of politeness, he would say: 'Je vous salue, Monsieur', or, with an extra glint: 'Je vous salue, Madame.' His voice was deep and he relished every syllable, as if turning the words over and savouring them on the tongue before delivering them. He would rise to his feet and shoot his cuffs with a theatrical flourish, stretching himself to the full extent of his small stature. There was a wryly appraising look in his eye. His spectacles were of a sort worn by few other people. They had rusty iron frames and slipped half-way down his nose. His ruffled hair was turning into a dirty shade of white. Deep ravines hollowed his cheeks. His tie, often little more than a black bootlace, straggled untidily at his neck. He wore a jacket of cheap, rough material and canvas trousers that corkscrewed baggily round the legs. A creation by Balzac, you would have thought, an actor down on his luck, an unfrocked priest, an impecunious bank clerk or an unsuccessful poet.

Often he was not to be found in his office. An invalid dog might have kept him at Fontenay and delayed his arrival by several hours. After lunch he sometimes did not return to his desk until four in the afternoon, having had urgent business in the nearby Jardins du Luxembourg where a stray, half-wild cat had been defying his kindly attempts to feed it. In the corner of the room lay the capacious bag, stained and crumpled, in which he carried the odd scraps he kept for strays. Occasionally chunks of mildewed bread were laid out to dry. The atmosphere was redolent of old books and animals. Vallette, at least to begin with, suffered in silence the unpunctual habits of his strange employee, and only objected mildly to the presence of food scraps. When, however, Léautaud asked him for a rise in later years, his reply would show that he had not overlooked the matter of eccentric time-keeping. He would also point out, coldly, that only two members of a publisher's office could expect to be well paid. These were the accountant and the production manager.

Léautaud soon became a well-known figure in the Latin Quarter streets that surrounded the Rue de Condé office. Each day his route led him from the Gare du Luxembourg across the Boulevard Saint-Michel, down the Rue de Médicis, through the Place de l'Odéon and its theatrical memories, and finally by way of the Rue Crébillon to the *Mercure* headquarters. In the street he wore a shapeless hat faded by time and weather, a few whisps of bedraggled hair peeping out from underneath. His bag of scraps in one hand, a dandy's walking-stick in the other, he picked his way along the pavement, eyes alert behind the rusty spectacles for any animal that might be needing help. In winter he twisted a moth-eaten woollen scarf round his neck and, for extra warmth, donned two coats of different sizes, one on top of the other, the sleeves hanging forlornly. One evening, at a smart Sacha Guitry first night, a friend jokingly observed that he and Léautaud were probably the poorest people in the audience. 'Very likely,' said Léautaud, 'but you can't deny that I'm wearing two coats. Find me someone else here who can boast as many.'

The friend to whom Léautaud made this remark was André Billy, then a young and ambitious journalist. Billy had arrived in Paris from his native Picardy at the age of twenty-one determined to make a name for himself in literature. He met Léautaud in 1908, by which time he was twenty-six and had already published his first novel. When he died in 1971 at the age of eighty-nine he was a celebrated figure, *doyen* of the Académie Goncourt, friend of every important French writer over nearly three-quarters of a century, and the author of thousands of articles and dozens of novels, biographies and memoirs. Widowed in old age and deprived of the companion who had been so much a part of his existence, he threw himself with even greater energy into the punishing routine of work he always set himself. It was the only solace left to him. Right up to the end of his life, despite the pain of arterio-sclerosis and the hindrance of acute deafness, he went on writing his weekly article for the *Figaro littéraire*, preparing his book reviews and planning new biographies. For the prospect of death appalled him.

He had been trained for the priesthood at the Jesuit college of Amiens. Soon after leaving he went through a spiritual crisis and lost his faith. His dilemma was that he never found anything to replace it, and his novels are a perpetual exploration of a question to which he knew he could not supply an answer. His fiction does not so much attempt to depict character and tell a story – though this he does with professional skill – as to resolve the enigma of belief. The shadow of his Jesuit formation was inescapable and it haunted him all the years of his life. Each of his novels approached the subject of faith in a spirit of resigned hope. Each of them, however expertly the subtleties of theological argument were deployed, was forced to leave the discussion unfinished. Billy could find no solution and his anguish remained unappeased. In the nineteen-fifties he made the personal acquaintance of Teilhard de Chardin, whose writings seemed to hold out a glimmer of hope. He resolved to write a biography of the Jesuit philosopher that would communicate his own feelings of joyful discovery. Over the years the documents and files mounted up. The book was never completed.

At the age of seventy he was asked to give his response to Marcel Proust's famous questionnaire. What, said the first question, is for you the depth of misery? Philosophically speaking, replied Billy, it is man's existence here below. What would be your greatest misfortune? said another question. To relive my youth, was the answer. The last question asked him what his motto was. 'Pretend to believe that life is worth living,' came the bleak reply. In his eighties he looked back on his life, which had been a successful one by any criterion, and dismissed it as of no account. His enviable reputation, his distinguished membership of the Académie Goncourt, his position as one of France's leading men of letters, were ashes in his mouth. They counted for nothing beside the approach of death and the terrifying prospect it implied.

But when Léautaud first knew him Billy was full of youthful optimism that overlaid his religious doubts and kept them for a time out of sight. Léautaud was ten years older and took an almost paternal interest in him. He found him sympathetic, without pose or vanity, frank, lively and gay. It was a pleasure to talk with a man who loved literature so much. Léautaud, whose own immediate youth was past, rediscovered something of it in his junior. One evening after the theatre they sat in a café and looked up the Avenue de l'Opéra, a dazzling perspective of light and bustle that thrilled Billy. His enthusiasm amused

Léautaud, the hardened Parisian, and he teased him by comparing him with Rastignac, Balzac's ambitious hero who, at the
end of *Le Père Goriot*, challenges Paris to a duel of wits. The
two friends often joked together at the comparison.

Though Billy may not have seen himself as a Rastignac, he
had his ambitions no less. He sought fame, women, and the
trappings of a successful career. He was ready to work hard
and long to achieve these things. It puzzled him that Léautaud,
who obviously had talent, was not prepared to do the same.
Léautaud, for his part, was horrified by the life Billy led. His
industry was amazing. Every day he wrote an article of one
sort or another. Every morning there was a book for him to
read and review. Lost in a whirlpool of activity he became
absent-minded to the extent that once, at the barber's, he stood
by the cashier waiting for his change, unaware that he had not
even paid the bill.

He had to be a diplomatist as well as a writer. Not only were
editors to be humoured but also the opinions of advertisers had
to be respected. One day, stuck for a subject, he wrote about
banking after a desperate search for ideas. At the last minute
his editor told him to scrap the article because it might offend
banks who took large advertisement spaces in the paper. Billy
then had to dictate a hastily improvised article by telephone.

This sort of thing shocked Léautaud. He did not envy in the
slightest the large sums of money Billy earned. They were no
compensation for the sacrifice of independence. Privately Léautaud believed that people like Billy were no more writers than
hired servants. It was pleasant to make money, but under such
conditions there was no true freedom, no opportunity for the
honest self-expression that should be the aim of writing, and no
scope for the luxury of saying what one really thought.

Billy chuckled at Léautaud's scruples. 'When you've done
this job for some time,' he said, 'you're ready and able to write
about anything – and you do, too!'

Yet Billy was not an arriviste. He enjoyed everything he did.
When Léautaud asked him if he were never bored by the great
quantities of novels he had to review, Billy was surprised at the

question. He set aside three hours each evening for reading them. Even cutting the pages was a joy to him. The action of slipping a well-sharpened ivory-handled paper knife between the pages, especially the fine textures of a de luxe edition, gave him a sort of physical pleasure which he compared with that of possessing a woman. So much did he prize this enjoyment that he insisted on cutting not only the pages of his own books but also of those his wife read.

As a literary journalist Billy was instructive and delightful to read. He was a keen-eyed chronicler and memorialist of the French literary scene from 1903 to 1971. He observed it with gusto. French literature he saw as a great adventure, a huge novel in episodes where the main characters were the great authors and the supporting players were the minor writers whose function was to throw into relief the work of the leaders. There could, accordingly, be no writer or work that was entirely negligible. Billy pointed to theologians who claimed that there was no such thing as damned souls because, whatever men may be, they all take part in God's creative activity. Just so, he argued, there were no damned souls in literature since all writers participated, directly or indirectly, in exalting the mind. When all was said and done, failures were as useful as successes, and even, sometimes, more deserving of merit. In this belief he was able to write just as interestingly on Stanislas de Guaïta, that obscure *fin-de-siècle* author who was the subject of his last biography written at the age of eighty-seven, as on Balzac.

Billy's enjoyment of the literary spectacle as a human drama makes for sharp writing and crisp journalism. There is no doubt that he was a superlative journalist. While Léautaud praised his clarity, his quick reactions, his gift of observation, he felt that Billy wrote too fast, that reflection and revision would have improved his work. This, however, is a small price to pay for his living portrait of, for example, Balzac. Here the turmoil of that prodigious existence is re-created and the boisterous hero dominates as in real life. Another of Billy's favourites was Sainte-Beuve, and his two-volume biography once again evokes the subject as an actual presence. He had a particular admiration for the great critic and always made a point of defending him whenever, as is frequent these days, he came under attack. The Goncourts, too, he presented with engaging briskness. He was just as good on Mérimeé and Stendhal. Although the nineteenth century was his chosen province, on the occasions when he strayed outside it, as with Diderot, he showed the same acuteness. His dozen or so biographies are not works of pure scholarship. They owe their value to his knack of making happy discoveries, his practical experience as novelist and critic, and above all his knowledge of men and women.

For many years, in fact until the end of Léautaud's life, Billy remained a close friend. Clouds sometimes overcast their friendship and there were disagreements, as was inevitable with such an unpredictable character as Léautaud. Billy was tolerant and understanding. He once even gave to Léautaud an overcoat inherited from an uncle which was too small for him. Léautaud was delighted and wore it frequently. He wrote Billy long, chatty letters over the period of their association, letters that reveal an esteem and a respect he felt for few people. Since he liked writing for writing's sake, he would often spend a whole evening corresponding with Billy. For Billy, writing was work. His busy career did not leave him much time for social letters, and his replies were scribbled in hasty moments snatched from other more important tasks.

Billy was tall and commanding. He had a habit of looking you up and down and spoke with a loud, barking voice, as if he were a preacher in some lofty pulpit rebuking a sinful congregation. Perhaps this was a remnant of the Jesuit influence. Soon, when you came to know him, you realised that the gruff exterior hid a sensitivity and a kindliness which made him the gentlest of men. His gift for friendship won him the intimacy of Guillaume Apollinaire, with whom he collaborated on a film script. Apollinaire's untimely death at the age of thirty-eight filled him with a sorrow that never left him. More than fifty years later the tears still came to his eyes when he told the story of Guillaume's death. 'Sauvez-moi, docteur, sauvez-moi! J'ai tant à donner. . . ,' he would end, repeating Apollinaire's last words with a catch in his voice.

Léautaud met Apollinaire in the same year as he made the acquaintance of Billy. At one of Rachilde's 'Tuesdays' he noticed a striking face which, anticipating Picasso's caricature, he described as a 'physionomie en cul de poule'. He started talking to the owner of these unusual features. 'Look,' said Apollinaire, placing his index finger to his chin and standing sideways, 'I've got Caesar's profile.' The remark both flabbergasted and enchanted Léautaud.

A month or so afterwards – he was still living in Paris – Léautaud took three of his dogs for their usual evening stroll in the Boulevard Montparnasse. He saw, coming towards him, the Caesarean profile of Apollinaire. They fell into a conversation that lasted an hour and a half while they walked back and forth many times between the Boulevard Raspail and the Port-Royal station, so absorbing was their talk.

'Why,' said Léautaud, 'don't you send some poetry to the *Mercure* ?'

'I did,' answered Apollinaire, 'a long time ago, but I've heard nothing since.'

Next morning Léautaud arrived at the office and went straight to the pigeon-hole where manuscripts sent in by would-be contributors were kept. There he put his hand on 'La Chanson du mal-aimé'. He read it and was, in his own words, 'transported'. Immediately he hurried over to Vallette: 'Look, Monsieur Vallette, here's some remarkable poetry by Apollinaire.' Without hesitation Vallette replied: 'Put it in with the accepted manuscripts.' This explains why, when 'La Chanson du mal-aimé' appeared in *Alcools*, it was dedicated to Paul Léautaud.

The copy of *Alcools* that Apollinaire gave to his friend bears the inscription: 'A Paul Léautaud poète son ami Guillaume Apollinaire.' Since by then Léautaud had not written poetry for many years, this suggests a subtle compliment on his perception in being the first to recognise the merit of 'La Chanson du mal-aimé.' Another acknowledgement, this time a humorous one, appears in *Les Mamelles de Tirésias*. At one point in Act II of this joyous buffoonery, a banner is paraded across the stage with the headline: 'Monsieur Léaut . . . d's dogs on strike.'

Léautaud was captivated by Apollinaire's genial personality. When he learned that the poet was fond of animals to the extent of keeping three dogs and a monkey at home, his approval was complete. (Strangely enough he never mentions the charming *Bestiaire*, which, one feels, would have appealed to him.) Closer acquaintance confirmed his favourable impression.

Apollinaire invited him to dinner. The hostess was the painter Marie Laurencin, that wilful and whimsical mistress who was to lead 'pauvre Guillaume' such a dance. Though Léautaud was not by nature sociable he enjoyed the occasion. The poet, he thought, had a curious personality, mysterious even. He decided that he liked him very much. Guillaume Wladimir Alexandre Apollinaire de Kostrowitzky, alias Apollinaire, had an equivocal air and sometimes gave the impression of being an adventurer. Intelligent, secretive, very cosmopolitan, he was a delver into rare books and a collector with a bower-bird instinct for arcane knowledge. 'That's what you put your books together with,' Léautaud afterwards accused him when he brought out *L' Hérésiarque*, a notably exotic work. Apollinaire denied the charge indignantly.

That evening at dinner Apollinaire, collarless and in shirtsleeves, helped Marie Laurencin with the cooking. When the dishes were ready he brought them to the table and afterwards cleared them away. Such unaffectedness pleased Léautaud. He liked Apollinaire both as a man and as a poet. Apollinaire was also a colleague, since he had started to contribute a regular feature, 'La Vie anecdotique', to the *Mercure de France*. This was another of Vallette's inspirations. 'La Vie anecdotique' provided the flavour of novelty which Jean de Tinan had supplied in his time, and which Vallette was anxious to revive.

'What an unusual character,' Léautaud thought. 'You feel he's full of mysteries.' Apollinaire satisfied his taste for the eccentric. At the same time he wrote in a way that was inimitable. In their conversations together Léautaud confessed that what prevented him from writing more was his lack of confidence in himself, his uncertainty as to whether his subject matter would be of interest. He was startled when Apollinaire stoutly replied: 'Ah, no! I never feel that, not a bit of it.'

When the war came in 1914 Apollinaire was urged by a foreigner's love of his adopted country to join the army. Next year he wrote to Léautaud from barracks: 'I wish you a Happy New Year, my dear Léautaud. You've always shown me so much friendship that I'd reproach myself for not wishing you in these troubled times all the happiness you deserve for 1915.' He gave news of his life in the army and, knowing the topic would interest Léautaud, told how one of his duties was caring for the horses. As a discreet afterthought he mentioned that he was short of money.

Léautaud himself was in dire straits at the time. The *Mercure* had shut down and he had to exist on a severely reduced salary of fifty francs a month. He was pleased to hear of Apollinaire's good spirits and replied: 'I'm only sorry to know that you're probably deprived of many things. I'm enclosing in my letter a small, very very small banknote. Don't thank me. I'm ashamed at doing so little in view of the great and true friendly feelings I have for you. Just tell me, in a note, if you've received it, simply so that I shall know.'

Apollinaire's death in 1918 was a shattering blow. Léautaud could not believe that this creature of fantasy, compact of mischief and liveliness, would never intrigue him again with his exuberant sallies and his roars of laughter. The combined effects of a head wound and Spanish flu had carried off 'a friend whom I adored as man and writer'.

A meeting soon afterwards with Apollinaire's mother, the formidable Madame de Kostrowitzky, showed that the poet had inherited from her his taste for the bizarre. She called at the *Mercure* to ask for copies of her son's books. Not a line of them had she ever read. Indeed, she did not know they existed and was unaware of his reputation. Léautaud did his best to convince her that Guillaume was held to be a fine poet and was much admired by good judges. She was astonished. Then she added proudly: 'My other son is a writer, too. He writes financial articles in a New York newspaper.'

In 1943, long after Apollinaire's death, his widow spoke of a notebook in which her husband had written his private opinions about people. She was unwilling to publish it or even to show it to anyone since many of those concerned were still alive. Was it here that Apollinaire, as a malicious acquaintance told Léautaud, had described him as a 'crapaud' (toad)? Perhaps Apollinaire has been upset by Léautaud's tactless witticism about the notorious episode when he was kept in the Santé prison on suspicion of having stolen the *Mona Lisa* from the Louvre. 'Eh! bien, cela va, la Santé?' Léautaud had said, making a clumsy pun on the double meaning of 'santé'. Though Léautaud always insisted that Apollinaire laughed heartily at the jest, the misadventure had caused him deep distress and he may not have appreciated such heavy jocularity.

At a time when Léautaud had long since been disabused of his early poetic enthusiasms, he was ready to make an exception for Apollinaire. 'Mallarmé is nothing beside him,' he wrote. 'Valéry even more so.' When Léautaud tried to define the quality of Apollinaire he had to admit that he was a minor poet, not a great one. He possessed charm, feeling, picturesqueness and evocative gifts, but he was limited in his range. The great poet was one who surveyed wide landscapes and dreamed universal dreams, one in whom every man could find himself. 'The "great" poet is Lamartine, who interests me not at all, or Hugo, whom I find extremely distasteful: the perfect combination of man and work is perhaps Verlaine in certain aspects.'

There was also something of the junk merchant in Apollinaire, the dealer in pretty but imitation gems. His poetry seemed to Léautaud a baroque collection of unusual objects, some pure and others false. Did he, as Marie Laurencin firmly believed, have Jewish blood? This, Léautaud thought, might account for the assimilations and borrowings in his prose, and, in his verse, for the gipsy element.

Yet Léautaud never forgot his first emotion on reading 'La Chanson du mal-aimé'. Each time he looked at it again he was conquered afresh by its ambiguous magic and its hint of mystery, often conveyed in the simplest of words. He knew it by heart and could recite it with intense feeling.

Apollinaire, he decided, had all the gifts of the born poet: fantasy, imagination and spontaneity. This 'cher ami que je regretterai toujours' represented the perfect literary conjunction: the man who expressed himself faithfully in his work. Léautaud's praise for Apollinaire would seem commonplace today when we know the immense growth in the poet's reputation and the elaborate scholarship his poetry has attracted. It must be remembered that Léautaud appreciated him at a time when Apollinaire, for the general public, was an obscure and ridiculous writer not worth reading. The novelist Georges Duhamel expressed the conventional opinion when, in his *Mercure* review of *Alcools*, he attacked it as second-hand rubbish. Thirty-five years later, in 1948, Léautaud noted with amusement that Duhamel was flattered to accept the chairmanship of a committee formed to honour the memory of Apollinaire.

Each November, on the anniversary of Apollinaire's death, a small group of friends used to meet at his grave in Père Lachaise cemetery. Billy would be there, so would the poet André Salmon, and the small circle of admirers would include Léautaud as well. He made a point of attending the little ceremony. Until the time when the fog and chill of the season became too much for him in old age, he was usually there at the tomb, exchanging memories with acquaintances, and afterwards, in some warm café, looking round the group and remarking the gaps caused by death and the passing years among those who had known Guillaume.

It is significant that Apollinaire was among the few friends with whom Léautaud never quarrelled. The year 1908, which introduced him to Apollinaire and Billy, also brought into his life the awkward personality of André Rouveyre, a man who had what amounted to a genius for provoking disharmony wherever he went. It was, again, at one of Rachilde's Tuesday gatherings that Léautaud made his acquaintance. Rouveyre had been introduced to the *Mercure* circle by Gourmont, whose protégé he was at the time.

Gourmont often took up promising writers and artists. His instinct for talent rarely went astray. Léautaud was curious to see what he described as 'Gourmont's latest great man'. He was not disappointed. Behind Rouveyre's façade of frivolity and cynicism he detected evidence of hidden depths. Rouveyre was intelligent, impatient of convention and healthily disrespectful.

Rouveyre was seven years younger than Léautaud. Against the wish of his father, an art publisher and antiquarian bookseller, he had enrolled at the École des Beaux-Arts. There he met Rouault, Matisse and Marquet, and led a typical art student's life. He also began contributing sketches of boulevard personalities to illustrated papers. In 1902 he became seriously ill and spat blood. He was told he would not survive. He recovered, but the experience left its mark on him. The caricatures he had begun to specialise in took on a new note of ferocity.

Three years later he married a woman twelve years his senior. She had much in her favour: she was an orphan who possessed a substantial fortune derived from coalmines in northern France. Rouveyre was able to save his father's declining business and support him for the rest of his days. He also inaugurated a domestic arrangement that suited him very well. Having set up his wife and daughters in a house some way outside Paris, he then took a room in the centre where he could work on his own and lead the Bohemian existence of his choice.

His caricatures attracted the attention of Gourmont, who published some of them in the *Mercure* and later wrote prefaces to three of Rouveyre's collections when they were issued as albums. After the initial shock, the victims seemed to take a masochistic pleasure in having been seen through his distorting vision. Apollinaire described his technique of scribbling a few strokes in his sketchbook while chatting with his subject and apologising for not revealing what he had drawn. Then, at leisure, he redrew the sketch ten, twenty times, always trying to avoid any resemblance between it and the model. Sometimes he took more than a year in the process. When a drawing seemed most removed from reality, he was content. The cruelty of the method, Apollinaire remarked, produced several surprising portraits which, though far from actuality, were astonishingly close to truth.

Struck by the similarity between Léautaud's face and a La Tour picture, Rouveyre did a sketch of him. It was the first of the half-dozen or so drawings he was to make of Léautaud at various times. Léautaud was puzzled by it: 'It's certainly me, it looks like me, you can't deny, but what a curious distortion.' He hung it in his office, where its harsh nervous lines contrasted with the soft and flattering portrait of him that Marie Laurencin had drawn in her most feminine manner.

In his literary criticism, as in his drawing, Rouveyre was pitiless and abusive. He had little respect for those he termed 'the leading literary puppets of the day'. His attacks on Valéry and others sometimes degenerated into offensiveness. There is a hint of shrill fury about Rouveyre that makes one uneasy. He had no reason to be discontented with life. His circumstances were easy, he had a reputation as an artist, and his wife, the provider of his material comfort, acquiesced with grace in the domestic arrangement he imposed upon her. He seemed to take a sadistic pleasure in effacing her and his two daughters from his existence, and he was ready, Léautaud noticed, to trample on his closest friend for the sake of the perverse enjoyment it gave him. It is possible that he hungered after literary fame and was disappointed when he found that his books, despite the laborious work he put into them, failed to gain attention. It was easier for him to win notoriety through attacks on established figures – though this may be too simple an explanation of his complicated personality.

For some people, however, Rouveyre was a man with few faults. Among those who had affection for him was Nathalie

Barney, the 'Amazone' to whom Gourmont poured out his unrequited love. She described Rouveyre as 'the most generous of men'. Yet his gift for caricature, which seized on a woman's beauty and deliberately twisted it into ugliness, showed an ingratitude towards life. Might it not be, she suggested, the result of a timorous defence against becoming a victim himself?

Such a diagnosis could serve to reconcile the confused elements of hypocrisy and frankness, affectation and sincerity, which made up the puzzling tangle. This fear of being a victim could have inspired Rouveyre's attacks on other people. He was anxious to get his blow in first because he was insecure and lacked confidence in his own powers. This would explain the sometimes unbalanced and gratuitous fury of his vendettas against Gide and Valéry. They were writers who, however dissatisfied they may privately have been with their work, knew that they had at least achieved something worthwhile. They did not need to declare war on others. Rouveyre lacked this consolation, since he found writing difficult and was unsure of himself. Perhaps his sense of inferiority made him believe that more experienced colleagues would scorn his efforts. The best method of defence was therefore attack.

The fear of being a victim was also to be found in Léautaud, though it expressed itself in a contemptuous indifference rather than in the belligerent form it took with Rouveyre. Léautaud had been treated so harshly as a child that ever afterwards his relationships with men and women were governed by distrust and suspicion. Few indeed were those who penetrated the barrier he put between himself and the rest of the world. Here was a common identity with Rouveyre.

For nearly fifty years the uneasy acquaintance endured. Rouveyre could be generous, embarrassingly so. At other times he was sullen and malicious. In the end, as we shall see later, they were separated by an unforgiving quarrel. The innocent third party to be involved was André Gide. Long before the final break came, Rouveyre had written a book called *Le Reclus et le retors*, a dual study of Gourmont and Gide. Gourmont

was the 'reclus' and Gide the 'retors'. In a moment of exaspera-
tion with Rouveyre's devious ways, Léautaud once said to him:
'Le retors, c'est vous.'

Devious Gide may have been too, though he was more
stylish than Rouveyre. As far back as 1897 Léautaud had been
an admirer of his work, though he did not specify which of
Gide's early publications impressed him. Personal acquaintance
does not seem to have come until 1903, the year of *Le Petit Ami*.
Gide's opinion of the book was not without reservations, but
Valéry's enthusiasm for it persuaded him to revise his judgement. From then onwards he gave Léautaud both sympathy
and encouragement. In 1908 a friend told Léautaud that Gide
ranked him highly among young writers of the day.

A mutual acquaintance was Charles Louis-Philippe, the
author of *Bubu de Montparnasse*, who died at the early age of
thirty-five. They both were present at the deathbed and the
funeral afterwards. Gide wrote in his journal: 'Léautaud, very
pale and with a very black beard, gulps down his emotion.'
Later, walking through a street fair, Gide came across the
bizarre figure of a fortune-teller: 'He was sitting in profile before an enormous Latin book propped up in front of him (I
couldn't see exactly what the title was – but only that it was in
Latin); he wore spectacles and looked the very image of
Léautaud.'

Gide often called on Léautaud at the *Mercure* and looked
forward to his visits as pleasurable occasions. Frequently he
borrowed cigarettes and never offered any. His conversation
was eternally punctuated by a nervous sniff as, in his nasal
voice, he complained about the hangers-on who crowded about
him elsewhere. Here, in the dusty clutter of Léautaud's room,
he felt he could relax, could drop the mask of the public figure
he was rapidly becoming, and could talk frankly of private
matters.

They were both, to a certain extent, refugees from the brilliance of Valéry. Gide confided in Léautaud the shattering
effect Valéry used to have on him. After hearing his conversation, Gide said, he was overwhelmed and lost all confidence in

himself. He would look with despair at what he had written. Sometimes he needed a week, a fortnight, to recover. Now he had learned to resist Valéry's masterly paradoxes, though for a long time exposure to them had plunged him into discouragement, intellectual paralysis even.

This was a feeling Léautaud had often experienced. It was not surprising that he should have been more at ease with Gide than with Valéry. Whereas Valéry inhabited the domain of pure intellect, Gide was concerned with problems of a more human nature. The social, political and sexual questions he discussed in his books were ones that Léautaud could appreciate, even though he may not always have agreed with the solutions proposed.

Gide's relationship with Léautaud had few of the ambiguitites that were to arise from the latter's association with Valéry. He regarded Léautaud with a mixture of respect and amusement. Once he called him 'le misanthrope généreux'. Another of his descriptions of him was 'l'homme du bon sens'. He was intrigued by Léautaud's appearance, by the courtly manner that contrasted so oddly with the dishevelled clothes, and by the face which he could not help comparing, as did so many people, with a La Tour pastel. Léautaud was an anachronism, a throwback to the Encyclopédistes of the eighteenth century. Gide delighted in his malice and his tenderness, his gusts of sarcasm or of generous indignation, his disrespect for convention and even his blind spots. He approached him with caution: 'I think that after a time I shall succeed in being perfectly natural with him,' wrote Gide. 'But I am still too careful to agree in everything he says, the better to put him at his ease and to obtain those great sonorous bursts of laughter which, as he led me to understand, do not proceed from a very joyful heart.'

Léautaud, Gide found, was as strict as an Academician in his defence of the purity of the French language. Gide noted his annoyance at misuse of the verb 'réaliser', which over the past few years has increasingly taken on the Anglo-Saxon meaning. A young lady who came to the *Mercure* office to consult files of past issues remarked innocently: 'Je n'aurais jamais réalisé que cela pût tenir autant de place.' 'Mademoiselle,' observed Léautaud icily, 'si vous vouliez bien parler français.'

As Léautaud admitted, Gide was unfailingly kind and helpful towards him. Gide attempted to enlist him as a contributor to the *Nouvelle Revue Française*, a rival magazine which he, Gide, supported in preference to the *Mercure*, where Gourmont's influence was too marked for his taste. At various times he offered to serialise Léautaud's writings, to publish his drama criticism under the NRF imprint and to send him books for review. As we shall see later, he finally succeeded in engaging Léautaud as theatre critic when 'Maurice Boissard' ceased to reign at the *Mercure*.

Gide's friendly feeling increased when Léautaud wrote what he called 'that *excellent* analysis of my *Porte étroite*' for the *Mercure* catalogue of new books in 1909. In one of his many digressions as 'Maurice Boissard', Léautaud had happened to attack Rousseau and Chateaubriand. What did they amount to, he inquired, compared with the sensitiveness, the superior intelligence, the spontaneity, the freedom of that admirable writer 'whom I shall not name and who has given me such intense pleasures that I would prefer to be alone in knowing him'. Gide immediately took this sentence to refer to himself and was confirmed in the opinion by others. He was profuse in his gratitude to Léautaud, who, much embarrassed, did not dare enlighten him by confessing that he had implied a reference to Stendhal. Fortunately Gide was allowed to continue in his happy illusion.

Though Léautaud recognised that Gide's writings were not wholly to his taste, he saw much there to praise. Gide fulfilled one of his basic demands: that a writer be true to himself. Gide also met another of Léautaud's requirements by insisting on his freedom to speak the truth as he saw it, despite the controversy he invited. This was shown in the case of *Corydon*, a plea for homosexuality which caused grave offence in the moral climate of the time. Léautaud told him that it showed 'great courage, great independence of mind'. In fact, his respect for Gide dated

17. Apollinaire, André Billy and Marie Laurencin

18. Léautaud, André Billy and André Rouveyre outside Billy's home at Barbizon

19. A snapshot of Valéry and Léautaud at La Vallée-aux-Loups in the nineteen-thirties

20. Léautaud writing with the famous quill pen in his office at the *Mercure de France*

21. 'Photograph me if you like, but don't forget to retouch it!'

from the time when the latter deliberately sold books bearing laudatory inscriptions from former friends who had denounced him for his homosexuality. The frankness of *Corydon* pleased Léautaud, and so did Gide's readiness to break with his intimate circle and to put a barrier between himself and Establishment honours.

Gide's nonconformist side appealed to Léautaud. He thought it commendable that the author of *Voyage au Congo* should have put aside his usual work and pleasures as a writer to campaign in the face of powerful interests on behalf of African natives under French colonial rule, and have knowingly stored up for himself all sorts of trouble. It was, presumably, the same impulse that led Gide to espouse Communism and the new Soviet Russia. Here Léautaud could not follow him. He was shocked by the naivety that landed Gide in such an embarrassing situation and brought about the volte-face of *Retour de l'URSS*. Gide's remark that he was prepared to give his life for the success of the new government appalled Léautaud. 'What childishness, what softness,' he protested. He did not hesitate to tell him so, and Gide, with his usual courtesy, heard him out uncomplainingly.

This was not the only occasion when Léautaud detected a tendency to humbug in him. He was irritated by Gide's affectation in complaining about his bad luck at having been born rich. His private income, lamented Gide, denied him the privilege of earning a living as did the majority of people. Such remarks aroused Léautaud's scorn. He was also repelled by Gide's feline dislike of Gourmont, a dislike that persisted long after Gourmont's death and verged on the fanatic.

Together with these flaws Léautaud noted Gide's disinterestedness, his acts of kindness, his disregard for popular acclaim. Gide, in short, was a very human person with all the contradictions the phrase implies. Léautaud's own character was a maze of warring elements, and he was anxious to do justice to Gide's complexity. Gide's conduct towards Léautaud was wholly consistent. Although his accommodating attitude may have sprung in part from a desire for approbation – he was reported to be 'terrified' at the thought of what Léautaud's diary might contain about him – his interest in Léautaud was genuine.

Although both Valéry and Gide fully realised that Léautaud was apt to be a dangerous friend, this did not prevent either of these more famous writers from treating him kindly. Pity, no doubt, entered into their feeling for him, and they were probably moved by his poverty and misfortune. Yet pity alone does not account for the keenness with which Gide sought to know his opinion of his work, and neither does it explain why Gide should write so warmly about him. There were traits in Léautaud that he recognised as his own: independence of accepted opinion and nonconformity. Léautaud was not a figure whose influence was to be solicited nor one whose opinion counted in the literary world. Gide was drawn to him because he valued his opinions and respected his views.

He knew Léautaud's character. He was aware that often Léautaud was disobliging about him in remarks to other people. It did not worry him. Shortly before his death, he said to an acquaintance: 'You see, Léautaud, such as he is, Léautaud, that . . . well . . . that treacherous man, who speaks badly of me and thinks badly of me, well . . . I'm very fond of him.'

═━X━═

THE SCOURGE

'The man who doesn't understand that you could strangle a woman doesn't know women.'

Paul Léautaud

So many things happened in 1908. It was the year when Léautaud started work at the *Mercure de France* and found himself involved in the literary world. It was the year he met Apollinaire, Billy and Rouveyre, and deepened acquaintance with Gide. It was also the year when he came within orbit of the tempestuous female who was to dominate his life for the next three decades or so and to make his existence by turns a heaven and a hell.

Of course, the most important woman for Léautaud was always to remain Jeanne Forestier. The story of his relations with women begins – and ends – with his mother. There were others in between, but over them all hovers the shade of this 'être de fuite', in the Proustian phrase, who by neglecting him, by treating him with callousness and by finally rejecting him, gained from him the love he was never able to give to any other woman.

She influenced, all unawares, his choice of mistresses. He liked them plump, as he thought she had been, and he was always attracted by women who looked like her, who reminded him of her eyes, her hair, her complexion. Sometimes he would see a woman in the train or in the street who resembled Jeanne Forestier. He would follow her timorously, knowing that he was wasting his time yet hoping that the unknown beauty would help him assuage the memory of Jeanne. Always he met disappointment and sometimes humiliation.

Jeanne Marié, his first mistress, had both his mother's Christian name and her type of figure. But with her, as with Georgette and with Blanche, he was never to find the impossible dream he sought: a replica of the woman he saw for the last time on

the Calais visit. In 1908 he met Madame Henry-Louis Cayssac.
Physically she looked like Jeanne Forestier. She had, he was
also to find, his mother's perverse temperament.

She was born Anne-Marie Galier in 1869, the daughter of a
concierge who worked in the Rue Saint-André-des-Arts. In
1896 she married Henry-Louis Cayssac who was then in his
fifties. He came of an old family in the Corrèze, was a man of
some education, read widely and had an informed interest in
music. He belonged to a higher social class than his 27-year-old
bride. Much of his spare time he spent playing Chopin, for he
was a good pianist. As a young man he had dissipated his inher-
itance on travel and the good things of life. Once his fortune
was gone he had to earn a living and took a clerical post
attached to the Ministère de l'Instruction Publique.

Monsieur Cayssac seems early to have realised that his marriage was a mistake. One day he complained to Léautaud, who
by then had become an intimate of the ménage, that life was
far too short to do all the things one wanted to do.

'Why did you get married, then?' Léautaud asked.

'To make life seem longer,' replied Monsieur Cayssac.

For Madame Cayssac her marriage was a triumphant step
up the social ladder. She never ceased to congratulate herself
on it. She prided herself on her position in society and on her
familiarity with the rules of polite behaviour. The couple lived
in a spacious five-roomed flat with a view over gardens at the
back. They kept a maid and spent their holidays in a villa they
owned at Pornic on the coast of Brittany. Their Paris flat was
in the Rue Dauphine at No. 24, and their neighbours in the
block were the writers Alain-Fournier and Jacques Rivière.
(At No. 44 in the same street is perhaps the oldest commemora-
tive plaque in Paris. It dates from 1673 and records the demoli-
tion in that year of the Porte Dauphine.)

Monsieur Cayssac's wife loved animals. In 1908 she became
aware of Léautaud through a mutual friend who belonged to
the Société Protectrice des Animaux, the French equivalent
of the RSPCA. She expressed a wish to meet him. He was
invited to a pleasant social evening in the Cayssacs' flat. In his

journal he noted: 'Madame Cayssac very pretty. Her husband much older.' The friendship grew to such an extent that in 1913 both husband and wife made wills in favour of Léautaud bequeathing him their property and laying on him 'the duty of continuing the sacred work of giving shelter to all the animals in my keeping'.

A year later they all three dined together and drank champagne to celebrate a successful piece of SPA business. Madame Cayssac reproached him: 'You're drinking without offering a toast. Let's toast the health of animals!' Léautaud clinked his glass against her and said in his most gracious manner: 'Your health, Madame.'

'Madame Cayssac,' he wrote, 'has a rare, yes rare, devotion to animals. Nothing is too much trouble for her: errands, bother, money, nursing, self-denial, putting herself out, etc. . . . She does things that few people, even real protectors of animals, do or should do. . . . '

There was another side to the medal. Though her care for animals showed an admirable unselfishness, she often annoyed him with her petty vanities, her boasting, her prejudices, her habit of praising herself and belittling others. He told her as much, frankly, on several occasions.

In spite of his reservations about her character he began to feel more than admiration for her kindness to animals. One day in her flat, as he watched her nursing a wounded cat she had rescued from the street, he said to her: 'You know, I'm beginning to like you very much.' Thus his 'cristallisation', to use Stendhal's term, took root in their common love for animals. On her visits to feed stray cats in the Jardins du Luxembourg she fell into the habit of calling to see him at his *Mercure* office. By 1914 she had decided not to do so any longer. It was dangerous for her as a respectable married woman, she explained coyly. He took the hint and acted accordingly. Her visits continued. On 25 March, while her husband was away, Léautaud seduced her at the flat in the Rue Dauphine. He was forty-two and she forty-five – 'a wonderfully well-preserved' forty-five, he noted.

In Madame Cayssac he believed that he had found the perfect mistress. She was passionate and lubricious. The techniques and pleasures to which she introduced him procured erotic delights he had never known before. All other women seemed dull beside her. How he had wasted his time with those inexpert girls, Jeanne, Georgette and Blanche! He had had to wait until his forties to enjoy the revelations of love at its fullest. Perhaps this was no bad thing, for by then he was of an age to appreciate them the better. The young did not know how to make love! This at least had been the case with him. He was shy, lost in his books, dreaming of literature. He had not known how to seize the opportunities offered. Even so, forty years did not seem a long time to wait if they were eventually to bring him Madame Cayssac.

The feeling was mutual. 'You know what you're doing, mon cher,' she told him of his performance in bed. 'Compared with you, my husband was a fool.' And with a shade of malice, she would add: 'You're not handsome, mon cher, but you've got lovely eyes and you're well built.'

Her use of the past tense in referring to Monsieur Cayssac was significant. He suffered from diabetes and was, she claimed, impotent as well. Léautaud was not quite sure about this second point. A sense of guilt at deceiving her husband might have urged her to make the remark in self-defence. In any case, there had never been much passion to their marriage. It was social ambition and financial reasons that had made her a bride. Monsieur Cayssac, wearied by the loneliness of a long bachelordom, wanted a home where meals were served regularly and where he was spared the tedium of domestic chores. Their strongest tie was a mutual love of animals.

As the affair between his wife and Léautaud flourished the two lovers grew more and more outrageous in their behaviour. While Monsieur Cayssac played the piano she would grimace behind his back, lift her skirts and make bawdy gestures in the direction of Léautaud. Sometimes, as the cuckold sat reading his paper after dinner, Léautaud would copulate briefly with her in the kitchen. A routine was soon established whereby

Léautaud came to lunch every day and often for dinner. When
he took her to a play with one of the complimentary tickets he
received as drama critic, he slept in a little room next to hers
to avoid the inconvenience of a late journey back to Fontenay.
On returning from the theatre they would find Monsieur Cayssac
dozing over a book. She would shoo him off to his own room.
Having accompanied him there on the pretext of seeing if he
wanted anything, she then gently locked his door from outside.

'That way we'll be quiet,' she sniggered. 'If he gets up, wants
to go out and is surprised to find the door locked, I shall say I
locked it by an oversight.' The little trick filled her with mischievous delight.

It would perhaps be wrong to say that she deceived her
husband, since he cannot for long have been under any illusions.
When others were present she made a point of treating Léautaud rather haughtily, of declaring that she only put up with
him for the sake of his devotion to animals. This seemed not
unlikely to outsiders, since Léautaud's wretched appearance,
his shabby clothes, his dirty and calloused hands, and the odour
of cats, vague but unmistakable, that hung perpetually around
him, did not suggest Don Juanism.

Monsieur Cayssac was obviously a philosopher. He must
have been grateful that someone else had attracted the attention
of his dominating wife and was diverting formidable energies
that might otherwise have made existence unrestful for him.
His age and his tastes called for a quiet life. He seems, indeed,
to have encouraged the liaison, for when Léautaud quarrelled
with her and stayed away in pique from the Rue Dauphine, it
was Monsieur Cayssac, genial and accommodating, who acted
as peacemaker by calling at the *Mercure* and urging him to
return. For his pains he earned a derisive nickname from the
two lovers. They had once seen a play in which a character
called 'le Bailli', a worthy but short-tempered man, was given
to exhibitions of rage and haughtiness until, at the appearance
of his wife, he changed his tune and crept humbly off. They
called him 'le Bailli' to his face. He laughed and accepted the
libel with good humour.

Monsieur Cayssac even had a sort of affection for Léautaud. He often took his side in disagreements with Madame Cayssac. Husband and lover eventually reached a point where confidences were offered. 'She's the sort of woman you ought to marry when you want to be sure of not being a cuckold,' joked Monsieur Cayssac. Though he knew the situation clearly, the remark contained a general truth.

In July, four months after the bastion of Madame Cayssac's chastity had fallen, it was time for summer holidays at the villa in Pornic. Both husband and wife invited Léautaud to join them there. The notion of leaving Paris for a fortnight at the seaside did not attract him.

'What about your husband ?' he asked.

'Oh, he's got his piano,' she shrugged. Besides Chopin there were the pleasures of astronomy, and Monsieur Cayssac would be kept harmlessly occupied with his study of the night sky over the Atlantic.

France was now in a state of war and the railway stations were full of troops recently mobilised and travellers hurrying back home. Trains were slow and disorganised. A band of ten dogs and four cats accompanied Léautaud on his journey. It was inconceivable for him to leave the dear creatures at home. The train started and frequently stopped. There were long halts in the middle of the countryside. Compartments were full to bursting point. For three days Léautaud stood surrounded by his animals in a lurching baggage van. Most of the time he quietly rolled and smoked cigarettes in an effort to forget his noisy, dirty fellow travellers who from time to time erupted into the van or trod on the paws of his charges.

When he arrived at Pornic he turned his back on the sea – a boring prospect, he declared, that made a din at night and kept him awake – in favour of releasing his cats and dogs and watching them frolic in the garden. The Cayssac villa was in Gourmalon, a district of Pornic some thirty miles from Nantes. The region is picturesque, despite the holiday chalets that disfigure it, but Léautaud the city dweller had no time for its beauties. His imagination was unstirred by the nearby castle of Gilles de

Retz, the infamous original of Bluebeard. Only the charm of the Breton place-names moved him: Préfailles, Sainte-Marie, Saint-Père-en Retz, La Bernerie, Saint-Michel-Chef-Chef. . . . 'Madame de Préfailles' – what a beautiful name for the heroine of a love story, he thought.

There exists a dim snapshot in which may be seen the strange trio that holidayed at Pornic in the long warm summer of 1914. At the rear is the villa, a small but solid construction with French windows looking out onto a white-railinged balcony. On the right, in the foreground, are seated the Cayssacs, he with legs crossed and a small dog on his lap. A larger dog nestles at his feet, and beside him sits Madame Cayssac, hands demurely clasped, an arch look on her face. A little way away, in the middle of the picture, stands Léautaud. He wears trousers so white that they have faded into the pale expanse of the path, with the result that the upper half of his body, in black coat and waistcoat, seems to hover like a ghost. The effect is oddly similar to that of a Chirico picture, timeless, frozen, without motion.

Léautaud's quarters were in an attic filled with old pieces of furniture, garden tools, potato sacks, rolled-up carpets and stacked chairs. There was just room for a little table where he could write. He liked it there. It reminded him of Paul-Louis Courier who also had written his pamphlets in a country attic surrounded by dusty sacks of wheat and spare furniture. Better still, there was no view of the sea. Here, when he was not running errands for Madame Cayssac, he scribbled at his ease, or, more often, just daydreamed.

Madame Cayssac was well known in the neighbourhood for her love of animals. Her reputation was not altogether an advantage, since the owners of unwanted pets frequently dropped them over the garden wall at dead of night. In the morning she would awake to find that her little colony of dogs and cats had unexpectedly increased. The new arrivals were adopted with good grace and joined the evening excursions when Madame Cayssac and Léautaud conducted the troop for a stroll along a rocky path near the villa. At the end of the

holiday care was taken to find a good home for the creatures
that had been thrust upon her.

The charm of Pornic for Léautaud did not lie in the sea or
the countryside, both of which bored him infinitely, but in the
opportunity of making love with Madame Cayssac more freely
and more often than in Paris. In the evening, as soon as
Monsieur Cayssac began to yawn and doze in his chair, the
lovers would exchange significant looks. Léautaud having said
that he intended to work late in the kitchen, Monsieur Cayssac,
remarking: 'I'm going to bed. Good luck. What an appetite for
work you must have. It must be a very fine piece you're working on', would vanish upstairs. His wife and Léautaud, chuck-
ling at the innocent double meaning (or was it so innocent?),
waited until they heard him snoring. 'Quick! He's snoring,'
Madame Cayssac would whisper. 'Put it up me.'

Sometimes their guilty pleasures were interrupted by a noise
from upstairs. Monsieur Cayssac moved about or stopped
snoring. Léautaud dressed rapidly and strained an anxious
ear. Then the snoring began again and the session could continue.

They were both proud of their ardour in love at an age which
is politely reckoned as mature. Madame Cayssac was insatiable
and used every trick, both verbal and physical, to encourage
Léautaud's desire. He kept a record of their sessions which
listed all the details. The *Journal particulier*, as it is called,
registers the number of times they made love, the positions
adopted, the techniques preferred, the obscenities uttered and
the dialogue spoken. This private diary has been described as
pornography. It is, on the contrary, a far from stimulating work.
As an obsessive commentary on his physical enslavement by a
woman whom he never truly respected or liked, it is a sad
human document.

For soon after the early raptures were over and they were
back in Paris from holiday he began to find that his first impressions of her unattractive personality were being confirmed.
If she possessed his mother's physique she also had, alas, her
temperament. 'What a perfect resemblance there is between

them,' he wrote when they had one of the quarrels that were becoming more and more frequent, 'in the way of harshness, rancour, obstinate silence, unwillingness to let bygones be bygones. All my life I shall never have any luck where love and tenderness are concerned.'

She was mean. At the height of passion she would suddenly break off, exclaiming: 'Put out the light. The electricity's burning away.' Or she would tell him not to mess up the sheets. Or she would rebuke him for sitting on the edge of the mattress – that was how things got worn and broken. Once, soon after midnight, while Léautaud awaited her in bed, she suddenly decided to do the housework. For an hour he heard her crashing about opening and shutting doors, filling coal buckets, shaking carpets. When eventually she joined him he gently chided her. 'Don't talk to me like that,' she snapped, 'or you won't come back.' Yet although she claimed to be house-proud, there were times when she slopped about happily in dirt and disorder, the floor covered with bits of coal, sawdust and shreds of cat food.

They never seem to have addressed each other by their Christian names. She prefaced her remarks to Léautaud with an imperious 'Dites donc!' In gentler moods she honoured him with the more familiar 'Dis donc!' Not once did she use the name Paul. He gave her a nickname which is self-explanatory: 'la Panthère'. As he came to realise the true nature of her scourge-like character he called her, with bitter humour, 'le Fléau'. Though he may not have used this uncomplimentary nickname to her face, it is probable that she knew about it, for whenever she had the chance she would search through his belongings and read what he had written.

She provided him, involuntarily, with copy for an article he wrote entitled 'Admiration amoureuse'. He began: 'No man is a hero to his valet, says a proverb. Not only to his valet! Here is the way I am appreciated as a writer by "the beloved idol of my heart", as romantic writers have it. . . .' He went on to give some choice examples of her invective. When she read it the inimitable 'beloved idol' claimed that she was entitled to a share of his fee for the article. Was it not made up entirely of her own sayings? 'You put on airs because you say everything you think!' she challenged him. 'Other people are cleverer than you. They write what they're asked to write and they pocket the money. You're much too stupid to do the same.'

In any case, she would say, writers made too much fuss about themselves. 'Writers are all scoundrels. They're fools who think they're somebody because they put things into black and white! . . . I don't write, and I'm a better sort of person than you are.' She felt she had the measure of even the greatest authors. 'How that Chateaubriand is like me! . . . As for Rochefoucauld, *I* could write Maxims too!'

When she read an article or review unfavourable to Léautaud, her comment was: 'All well and good. There's a man who knows you. He's been able to see through you.' By way of postscript she might add: 'You were lucky to have found the *Mercure de France*, a place where people stand up for each other. Nobody would have wanted you anywhere else.'

And what did his style amount to, that plain, simple style he thought so much about? It showed his hardness of heart, his lack of feeling, his abominable character. All he could do was to criticise and mock at everything. Talk of his 'literary reputation' made her laugh. He had no friends. People spoke well of him to his face, but if only he could hear what they said behind his back! He was a man to be pitied.

What he did not print in his article was the insults she flung at him when they had one of their quarrels. These would arise from some trivial cause and flower into scenes of violence. He was a pimp! He was a thief! He was the son of a whore! (Though this last statement was more veracious than insulting.) He tried to kiss her and she scratched his chin, drawing blood. When he tried again she brought her knee sharply up into his groin. Her hand flashed out and tore open his lip. Grasping both her wrists he threw her to the floor. There they grappled while he fought for mastery. She sprang up and rushed to the kitchen. Once again he caught hold of her, dragged her away, pushed her down, and this time succeeded in possessing her as she squirmed and hurled abuse at him. No doubt she secretly enjoyed the pattern of events.

Although she treated him with contempt and never lost an opportunity of belittling him, she was bitterly jealous. She prowled in the Rue de Condé and spied on visitors to the *Mercure* office, hoping to catch him out in affairs with other women. She was jealous even of the animals that took up so much of his affection. The thought of his having a flirtation with anyone else drove her into spasms of rage. Whenever she heard of something like this going on – and the network of spies that provided her with information was remarkably accurate – Léautaud would receive anonymous letters full of threats and gibes. Coming home to Fontenay in the evening he would realise that someone had been there during the day working through drawers and investigating his papers. On occasions when he lay in bed at her flat in the Rue Dauphine he knew that in the next room she was turning out the pockets of his clothes.

Her scenes were not confined to indoors. One evening, as she accompanied him along the Rue de Médicis on his way to the Luxembourg railway station, an argument began over money. She raised her voice. Seeing a policeman, she commanded: 'Take this gentleman to the police station. It's about a financial matter.' The policeman, believing she was a prostitute cheated of her fee, took her by the arm. Léautaud intervened. 'Don't do that. She's a very respectable woman.' The grotesque procession started back down the Rue de Médicis towards the police station in the Rue Crébillon, Léautaud and the policeman in front, Madame Cayssac behind. A few minutes later the policeman turned round.

'Where's the lady, then?' She had vanished, probably embarrassed.

'Don't you know what women are like?' said Léautaud resignedly. His companion's face lit up with understanding. 'So that was it!' None the less they went on to the station and Léautaud, for the sake of form, made a statement which was duly signed and witnessed.

In that same street a little later she suddenly attacked him with fury. He staggered under her blows. She ripped the collar of his shirt and coat, tore off his tie, and scratched his cheek until the blood ran. He held in his hand the proofs of a drama criticism he was taking home to correct. She seized it and tore it to pieces as she stamped off. 'This is important – it's work,' he protested. 'I couldn't care less about your work,' she snapped. Next day, contrite, she handed back the torn shreds.

Sometimes she pursued him beyond the railway station and even climbed into his compartment with him. Sitting opposite him she pointed him out to the bemused commuters. 'Do you see that man? A fine sort of fellow. He's slept with his mother,' she bawled again and again. Throughout the whole of the journey her objurgations would continue. Léautaud sat without speaking a word, as if lost in peaceful meditation. She had lost all control. At Fontenay station she got out and followed him home. Still screaming at the top of her voice she clutched her side and felt faint. She begged for a glass of water. He watched her silently, not caring whether she lived or died.

At other times these monumental scenes ended happily. She lay in his arms and he said softly: 'Why are you so unpleasant, only to be so charming afterwards?' She began to cry. 'You mustn't take any notice of what I say when I'm angry.' She was never so attractive, so amorous, as after a violent explosion of temper.

Without jealousy, he mused, there can be no real love. Her unreasonable possessiveness showed that she must love him. This was a thought that he was too modest to have had himself. It was suggested by another woman with whom he discussed his tumultuous love life. Perhaps, too, her contradictory behaviour was influenced by an exchange they once had which, as she never referred to it again, must have gone deep.

'If my husband died would you marry me?' she asked at the beginning of their liaison.

'No,' he replied. It was the answer he would have given to any woman had she put him that question.

Ten years later, in 1924, the poor 'Bailli' did in fact leave this world. He had been a gentle and pacific man. In literature he enjoyed everything Léautaud did not – Corneille, Hugo and Anatole France. In music it was Chopin who had helped to ease the strains of his married life. 'People should never marry below their station,' he once told Léautaud regretfully.

Towards the end of August Monsieur Cayssac returned from Pornic, leaving his wife there to continue her holiday. At midday on 5 September Léautaud called at the flat in the Rue Dauphine to have lunch, a habit he had acquired over the past few years. All was silent. On his way to the kitchen he glimpsed Monsieur Cayssac sleeping in the dining-room. On the kitchen table was a bowl of coffee ready to be drunk. This surprised him. He went into the dining room and looked closely at 'le Bailli' in his armchair. His eyes were closed and his hands neatly folded on his lap. His face looked waxy and there was no sound of breathing. Léautaud felt his hands. They were still warm. He must have died no more than a quarter of an hour ago. Léautaud took one of the dead man's handkerchiefs and put it over his face.

He called the doctor, notified the police, warned the concierge, sent a telegram to Madame Cayssac, and, not least of the duties he voluntarily undertook, fed the animals. It was odd: this sudden death plunged him into a child-like mood of excitement. There was novelty in the air, despite the sadness of the occasion. How would his relationship with Le Fléau be affected? He met her off the 6.10 morning train from Pornic.

'Is my poor husband dead?' she queried.

'Mon Dieu, oui.'

There were floods of tears. He told her about his discovery the previous morning.

'Now I'm alone in the world,' she lamented.

'Well, I'm still here,' he sought to comfort her.

'You don't count for much,' was the tart reply.

Monsieur Cayssac was still in his chair. More tears followed, more praise for the dead man whom, in life, she had rarely ceased to denigrate. He became a paragon of all the virtues, a model husband and a perfect gentleman. While Léautaud scuttled about on various errands, he found time to note the comment: 'It's not very amusing for a lover to lose his mistress's husband.'

At the funeral she ordered him not to ride in the hearse carrying the coffin. The 'clown's hat' he wore made him look out of place there. So he went to the cemetery by bus. That evening she was in a better mood, and they enjoyed a superb bout of love-making. The same thing happened on the two subsequent evenings. Her husband's death had infected them both with a sort of exhilaration.

Of course she made many comparisons between Monsieur Cayssac and Léautaud. Sometimes she bewailed her lot – she'd been unlucky, she said, both in her choice of husband and in her choice of lover. 'You only appreciate people when they're dead,' complained Léautaud. 'You'd probably regret me if I died.' She answered: 'That could well be.'

This period of amity was short-lived. By the middle of October they were engaged in open battle again. She reproached him for not having offered to help her financially. She was now a poor widow with no one to defend her, no one to cherish her. He was a parasite, a mean and selfish hanger-on only interested in what he could get out of her. She could no longer afford to give him lunch every day. Few were the encounters between them now that did not end in blows and scratches.

He was too poor to afford decent restaurants. During the lunch hour he wandered miserably through the streets of the Latin Quarter in search of somewhere to eat. Usually he ended by making do with a few cups of coffee on a terrace. It was a trial for him even to enter a restaurant, so shy was he, so convinced that people were mocking his shabby clothes. The only places he could afford served disgusting food that upset his stomach.

Yet he still wanted her, still lusted after her, however much he abominated her character. What a fool he was, he told himself, to be so completely in the thrall of a woman fifty-six years

22. Mademoiselle Marie Dormoy, to whom Léautaud owed more than he ever admitted

23. The house at Fontenay-aux-Roses

24. A part of the overgrown garden at Fontenay

old. He had noticed, had even told her, that he could see her charms were fading, that her breasts were becoming stringy, that her skin was coarsening. Too late he realised that perhaps he should have reacted to her high-handed behaviour with toughness instead of resignation. On the occasions when he nerved himself to treat her roughly she had capitulated with surprising swiftness. But it was not in his nature to dominate anyone, and he could not bring himself to act the masterful lover. Encouraged by this apparent weakness she piled enormity upon enormity. He was baffled.

He could not resist the sensual pleasures which, in moments of calm, she was prepared to allow him, and he found himself drawn back to her despite his hatred. It was impossible for him to do without her. When, for financial reasons, she took in a lodger, he was tortured by jealousy. Trapped in a prison of sensuality he had come to love his chains. She could call him anything she liked – ugly, weak, crude, mercenary – and he even heard in silence the most poisonous charge of all: she allowed him to make love to her only because she pitied him.

Although he remained under the shadow of this termagant, who doubled with monstrous ease the roles of virago and courtesan, he was always ready for adventures on the side. In the year of Monsieur Cayssac's death he received an appreciative letter from one of his readers. This sometimes happened. His literary reputation may have been small, but those who enjoyed his writing tended to be fanatical in their admiration. He replied gratefully with an invitation to his correspondent, who lived in Bordeaux, to visit him in Paris. There walked into his office one day an attractive girl of twenty-three.

Mademoiselle Véronique Valcault had left Bordeaux in protest against her family's wish to marry her off to a carefully chosen young man with excellent prospects. It appeared that she was fond of literature and especially of Remy de Gourmont. She read an article of his about Guillaume de Machault and Péronnelle d'Armentières, and the account of a young girl's love for an old man moved her. Then she read Léautaud's reminiscences of Gourmont and became fascinated by his style. *Le Petit Ami* was out of print by then, so she borrowed a copy and, as a labour of love, typed the whole thing out.

Léautaud was flattered by the respectful admiration of a fresh and innocent girl. He gave her copies of his books and engaged in a libertine correspondence with her. When she came to see him at the *Mercure* he grabbed at her hand and kissed her. They went for walks together. She felt a strange emotion towards him. It was love, but a love that existed only in the mind and one that was infinitely stronger than the physical sort. Whenever she saw him her legs shook so much that she was ready to drop. Platonic passion had little appeal for Léautaud, and gradually she gave way to his more common-place urging. Had he known the reason for her capitulation he would have been deeply humiliated: she felt an overwhelming pity for what she took to be a life in decline.

For fear that his letters to her might be intercepted by Madame Cayssac he neither headed nor signed them. It was a useless precaution. Le Fléau's espionage system quickly found out what was going on. As he walked down the street one day with Véronique there was a sudden commotion. A hand from behind seized him by the collar, a voice screamed, 'Ah! I've caught you at it!', and Madame Cayssac, foaming with rage, separated the two lovers. While Véronique stood deserted on the pavement, the unresisting Léautaud was marched off into the distance for a hearty scolding. After that they arranged their meetings with cloak-and-dagger precaution.

Véronique's concierge received a visit from Le Fléau who warned her that Léautaud was a dangerous and dirty old man bent on corrupting her tenants. Anonymous letters, sometimes two or three a day, blackened his character and portrayed the dreadful results that must ensue should the affair go on. The girl was perplexed. Wherein lay the power of this unruly old woman who had bad teeth, wrinkled skin spotted with ugly freckles, and greasy white hair? How could this creature with her dirty nails and muddied shoes exercise so strong an influence over Léautaud?

During the few intervals of peace allowed them by Le Fléau, Véronique and Léautaud even talked of marriage. She proposed to take him to the country and there to settle on a farm owned by her father. She heard him discuss literature and paid what he said the tribute of eager attention. She closed her eyes to his repellent and all but toothless physical aspect.

The most bizarre element in this episode was that, despite everything, a peculiar sort of comradeship grew up between Véronique and Le Fléau. These two completely different women, though opposed in all else, were united in their absorption in Léautaud. The girl was honoured with an invitation to Pornic, and in those pleasant surroundings Le Fléau indulged herself in long tirades against him. Refreshing her memory with the aid of many papers and documents, she enjoyed herself vastly in detailing his villainy and baseness, and in pointing out to Véronique how foolish she would be to let herself be deceived by his nasty tricks. Véronique returned to Paris convinced that Le Fléau had conceived an affection for her, distorted though it might have been by her wish to do Léautaud down.

The crazy situation could not last. In any case, Véronique was unable to give Léautaud the mature pleasures he was accustomed to receive with Le Fléau. For all his complaints about his 60-year-old mistress, for all his dislike of her odious character, no one else could satisfy him so completely as she could. Véronique drifted out of his life. A little later she happened to see him in the street. He looked worn and battered, much older than his age of fifty-four. He could not live much longer, she thought to herself. Twenty years after, in 1946, she saw him again. Although he was in his mid-seventies his appearance had not changed much and the old magic still worked. 'I went home,' she wrote. 'I noted with astonishment that my legs could scarcely carry me.'

Le Fléau had triumphed. Once again she had put a stop to Léautaud's philandering activities. Their stormy relationship continued throughout the nineteen-thirties, by which time she, getting on for seventy, remained still as virulent as ever. Despite the volcanic nature of their perpetual disagreements few of

Léautaud's acquaintances knew of her existence. They sometimes saw him in the company of this cantankerous, ill-dressed,
grubby old woman, and they dismissed her as yet another of
the quaint animal-lovers with whom he often associated. In any
case, he already looked an old man himself. His face was
ravaged and seamed with deep wrinkles. Only his eyes and
voice retained their attractiveness. No one suspected that an
ancient mistress was often stationed in the Rue de Condé
inspecting callers at his office and imagining that every woman
who met 'her' man had no other design but to snatch him away
from her. The secretive Léautaud kept it all to himself and
confided his thoughts to paper.

Le Fléau was the inspiration of the bitter aphorisms he published in a small volume called *Amour*. 'Love,' he wrote, 'is
physical, is sensual attraction, is pleasure given and received, is
mutual enjoyment, is the union of two human beings made for
each other sexually. The rest, the exaggerations, the sighs, the
"soul's uplifting", are jokes, sayings for fools, the dreams of
minds that are refined and impotent.' Every man and every
woman, he believed, had a perfect partner in love. Some found
this partner late in life, as he had. This was all to the good since
the pleasures of love could only be savoured in maturity. A man
of twenty did not know how to enjoy a woman fully, nor could
a mere girl be expected to perform with the accomplishment of
experience.

'I like woman,' he wrote. 'I don't like women.' It was inevitable that one day they would reproach you for the favours
they had granted you. They despised men who were faithful to
them and were really only interested in the ones who deceived
them. The charm of women lay not in their moral qualities nor
in the distinction of their mind or taste: it lay in their physique.
The greatest love, he declared, could very well exist without
affection. He always affirmed that he would not have been
unduly upset had Le Fléau dropped dead while making love.
'One must have been very fond of women to detest them,' he
concluded.

He summed up Le Fléau:

'If she was, for me, the partner I had dreamed of, a being made for love such as I have described it, possessing to the highest degree what I call the spirit of love, that is to say extreme licentiousness in word, attitude and gesture, which is very pleasant in the woman you love, I owe to her as well most of the very small respect I have for women.'

There are two sides to the question, though Léautaud would not admit it. We have never, after all, heard Le Fléau's version of the affair. He enjoys the inestimable advantage of having had the last word.

⟶ XI ⟶

THE JOURNAL

'I wrote one day that I have lived certain moments of my life twice over: first on experiencing them and then on writing about them. I've certainly lived them more profoundly in writing about them.'

Paul Léautaud

The declaration of war in 1914 did not find Léautaud among the excited crowds who filled the Paris streets with their shouts of 'A Berlin!' He was supremely unenthusiastic. 'Marriage produces cuckolds,' he had once said, 'and patriotism fools.' The raucous jingoism of his fellow countrymen disgusted him. He did not care a brass button whether Alsace and Lorraine stayed under German rule or came back to France.

'France,' he wrote with irony, 'is the greatest country in the world. The French are the greatest people in the world. What a pity Napoleon didn't succeed in conquering the whole of Europe and making Frenchmen out of all those inferior races called English, Italian, German, etc. etc. At last, perhaps, we'd have had peace. And then we could have started thinking about the Chinese and the Patagonians.'

The chief result of the war for Léautaud was that his salary dropped to fifty francs a month and he lived in poverty. He did not care for himself so much as for his animals who had to go short of food. The plight of horses worried him too, since large numbers were required not only for cavalry regiments but also for the transport needs of an army not yet fully mechanised. In the horrible conditions of warfare men could look after themselves. Horses could not.

In the second year of the war his old friend Remy de Gourmont died. The author of *Le Joujou patriotisme*, the attack on militarism that brought about dismissal from his post at the Bibliothèque Nationale and threw him onto the risky seas of freelance authorship, had become with age a conventional patriot. Forgetting his early independence and his refusal to go with the crowd, he now joined in the flag-wagging. 'C'est tout de même beau, la solidarité,' he wrote to Vallette. The war closed down the magazines and reviews that were his source of income. Sometimes he literally starved. An English admirer, Richard Aldington, helped him by placing translations of his work and sending him the fees. There was also a little money to be gained by selling his manuscripts. During the first year of the war he contracted uraemia. In September 1915 he was very ill. Taken to hospital in a coma, he died soon afterwards. Léautaud went to see the body. Gourmont's face was pinched and bloodless. The patchy discolorations caused by the lupus had blended into a uniform pallidness. He was a casualty, both intellectual and physical, of the war.

Léautaud put a bunch of roses on the sheet. He walked back to his office full of memories. He remembered Gourmont saying, 'A . . . à . . . revoir!' with his slight stammer and crossing the Rue de Condé, umbrella under his arm, head held high, his large bottom undulating beneath the overcoat. What irony that in the hospital ward, hidden from the view of Gourmont the ferocious disbeliever, there should have hung an enormous gilt cross! Even more so were the church funeral, requested by his family, and the religious ceremony which Gourmont himself had described as 'laughable'. For months afterwards his companion Berthe de Courrière was to haunt the *Mercure* and other publishers' offices battling for the meagre royalties on his books. When it was suggested that perhaps his brother might have an interest, she snapped haughtily: 'Jean de Gourmont doesn't count. I'm the one you have to deal with.'

Next year, on 17 March, the Cayssacs handed Léautaud a copy of the *Journal de Genève*. It contained an announcement of his mother's death on the 15th. Some time previously she had been attacked by an Italian servant girl, who, annoyed at being given notice, savaged her with a kitchen knife. Bleeding copiously from many wounds she was taken to hospital and lay there in a serious condition. She never really recovered from the incident. The stark newspaper report brought back to Léautaud a flood of recollections.

Prompted by Le Fléau, whose practical instinct foresaw possibilities in the will, but moved chiefly by the wish to find out as much as possible about his mother, Léautaud wrote to the widower. A week later there arrived a precise and courteous reply. Dr Oltramare reported that he had been vaguely aware of Léautaud's existence, but his wife had at no time wished to dilate on the subject. Although, these last months, she knew that death was near, she had never spoken of her mysterious son and there was nothing in her papers relating to him. Neither was Dr Oltramare very well acquainted with his mother-in-law, Léautaud's grandmother, who died in 1909. Mother and daughter had had frequent disagreements and he had discreetly taken no sides, limiting himself to responsibility for Madame Forestier's board and lodging with a local family. His mother-in-law and his wife had not, to his knowledge, possessed money of their own. Indeed, after his wife's death there were many bills to be paid which he had not known about. Dr Oltramare concluded by asking Léautaud to accept his most respectful sentiments.

The news of his mother's death reawoke all the old disappointments and bitterness. Léautaud spent the afternoon of the following day talking about it with friends. They listened, sympathetically, while he spoke with emotion of her beauty, her vivacity, her attractiveness. He mentioned also her indifference and her duplicity. Until evening came he exhausted himself in an endless catalogue of her faults and her merits. Then he went away.

Next morning one of the friends who had sat through this painful spectacle called at the *Mercure*, anxious to comfort him after what she imagined must have been a distressing night spent alone with his thoughts. He looked up from his desk. At her first words he hissed: 'My mother? I couldn't care less!'

She went in astonishment to Vallette. When she told him of her surprise at this sudden about turn, Vallette replied: 'He's put on his mask again.'

Two years after the war ended Léautaud heard of yet another woman who had played an important part in his early years. The husband of Jeanne Marié, his first mistress, died at the age of seventy-one. He thought of the widow, now fifty-four, shapeless, gross, her youthful prettiness faded into the unappetising contours of a tired elderly housewife. For some time she and her husband had run a tavern on the outskirts of Paris. Life could not have been easy for them. How fresh and amorous and sensual she was at the time of their love! Age and death were creeping up on everyone he knew. He looked in the mirror and contemplated, anxiously, the wrinkles that were invading his own face.

Gourmont, Jeanne Forestier and Jeanne Marié had all been a part of his youth. So had Valéry, and even the link with him was to be eroded before the war ended. For some time their ways had drifted apart. They came together again in 1915 when Léautaud received from Valéry a lunch invitation couched in whimsical alexandrines that began: 'Mardi, sombre Boissard dont le cerveau travaille. . . .' Alone at table they spoke of their memories, of the days already far off when they walked arguing through Paris and continued their discussions on the upper decks of omnibuses with never a glance at the streets rolling by outside. They returned to an old theme when, at the mention of careerist acquaintances, they agreed in condemning the rat-race for fame, decorations and the Académie Française.

After lunch they took the air: Voltaire, Diderot and Talleyrand were the subjects of their conversation. The streets in wartime were virtually free of traffic, and Léautaud delighted in the atmosphere of a small provincial town that seemed to have descended on a Paris that somehow, after all, remained Paris. He left Valéry at half past four in the afternoon. Their talks about eighteenth-century authors sent Léautaud into a mist of reverie, and that evening, suddenly catching a reflection of himself in a glass, he felt a shock of surprise at seeing that he wore modern clothes and not the buckles and flowered waistcoat of his favourite period. It had been a charming day and Valéry had

shown himself to be as engaging a companion as in the eighteen-
nineties when first they met. Only one little flaw in the day's
enjoyment worried Léautaud: why *did* Valéry keep on writing
that 'obscure and precious verse' for which he had shown a
taste when young? Nearly twenty years later he was still con-
fecting these 'artisteries'.

In 1917 Valéry published *La Jeune Parque*, the work that was
to establish his reputation and make him a social lion. It was
reviewed in the August issue of the *Mercure de France*. Valéry,
said the anonymous reviewer, was the only true disciple of
Mallarmé. Twenty years had passed and he was still haunted
by the same dream, the same images, the same beauty. He remained a loyal worshipper of Mallarmé. 'Loyalty is a beautiful
thing. It is a great thing. It is one of the finest virtues. It is often
a strength. It is also perhaps, in literature as in love, the most
disastrous of weaknesses.'

Valéry read the article and confided to Gide: 'It hurt me, if
the author is the man I guess him to be. In which case it's a very
unexpected piece of treachery and one without cause.' As
Valéry divined, his critic was Léautaud. It was chance that had
made Léautaud for a short time poetry reviewer at the *Mercure*
in the absence of the magazine's regular contributor. As was
usual in such cases, the deputy signed off as 'Intérim'. The
anonymity of the review had nothing sinister about it.

Even so, the harm was done. When Léautaud heard of
Valéry's distress he was genuinely surprised. He did not understand why an old friendship should prevent him from saying
what he honestly thought. Valéry was a dear friend, a man
whose company he enjoyed and whose intellect he admired,
but that was no reason for concealing his opinion that Valéry's
poetry was mannered rubbish. He could see in it nothing that
was human or alive. It was freakishness, mere playing with
words. Valéry, though deeply hurt, preserved a dignified
silence.

Léautaud viewed with cynical astonishment Valéry's rapid
ascent in the post-war years. The Valéry he knew when young,
poor but contemptuous of worldly honours, became a noted

figure, a sought-after guest. It seemed that the whole of society was infected with what Léautaud called 'la maladie valéry-enne'. 'The buffoonery goes on,' he noted when Valéry took the inevitable step and was elected to the Académie Française, that institution he had so often derided in the past. Out of curiosity Léautaud waited beside the Institut on the day of Valéry's ceremonial reception. He saw him emerge wearing his Aca-demician's uniform, stiff and ill at ease in the pompous clothes. He looked tired and aged. His face was worn, his cheekbones stood out sharply. Léautaud thought of Mallarmé, obscure and mocked throughout his life, and contrasted him with his disciple Valéry, famous, courted, a member of the Académie and on the top rung of the social ladder.

Yet the Valéry Léautaud had always known never changed. The affair of *La Jeune Parque* does not appear to have been mentioned by either of them, and soon Valéry started to call at the *Mercure* from time to time. Perhaps he felt, as Gide did, that with Léautaud he could relax and speak freely with an old friend. Léautaud was not a rival, he was not one of the camp-followers who swarmed increasingly around him, and he would certainly not ask him for favours.

Valéry's confidences about his life as a famous writer made Léautaud thankful for his own relative obscurity. Morning was the only time when Valéry could work undistracted, and from dawn until ten o'clock he concentrated on what really interested him. After lunch he spent the afternoon more or less in a daze, and in the evening he went out to the receptions, the dinners and the public functions where his presence was incessantly demanded. Often he fell asleep. As a young man he had been full of ideas and projects. As a writer who had 'arrived' he found that the literary life became a profession like any other, a matter of contracts and agreements and negotiations.

He was assailed with requests for prefaces, speeches, lectures. It would have been foolish to reject them since he had family commitments and many expenses. Besides, he never wrote anything that had not been commissioned beforehand. His talk was of royalties and of deals concluded. He needed money and only a saint would have turned down the opportunities that flowed his way. As his fame grew so did the cost of his way of life. The birth of a child, normally an occasion for happiness, was of necessity translated into the need to seek new commissions, to write still more and eventually to earn more. The irony was that he did not really enjoy writing.

The modest fee of eighty-three francs Valéry received each month as a member of the Académie was gratefully pocketed. After a youth deprived of many things for lack of money, he could be forgiven for making the most of his successful maturity. He rarely rejected an invitation to lecture, even on a subject of which he knew little. The Goethe centenary cast him as principal speaker at the Sorbonne celebrations. He had never read a line of Goethe and did some hasty homework for the occasion. There were coughs and fidgets among the audience as he read, from a thick bundle of notes, in a low and monotonous voice, dull and motionless. Never mind – it helped pay the rent. As for Goethe himself, Valéry told Léautaud with his usual freedom of language, enunciating each syllable with emphasis: 'Il m'emmerde.'

Léautaud's review of *La Jeune Parque* was not the only factor to have altered their relationship. Like many of Valéry's friends he possessed letters from the poet and first editions of his books containing personal inscriptions. Now that Valéry was famous there was a profitable trade in such things. Not only were his letters sold for high prices. Extra dividends were reaped by publishing them in limited editions 'hors commerce', a device that prevented Valéry from doing anything to stop the practice. Léautaud himself owned seventy letters Valéry had written him between 1897 and 1907, as well as valuable association copies. Genuinely troubled by scruples but impelled by an equally pressing need (he had depended on a tiny grant from the Ministère de l'Instruction Publique to survive the war), he at last sold them for 22,500 francs to a dealer.

He always felt a little guilty thereafter when he met Valéry. It was annoying for Valéry to see his intimate correspondence made public, and on occasion it was embarrassing as well, especially when some indiscreet exchanges with the ambiguous writer Pierre Louÿs came into the light of day. Léautaud was never quite sure whether Valéry knew of his action. If he did, he refrained from speaking of it, just as he did of the *Jeune Parque* incident. Indeed, in his dealings with Léautaud he emerges with credit as a man who, despite the wounding things the friend of his youth said about him, continued to see him and, in later years, used his influence in an attempt to help him financially. It cannot, after all, be very congenial to spend your time with a man who you know despises your work. The tone of their conversations together – gossip about the Académie, nostalgic recollections of early days together, chit-chat about publishers – shows that what Valéry cherished in Léautaud was the young man he had known at the turn of the century. Léautaud was one of the very few people with whom he could laugh at the more absurd aspects of his unique success story. Among these was the story of a magnificent umbrella presented to him in admiration by an umbrella manufacturer. Upon the handle was engraved the legend, 'Paul Valéry, de l'Académie Française'. It was stolen from him twice in London. Back in France it was appropriated by someone else. A second time it was stolen by Pirandello. Now he had lost it again at the *Mercure*. 'Perhaps,' said Léautaud, 'you'll be able to say it's been stolen a third time . . . by me.'

Their meetings were limited to the *Mercure* and publishers' offices. Valéry no longer invited Léautaud home. The reason, Léautaud guessed, was a remark of Valéry's passed on to him by a third party: 'Cet homme met tout sur ses papiers.' Like everyone else in the literary world, Valéry knew that Léautaud kept a diary which might, some day, be published. Had he also known what Léautaud was recording about him their meetings would probably have been even less frequent. For everything that Valéry told him – the indiscretions, the anecdotes he recounted with his Italian vivacity, the crude language and obscene epithets that continually larded his talk, his habit of leaving a sentence in mid-air – was faithfully retailed in the diary.

This *Journal littéraire*, as Léautaud called it, was started in 1893. Keeping up the *Journal* became in time an obsession with him. 'This need to note down everything of one's slightest ideas, acts and deeds is absolute slavery,' he wrote. 'I can't resist it.' It often led him, in the middle of conversation, to take lengthy notes. The habit was not of a nature to reassure acquaintances.

In many ways the whole of Léautaud's work may be regarded as one vast 'journal'. The articles, the essays, the slim volumes, the brief paragraphs in the *Mercure de France*, can be seen as instalments in a continuing day-by-day autobiography. The *Journal littéraire* occupies a central position. It was both a ready-made source of material for other writings and a 'workshop' where, as events turned out, he was able to record the thoughts he would later present in a form suitable for publication in a magazine.

At first Léautaud seems to have looked on it rather as a notebook in which to jot down ideas and observations. A regular chronology does not appear until 1895, the year when he made the acquaintance of Vallette. By 1900, when he had begun to move in the literary world, the entries are more frequent and start to constitute a regular account. In 1903, with its story of his affair with Georgette, the *Journal* gains the status of a diary proper. This is a significant year, for it saw the publication of *Le Petit Ami* in book form. His experience in writing *Le Petit Ami* had convinced him that he had neither imagination nor invention: 'I can only write about real subjects.' The topic with which he was most intimately familiar was himself.

'I talk a lot about myself in what I write. This is nothing to do with vanity. (I only wish it were.) It is solely for the pleasure of getting to know myself. I look at myself, I examine myself, on every occasion, as if I were someone else. I think: "That's how you are." I've spent my life doing this. I can say that certain parts of my life I've lived twice over: in living them and in watching myself do so.'

What more appropriate form could his writing take, then, than the very personal one of the diary?

To begin with he wrote the *Journal* on paper torn from school exercise books. In the last years, when paper was short, he wrote on whatever came to hand: backs of letters, used envelopes, torn-off wrappers and scraps of many descriptions. Certain fragments which he prized he stuck together in rolls a yard or so long. The material was stored in a haphazard way. Some was inevitably mislaid, other portions were removed by Madame Cayssac while he was away from home, as she suspected, rightly, that they contained unflattering remarks about her. The entries were written each evening, by candle-light, with a spluttering quill pen on material that often had the consistency of blotting-paper. His handwriting was execrable, and as he grew older and his eyesight dimmed it became increasingly illegible.

In the matter of personal character Léautaud was supremely qualified to keep a journal. Charm of personality does not seem to be an essential. Saint-Simon cannot have been a nice man to know and one would soon have become wearied by his excessive snobbery. Much the same might be expected of Edmond de Goncourt with his finicky airs and literary pretension. Although Renard was loved by his family and a small group of friends, most people regarded him as thoroughly detestable. One quality possessed by all these writers of 'intimate' works is a monstrous and devouring egotism. Léautaud was no exception. The diarist is his own most important character. Everything is seen and experienced through himself. Egotism, moreover, supplies the powerful urge that makes a writer sit down alone in the evening after a day's work, when he might be spending his leisure in any one of a dozen pleasanter and less demanding ways, to start the tiring business of putting words on paper.

Curiosity is equally important. It is, said Léautaud, an aspect of intelligence. Only fools and bird-brains are without curiosity. One should be as curious as possible, even to the extent of prying into affairs that do not concern one, listening at doors, peering through windows, following people in the street to overhear what they say, reading letters that happen to lie about, soliciting confidences, spying, watching, surprising and discovering. In the diarist this trait must be developed to a high degree. Without it we should not have had the works of Tallemant des Réaux or Boswell.

Curiosity is not much use if it cannot be exploited by an aptitude for detailed observation. Léautaud possessed this also. His *Journal* is crammed with detail. His eye took in everything. This quality was supported by a memory that allowed him to recall facts and conversations word for word at times when he was unable to take notes on the spot. He prided himself on his memory, and people were often surprised by the accuracy of his recollections. Events that had happened forty years ago remained clear in his mind. Only when he was very old did this power begin to falter.

One of the first things to strike us about Léautaud's *Journal* is its documentary nature. This is reinforced by his indignant rejection of a comparison André Billy drew with the Goncourts. They were 'artists', Léautaud protested, and he was not. They moved in distinguished society, whereas he lived in a very small circle. Instead of Flaubert, Zola, Verlaine and Hugo, he had to make do with Gide, Valéry, Duhamel and Apollinaire. His 'restaurant Magny' was an occasional cheap café in the Latin Quarter.

Léautaud's *Journal* gives a unique picture of over fifty years of Parisian literary life, more miseries than splendours, as it appeared to an acute observer living at the centre of what François Mauriac has called 'a culture medium where black insects, in the reek of paper and ink, rub their antennae together and turn their back on everything in the outside world except for the gossip in editorial offices, academies, backstage intrigues . . .'. In his pages we meet hosts of minor literary men whose names, once quite well known, are now but dimly remembered by virtue of the yellowing covers on books that clutter up the dusty shelves of second-hand booksellers.

Always conscious of man's mortality, in his evocation of these figures Léautaud provides an involuntary reminder of the transitoriness of reputation. He shows how cruel a mistress literature is. He records many pathetic cases of writers who, having known a brief glory, ended their days in destitution and suffering. Even those authors who surmounted the misfortunes of the literary life were not always to be envied. Léautaud's friend André Billy sometimes complained of the treadmill to which he was bound. The price he paid was high. Always to be writing, to be blackening paper: that wasn't what you'd call really living! He knew that if he once allowed himself to slacken the pace, misfortune would follow.

As for writers like Valéry who enjoyed the best of both worlds – critical esteem as well as a good living – they had their problems too. Valéry's conversations with Léautaud were full of complaints about the wearying existence he led. His principle, a sensible one in theory, was never to turn down an offer. So, for example, he found himself writing for a wealthy pharmaceutical manufacturer whose hobby it was to commission a book a year from some distinguished writer in the same way as other rich men buy themselves racehorses. After three months' hard work at his typewriter – like T. S. Eliot, Valéry never wrote by hand, finding that typing eased the tedium involved – the book was ready. Then complications arose. The deal nearly fell through. In the end all turned out happily and Valéry was able to utilise the material for other purposes as well. In the meantime his nerves had been severely tried, a few more white hairs had been added to his untidy shock, and he had smoked many more cigarettes than his usual already high quota.

If a writer did not win a just return from his work during his lifetime, could his family expect to benefit from the posthumous recognition he received? Apparently not. In 1927, nine years after Apollinaire's death, Léautaud asked Billy what sort of royalties were coming in to the poet's estate. 'Do you know what his wife collected in royalties from the NRF last year?' demanded Billy. 'Thirty-six francs! . . . thirty-six francs.'

The depths of pessimism were touched in a discussion about death which Vallette had with Léautaud. He spoke of Gourmont, who had lived a full intellectual life and produced a body of work. Then he compared him with the caretaker at the

Mercure who had recently died, a simpleton and a drunkard. 'It's true,' Vallette went on, 'that Gourmont profited from the knowledge he acquired and from the work he brought out. But he's dead. All that means nothing to him. The result is the same for them both.'

Long association with Vallette and the *Mercure de France* taught Léautaud a great deal about publishing. By 1908 the days of big sellers like Zola and Daudet were over. A book with a print order of more than 30,000 was a rarity. One reason lay in the absence of authors of Zola's calibre. Another, offered by Vallette, was the new craze for bicycling which had seduced people away from reading. In later years the stock excuse was to be motoring, then films, then radio, then television.

In the nineteen-twenties publishers were trying to make up for the lack of giants in the Zola mould by using unscrupulous publicity tricks. Gaston Gallimard launched Paul Morand's *Ouvert la nuit* with loud trumpeting and claims of a 30,000 sale. Since the time for awarding the Prix Goncourt was at hand, Gallimard sounded the committee about Morand's chances. It was pointed out to him that Morand hardly qualified because he was a successful author with big sales. Gallimard then had to confess: the print order for *Ouvert la nuit* was a modest 7,000. A few months later Bernard Grasset tempted Morand away from Gallimard with an advance of 50,000 francs plus a monthly allowance of 3,000.

Authors sometimes went so far as to sacrifice a large part of their royalties in return for heavy publicity. One of them claimed sales of 100,000. Another announced sales of 250,000. The name of the first was Alfred Machard, and the name of the second was Raymond Machard. Posterity does not know of them. With Claude Farrère boasting of 115,000 sales and Victor Margueritte announcing over a million copies sold, it was only necessary for Vallette to apply his expert knowledge of publishing economics to show that the figures were pure invention.

Another shady aspect of the publishing trade was that of bringing out books at the author's expense. One day Léautaud mentioned to Vallette that unwanted books made excellent

fuel. After soaking them in water and then drying out and pressing them, he had 'briquettes' of a high combustible quality.
This reminded Vallette of Sansot, a well-known publisher in his
day. Sansot never asked for money from writers anxious to
publish books at their own expense. He would say: 'I'll publish
your book at *my* expense.' The effect on hopeful authors of this
unexpected remark is easy to imagine. 'All I ask,' Sansot went
on, 'is that you buy 300 copies from me.' Three hundred copies
at pre-1914 prices including Sansot's profit margin represented
a handsome figure. The transaction was neat: Sansot owed
nothing to his author and the author owed nothing to him. As
for the books left over, he used them to fuel his fires. They kept
him warm throughout the whole of the war. 'He'd hit on a good
dodge,' chuckled Vallette.

Not so amusing was the story of Bernard Grasset's dealings
over the novel *Maria Chapdelaine*, a tale of settlers' life in French
Canada which became a sensational bestseller. When it was
first published it had only a moderate success. The author, Louis
Hémon, had died three years earlier, and his widow sold the
rights for a modest 1,500 francs. Grasset bought them outright
from the original publisher for 2,000. Despite the subsequent
very high sales, Hémon's widow never received a penny from
Grasset.

On a lighter note the *Journal littéraire* chronicles the activities
of some of the more exotic fauna who inhabited the publishing
world between the two wars. Among them were the notorious
Fischer brothers whose antics entertained Paris for many years.
They had begun as advertising agents for a tea firm and made
large sums of money by insisting on payment for articles in
newspapers where they bought advertising space. From this
they graduated to the posts of literary directors of the firm of
Flammarion. When they wrote to authors they addressed them
as 'Notre cher ami', or 'Notre cher poète'. Jules Renard used
to tell an amusing story about them:

'I went to see a publisher this morning. The Fischer brothers
were there. At eleven o'clock I was at another publisher's. The

Fischer brothers were there too. In the afternoon I had to see three more publishers. Each time the Fischer brothers were present. I decided to say to them: "Look, since this morning I've called on five publishers and each time you were there. How do you find time to do your work?" So they explained to me, in a low voice, as a secret: there's a third Fischer in the provinces whom nobody knows and nobody ever sees: he's the one who does the writing.'

The insincerities of literary life gave Léautaud much valuable copy. He was amused, for instance, by Gourmont's habit of writing charming letters to authors whose books he adversely criticised in everyday conversation. Those whom he praised in his articles, such as Mirbeau, he privately denigrated. A more diverting example of malice was provided by Jean Paulhan, that unusual stylist, inspired critic and discoverer of talent. As editor of the magazine *Commerce* he had published a typical Léautaud article about the disreputable Firmin. The result was a furious letter from Paul Claudel declaring that after reading what 'le sieur Léautaud' had written he wished to break off all connection with the NRF who owned the magazine. Paulhan gleefully asked Léautaud for another article. 'I'd very much have liked you to give me something for the next issue of *Commerce*,' he said, 'so as to annoy him.' The abominable Claudel got his own back. A little later he offered Paulhan the first rights to a new poem. Paulhan had it set up and printed with due prominence. On the day the *Nouvelle Revue Française* was ready for distribution, the poem suddenly appeared in *Le Figaro*. A jubilant letter arrived from Claudel: 'It was a surprise, wasn't it? Well, you gave me another, no less pleasant, by publishing that Léautaud article in October. . . .' The incident confirmed Léautaud's opinion of Claudel. Claudel was justified in protesting to Paulhan. But he was not entitled to play such a nasty little trick on him. Did he imagine that what the NRF chose to publish was his responsibility? He was a fool.

In the *Journal* Léautaud gives a unique panorama of the world of letters. At its lowest level it may be read purely for entertainment by anyone interested in the period. On a different plane it is a fascinating study of human nature as embodied in the literary man – the vanities, the cruelties, the ambitions, the disappointed hopes and the injustices that fall to anyone who seeks to make a name for himself in the profession. Already it is proving to be a valuable source of research, for in general the facts, where they can be checked independently, are shown to be accurate. Only in old age, when Léautaud's memory began to fail, do errors stand uncorrected.

The picture he draws is black enough to repel any aspiring littérateur. Rewards do not necessarily go to those who most deserve them, and disappointments are apt to bruise the spirit with a sharper pain than is caused in more humdrum walks of life. Kindness, industry, tolerance, disinterestedness and all the other qualities of heart that ought to be prized count for little. It is a narrow and embittered atmosphere that he evokes, a world where men will stoop to degrading shifts for the sake of being appointed book reviewer at a handful of francs a page.

Yet there is something that ineluctably binds its inhabitants to this depressing world, something that holds them, as Léautaud was for ever held, in its thrall. This is an intense fascination with literature. It means more to them than money or position. They may be poor and despised, obscure and rejected. Their wives may disdain them and their mistresses contemptuously drop them because they cannot afford expensive presents. They may live in fearful dependence on the caprice of an editor and end their days in poverty. All that sustains them throughout humiliation is a belief in their work. Like actors, they deserve to be forgiven their pompous airs, for it is a cruel and insecure calling to which they are pledged. There is something comic, but also something very moving, in the letter the poet Francis Jammes once wrote to Vallette, thereby causing much hilarity at the *Mercure*: 'Enough time has now elapsed for me to see that the whole of my work can stand up to posterity.' Jammes was then in his early sixties and was to die eight years later in 1938. Surely, after a life devoted to literature in return for small reward, he was entitled to this little display of vanity?

For, after all, the writer's only justification, his only defence against a hostile or indifferent world, lies in his *œuvre*. He must be content with the support and comfort of a few choice spirits who are enlightened enough to appreciate his worth. This, the only certain reward literature can bestow, is touchingly shown in a conversation Léautaud had with the veteran Symbolist poet and novelist Édouard Dujardin.

Dujardin in his youth had been a disciple of Mallarmé. Now Léautaud, despite his dislike of Mallarmé's poetry, admired the man, as a matter of principle, for his sincerity, his dedication, his complete disinterestedness. He listened to Dujardin's reminiscences with sympathy.

'This old man talked about the time of his youth with such freshness, eloquence and delightful feeling. It was rather like a woman grown old, recalling her love affairs and saying: "I loved that man!" Such loyalty, still so keen, does great honour to Dujardin. As we were talking about the destiny of Mallarmé's work, he made this very apt remark: "It doesn't matter! You must think of what he had during his lifetime. He was mocked, scoffed at, ignored, poor. We young people, who weren't exactly fools, surrounded him with our admiration, our respect, our affection, we listened to him as to a master and we never deserted him. Compare this with other poets of his time: Mendès, Coppée, Sully-Prudhomme. He was the only one to deserve this following. Do you think this a small thing?"'

Here, it may be, is the most important moral to be drawn from the *Journal* which its author described as *littéraire*.

—XII—

THE END OF THE AFFAIR

'It's the same with love as with everything else. What you have is nothing. It's what you haven't got that counts.'

Paul Léautaud

When Vallette took away the *Mercure* drama criticism from Léautaud in 1920 and shunted him off to what he hoped was the backwater of the 'Gazette d'hier et d'aujourd'hui', the voice of Maurice Boissard was by no means stilled. He was too well known, too stimulating a commentator to be silenced. Or at least, that is what other editors thought. Almost immediately Jacques Rivière of the *Nouvelle Revue Française* invited Léautaud to revive Boissard in his pages.

The NRF was then at the peak of its influence. It started publication in 1909 and had become a serious rival to the *Mercure de France*. Gide was a leading light. Kept away from the *Mercure* by his strong dislike of Gourmont, he threw all his energies into the NRF. It prospered and soon, like the *Mercure*, added book publishing to its activities. Despite its initial rejection of the manuscript of Proust's *A la recherche du temps perdu* – a blunder at which Gide connived – the firm later took it on and gained in prestige accordingly.

Gide was insistent on Léautaud's writing for the NRF. He kept badgering him for articles and offering to serialise a new version of *In Memoriam* or whatever Léautaud happened to have in mind. Now he returned to the charge. In reply to his arguments Léautaud said that his style would be out of place in the NRF. There was a well-defined spirit to the magazine, and he felt that what he wrote would jar with it. Gide seized on this: 'We all suffer from it there. We're wondering what we can do to get away from it. That's why we thought of you. You're the sort of man we want. And it's so true what you say

about the spirit of the paper. Everything we're offered is written
in that spirit.'

Finally Léautaud agreed. In October 1921, he began his new
engagement. There was great excitement at the NRF over the
capture of such a celebrity. Gaston Gallimard, head of the
NRF, was anxious to print a selection of Léautaud's *Mercure*
criticisms in two volumes. It was typical of Léautaud that he
only provided the text of the first volume in 1926 and that of the
second in 1943.

For just over a year all went well. The NRF congratulated
itself on the fresh new tone Léautaud brought to the magazine.
Then the inevitable happened. He chose to drench with a cold
sarcasm the author Jules Romains, alias, he was careful to
point out, Louis Farigoule, the name with which he was born.
The occasion was a review of Romains's play *Monsieur le
Trouhadec saisi par la débauche*, and it offered Léautaud the
chance he sought of chastising absurdity. Romains gave lectures
on how to write poetry. So, Léautaud mocked, poetry could
be taught in the same way as drawing, playing the piano and
accountancy. Did Monsieur Romains teach his pupils inspiration, sensibility and the art of assembling words to move the
heart with beauty? Perhaps he, Léautaud, should give some
lessons in drama criticism. It was all part of the mania of the
age for instruction. You couldn't move for pedagogues these
days. All of which was a lengthy preparation for a slashing
attack on Romains's play. It was cold, monotonous and pre-
fabricated. Had Monsieur Romains 'learned' to write plays in
the same way as his pupils 'learned' poetry from him?

Romains was furious. Fifty years later, as his memoirs show,
his anger still simmered. What complicated the situation was
that he then occupied an important place in the NRF catalogue
as one of their principal authors. It was unthinkable that the
magazine should, by publishing the criticism, harm a valuable
commercial asset. Jacques Rivière asked Léautaud to suppress
the offending passage. The critic refused. He insisted on complete freedom in what he wrote. There was no alternative, in
his own words, but to put on his hat and walk out. Gide was

very upset by the incident. He told Léautaud that he wept on hearing the news. The management lacked guts, he went on. Then, whispering maliciously in Léautaud's ear, he said: 'It was probably the best drama criticism you've written!'

Maurice Boissard did not stay mute for long. Two days after Léautaud separated from the NRF he was asked to contribute to another magazine called *Les Nouvelles littéraires*. This had been founded in 1922 by Maurice Martin du Gard. Maurice was the cousin of Roger Martin du Gard, author of the Thibault family chronicles which, between the two wars, delighted large audiences and have since been reborn through the ministrations of television. The two cousins, for some reason, were not over-fond of each other. Perhaps Roger felt that Maurice, as a literary journalist, did not do enough to publicise his novels.

Maurice presented an amused, nonchalant face to the world at large. He was something of a dandy and walked with a light, mincing step. During the 1939–45 war he spent much time in Vichy, and his recollections of that bizarre milieu are very readable. Léautaud appreciated his cheerful cynicism. Although Maurice well knew the risk he took by engaging a critic whom, in his memoirs, he was to describe as 'un collaborateur difficile', he was ready for the consequences.

'Léautaud has little to say, sometimes nothing, but he says it well,' he wrote. 'He sees people not as they are, but as he is. In spite of all the inconvenience and quarrels his bearishness has already brought upon me, I remain attached to this odd and spontaneous man who is free of hypocrisy, peevish, not always as bad as he wants to appear, and basically free – which is easier when you insist on living alone. . . . At last here he is: he puts his article on my desk, ashamed, lowering his eyes as if he had stolen something and was returning what he brings me, which is never properly typed copy but always a manuscript. And what handwriting! tiny, cramped, but fortunately the letters are well formed.'

When Léautaud appeared before him sporting the finery he wore on evenings at the theatre – slim tie, new overcoat, fresh powder glinting on his cheeks – Martin du Gard exclaimed: 'You're a Chardin revised by Manet!'

The quarrels to which Martin du Gard referred were not long in coming. Although he had accepted Léautaud's stipulation that his first article for the *Nouvelles littéraires* should be the Romains piece which the NRF refused to print, less than three months later editor and contributor were hopelessly opposed over a phrase Léautaud wished to include in another article. It was a mild quip about militarism. Once again Léautaud picked up his hat and walked out. He realised now, more than ever before, that the *Mercure de France* was his true spiritual home. Nowhere else could he enjoy the freedom of expression he demanded.

Léautaud remained on good terms with Martin du Gard and continued to write occasional pieces for the magazine. One of these was a sardonic account of a stay with Le Fléau at Pornic. Another was a little anthology, with dry comments, of the insulting remarks that his terrible mistress hurled at him. He also wrote often for the *Mercure de France*. The 'Gazette d'hier et d'aujourd'hui' was a congenial form. It could be short or long, depending on how he felt. Unlike drama criticism, it did not force him into the straitjacket of deadlines and set subjects. He could fill it as he pleased with epigrams, anecdotes and topical commentaries. When van Bever died in 1927, the event was easily encompassed within a 'Gazette'.

Adolphe van Bever was his oldest friend. His life had not been easy, despite a busy and successful literary career. When he was a young man he already showed the symptoms of the disease from which he eventually died. This was tabes, a form of consumption that results in slow but progressive emaciation of the body. Léautaud believed it was caused by a syphilitic ulcer van Bever left untreated. The syphilis may well have been hereditary, since van Bever was thought to have passed it on to his son, a degenerate who, to round off this macabre passage, became a victim of the wartime mass-murderer Dr Petiot.

Van Bever's malady gave him constant pain. In order to find the temporary relief necessary for work he took a variety of medicaments including opium. Over the years these produced abscesses on various parts of the body. He did not complain and did not envy others their good luck. Sometimes the pain was too much for him, and his shrieks of suffering startled passers-by in the street outside. Rather heartlessly, Apollinaire wrote:

> 'Enterrerons-nous cet hiver
> Le pauvre monsieur van Bever?'

When he received visitors at home van Bever took care to be spruce, well shaved, and dressed in his best clothes. Only the twitches of his face revealed the suffering he endured. Léautaud was astonished that his frail little body could put up such a resistance to illness. He even forced himself to travel, and, with André Billy, made a journey to England.

Friendship, mused Léautaud, was a curious thing. He was linked to van Bever by memories, by habits shared, by common experiences. Yet in spite of forty years' acquaintance their tastes were entirely different. Léautaud was not at all interested in van Bever's researches, his enjoyment of collating texts and checking dates, scholar's work that bored Léautaud immensely. It was doubtful whether van Bever read anything Léautaud wrote. They had, none the less, affection for each other. 'You're a foul-weather friend,' van Bever told him warmly. 'When there's nothing to eat, you're always at hand to share your dinner. As soon as I'm in luck, you're off.'

Van Bever's last illness brought out some of Léautaud's most typical characteristics. He was a reluctant sick visitor and could not bear to hear yet again the agonising cries of pain and to see once more the frail body twisting feverishly on its bed. At the moment of van Bever's death the complete egoist remained unmoved. Death was a deliverance, and the best epitaph would be the concluding lines that graced the cripple Scarron's tomb:

> '. . . Voici la première nuit
> Que le pauvre Scarron sommeille.'

Moreover: 'Sorrow for the dead is foolishness. An illusion, too.

The tears we weep are for ourselves, for the feeling of emptiness or of being deprived that we are left with. They're dead, in other words: they are nothing now. To lament them doesn't make sense.'

Another comrade of his youth, and one with whom he drifted into an Indian summer of friendship during the nineteen-thirties, was Paul Valéry. They met on neutral ground, as it were, in the home of Dr Le Savoureux, a medical man of literary sympathies. Dr Le Savoureux, who died in 1961, had taken over Chateaubriand's old home, La Vallée-aux-Loups. 'When I returned from the Holy Land', wrote Chateaubriand, 'I bought, near the hamlet of Aulnay, a gardener's house hidden among hills covered with woods.' The ground was sandy and uneven. Upon it grew a wild orchard ending in a copse of chestnut trees and a little stream. Chateaubriand planted here a variety of trees and tended them with his own hands. In this house he wrote the words that occupied him between 1807 and 1818. The neo-classic facade, with its caryatids in stone draperies, looks out on a tangled garden and trees which, mere saplings in Chateaubriand's time, now reach in lopsided majesty to the sky. The scene is the essence of Romanticism.

Dr Le Savoureux restored the house and set up there a small Chateaubriand museum. Another part of it he turned into a clinic. A nearby Rue le Dr Le Savoureux commemorates his rescue of the place. Today it is a national monument.

Dinner parties at La Vallée-aux-Loups were noted for the quality of the food and the brilliance of the conversation. Valéry, Léautaud thought, sometimes looked like a candidate for the doctor's clinic. His face was heavily wrinkled, his head nodded often like an old man's, and when he rolled his unending cigarettes his hands shook. His mind, though, was as agile as ever.

'He's still unaffected, humorous, friendly,' wrote Léautaud. 'He still speaks with his teeth slightly clenched. As in the days of our youth he is full of crude words in conversation. Fame and the Académie, in this respect at least, don't seem to have changed him. I don't like his poetry or, in general, anything he writes. For me, it's making a lot of mystery about things that are often very ordinary. But I enjoy seeing him again, with all his little ways, such as I used to know him.'

Why had Valéry aged so rapidly? Dr Le Savoureux imagined it was due to his diabetes. The physical effects of growing old depressed Valéry. He confessed that he never looked in a mirror except when shaving. He remained a lively and amusing talker. When a fellow guest congratulated him on a lecture he had recently given about Pushkin he blithely explained that, as in the case of Goethe, not knowing the language he had never read any of his works.

Valéry had many good stories to relate. He told of a dinner abroad at which he was guest of honour. When coffee appeared he saw the hostess approaching him with her autograph book. He realised that now he had to pay for his dinner. It being a Sunday, he wrote in the book: 'Les pensées sont fermées le dimanche.'

There was also the incident when, as a candidate for the Académie, he made the ritual calls on existing members to solicit their vote. He was received by Marshal Foch who listened to him for a moment as he outlined his chances, and then exclaimed: 'I see what the situation is. The left wing is crumbling, the centre is advancing, we're on the right wing, we make a turning movement and we overcome then.' And, making all the gestures as if he were actually on the battlefield: 'We've won in advance.'

Among other guests at La Vallée-aux-Loups was that unusual cleric the Abbé Mugnier. He had never gained the position in the Catholic hierarchy his intelligence merited. It could be that his wit and his love of society did not endear him to more austere colleagues. His home was a very modest lodging in an unfashionable quarter. Most of his evenings were spent at the dinner tables of the rich, who enjoyed his amusing talk and looked forward to the occasions when he visited them. He knew why he was invited: they regarded him as a curiosity, an entertainer with an unfailing stock of anecdote and epigram. His success in great houses did not blind him to the main purpose of life. As the spiritual guide of many social figures he was instrumental in obtaining conversions. For not only the poor have souls.

Between the witty Abbé and the atheistic Léautaud there grew a bond of affection and respect. 'Let us speak no ill of sinners,' observed the Abbé. 'Sinners are the bread of the Church.' When attacked on the subject of Hell, he replied: 'Of course there is a Hell. It's absolutely certain. The only thing is, there's nobody in it.'

Léautaud's companion at La Vallée-aux-Loups was often a lady called Marie Dormoy, who drove him there in her car, did him many services and was eventually to play a very important part in his life. As librarian of the Bibliothèque Littéraire Jacques Doucet she hoped to buy the manuscript of his *Journal* for the collection. Valéry abetted her in this, as he knew how desperately Léautaud needed the money such a purchase would bring. Nothing, in the end, came of their friendly effort. The library committee saw little reason to expend a large sum on the manuscript of an obscure writer, and Léautaud, fiercely proud, rejected what looked suspiciously like charity.

Marie Dormoy was the daughter of a financier. He had deeply religious feelings and conducted family prayers at which God was invoked with exaltation. Each member fervently believed that an angel scrutinised every thought and every action, for which he or she would be accountable at the day of judgement. The seasons of the year were marked by the great religious festivals in a blaze of light, incense and music which profoundly impressed Marie. Since riches were, for her father, an obstacle to saintliness, he deliberately restricted his earnings to an amount that would keep the family at a certain level of comfort. As a result he took three months' holiday a year, the better to appreciate the divine attractions of the countryside that the Creator had made.

Her parents' absorption in things of the spirit tended to

deprive Marie of the more commonplace tenderness of family life. Sensitive to the charm of art and music, she found in the organist Lucien Michelot, for many years director of music at the church of Notre-Dame-des-Champs, the father-figure she was seeking. He was a novel character to inhabit churchly precincts. Each time he fell in love with a woman he wrote a mass. On one occasion he narrowly escaped becoming entangled with that predatory composer Augusta Holmès, the object of César Franck's affection and mistress of the poet Catulle Mendès. His Curé once observed him carrying large bundles of paper and asked him what they were. 'My love letters,' replied Michelot proudly.

Michelot also happened to be a great teacher. He would be carried away by enthusiasms of the moment, would plan vast undertakings such as a commentary on the *Divina Commedia*, a listing of all the medieval churches in France, a life of Michelangelo. Voluminous notes were made and then left to gather dust while he took up some other new interest. Yet his mercurial reactions were part of a genuine talent he had for opening the eyes of his pupils to the beauties of art, literature and music.

Marie Dormoy was grateful to him ever after for his teaching. In John Donne's words, she thanked 'not him only that hath digged out treasure for me, but [him] that hath lighted me a candle to the peace'. Michelot also introduced her to the writer André Suarès. Another friend was Romain Rolland. Soon she had a circle of acquaintances that included the organist Marcel Dupré, the architect August Perret, the sculptors Bourdelle and Maillol, the composers Darius Milhaud and Olivier Messiaen, and the art dealer Ambroise Vollard. There were, in time, few people whom she did not know in the literary and artistic worlds of Paris.

The man who had the most decisive effect on her career, and who gave her the opportunity of following what became her life's work, was the dressmaker Jacques Doucet. In the nineteen-twenties he was a legendary figure. From small beginnings he built up the celebrated firm which made him a colossally rich man and a leader in women's fashion. Business had left him no time for culture. He did not, for example, become aware of Molière until he was nearly sixty. What this untutored man lacked in education he made up for with flair, the flair that enabled him to appraise exactly the shapes and colours on which his fortune as a couturier was based. It served him equally well in buying pictures, furniture and art objects. He trusted to an instinct that never let him down, whether he was choosing a horse or a piece of sculpture. Edmond de Goncourt, who prided himself as a collector, was envious of Doucet's brilliant raids in the sale-room. He saw him as a formidable rival.

Women, too, he collected. At a fitting one day he overheard a beautiful and famous client exclaim: 'When I listen to *Tristan* I'm so moved that I'd do anything.' He took a sumptuous apartment, furnished it lavishly and engaged musicians. Then he invited the lady to a private hearing of extracts from the *Tristan* she admired. She arrived and was soon overcome by the potent music. 'Won't they go and leave us in peace?' she inquired. The musicians packed their instruments and left. Doucet was able to prove for himself that what she said about the effect of Wagner's music on her was correct.

The great romance of Doucet's life was inspired by a married woman. After long years of waiting, a divorce was arranged. In preparation for this moment he built a house in the Rue Spontini and filled it with the loveliest things he could find among the treasures of eighteenth-century French art. The divorce was about to be granted and he believed himself the happiest of men. Suddenly and mysteriously the woman died. No one ever knew the circumstances. Doucet could not bear to revisit the house he had lovingly prepared. He put up the contents for auction. They fetched the equivalent of 7 million gold francs. This money he put towards buying a magnificent art collection which later became known as the Bibliothèque d'Art et d'Archéologie, Fondation Jacques Doucet. It was open to the public and maintained at his own expense. During the 1914–18 war, annoyed by the fact that the authorities demanded

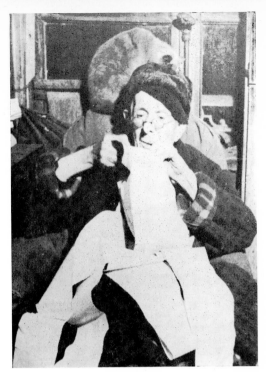

25. Reading proofs

26. At lunch with Madame Gould, Avenue Malakoff

27. 'Guénette', the monkey

28. 'Mademoiselle Barbette', who had 't[
loveliest eyes in the world'

29. Feeding time

tax on it, despite its philanthropic nature, he made a gift of the entire collection to the University of Paris.

Now he turned to literature. In his country house he entertained hungry writers to dinner. Pierre Louÿs, Henri de Régnier and Paul Valéry learned to appreciate the exquisite dishes, the fine wines and excellent cigars they enjoyed as his guests. He engaged André Suarès to write him, each week, a letter about some literary subject. And each week, in Suarès's banking account, a cheque for several thousand francs was deposited. During the nineteen-twenties Doucet patronised the young Surrealist writers. He subsidised the *Revue surréaliste* by purchasing their manuscripts. Others he helped by employing them on a salary to catalogue his library and to choose new books for it. Blaise Cendrars and Pierre Reverdy were among those whom he paid, as he did Suarès, to write him weekly letters.

In 1925 Marie Dormoy's father died, leaving his wife and daughter in financial straits. Doucet invited Marie to lunch the day after the funeral. He asked her if she would like to look after his books and named a handsome salary. She had no degree or qualifications. His generosity left her speechless.

The vast collection of books and manuscripts which comprised the Bibliothèque Littéraire Jacques Doucet, now administered by the Bibliothèque Sainte-Geneviève in the Place du Panthéon, helped to take his mind off the problems that clouded his last years. Devaluation had eaten away much of his fortune and a defaulting secretary embezzled a lot of what remained. When he died in 1929 his bank account did not hold enough to cover the funeral expenses. The future of the two great libraries he founded was assured, however, for he had bequeathed them to the State. The curious thing about them was that they had been created by a man who, knowing little, bought the items they contain simply for his own pleasure and with caprice as his only guide.

For the rest of her career Marie Dormoy remained there as librarian. The manuscripts the library houses – invaluable pieces by Verlaine, Baudelaire, Rimbaud, Gide, Valéry, to mention

only a few – have made it a centre of research in modern literature. The nature of her work brought her into contact with
many contemporary writers. Her acquaintance with Léautaud
did not happen, though, for professional reasons. For a long
time she had read and enjoyed his writing in the *Mercure de
France*. Once she asked Louis Dumur, Vallette's lieutenant,
about the identity of Maurice Boissard. 'He's one of our employees,' he replied. When she afterwards told this to Léautaud
he was delighted.

She was introduced to him by a mutual friend. He intrigued
her: a thin face, a meagre body lost in voluminous clothes too
large for him, a mouth with few teeth, big and muscular hands.
But he had appealing eyes, gentle and expressive. It was her
idea to issue an illustrated de luxe edition of *Le Petit Ami* commissioned by Ambroise Vollard, who produced many successful ventures like this between the two wars. Léautaud detested
limited editions and, furthermore, did not want to republish the
book until he had revised it. Though it would have been easy
to accept 25,000 francs for doing nothing, which was all the
proposal entailed, he turned it down.

In 1932, with the aid of Valéry, Marie Dormoy tried to persuade the Bibliothèque Doucet to buy the manuscript of the
Journal littéraire. As we have seen, the attempt was unsuccessful. Their acquaintance continued with little encouragement
from Léautaud. Her kindness was met with surliness. Offers to
lend him money were rejected with contemptuous anger. He
was incapable of showing gratitude. His remarks about her
were rough and uncomplimentary.

Invariably her thoughtfulness towards him was misunder-
stood. If a woman was nice to him he concluded, poor as he
was and able to offer neither money nor presents, that she must
have amorous intentions. Unaware at the time of his affair with
Madame Cayssac, Marie Dormoy could not imagine him having any kind of love life at all. She felt compassion, affection,
even tenderness for him, as well as respect for his literary work,
but nothing else. He, who had known so little tenderness in
his life, especially from women, found it hard to appreciate the

disinterested companionship she offered from the fullness of her heart.

She typed his articles for him. She helped look after the overgrown garden at Fontenay. In every way she sought to lighten the squalor of his daily life. He grumbled about her 'interference', complained of her well-intentioned efforts and rudely criticised her looks and figure. She commissioned the artist Vuillard to draw him for the frontispiece of a special edition of one of his essays. When he saw, among the list of subscribers, the names of Matisse and Auguste Perret he flew into a wild rage, declaring that he did not wish to be associated with men whom he regarded as impostors and charlatans, or to accept charity from them. His share of the proceeds was large, and she hoped he would buy himself some badly needed clothes. He pocketed it without a word of thanks. Later she learned that he spent the money haphazardly on two inferior reproductions of Louis XVI chairs and a paper screen in eighteenth-century style which his cats soon reduced to shreds.

His off-handed attitude towards her was partly due to a fear that Madame Cayssac might find out. When Marie Dormoy came to visit him in his office he was nervous. Somewhere down the street, he felt sure, lurked the vengeful shape of Le Fléau or one of her spies. Early on in their acquaintance he had told Marie Dormoy that 'a certain person' might be put out by her visits to Fontenay and the letters he wrote to her. She laughed and asked him if he were mad. She pointed out that it was not her custom to pry into other people's affairs.

A few years later she actually saw this 'certaine personne'. Léautaud was feeling ill and had gone home. Marie Dormoy went out to Fontenay, thinking him alone and without help. There in the kitchen, she found an elderly, ugly, dirty female. 'Is Monsieur Léautaud here?' asked Marie Dormoy. 'You only have to go up,' said the apparition shortly.

Léautaud was upstairs, lying on a bed. 'Did you see Madame Cayssac?' he asked anxiously. 'Yes.' 'Did she say anything to you?' 'No – she only told me to come up.' He breathed a sigh of relief.

She went downstairs. Le Fléau was still on the watch. Did she, the unwelcome caller asked, want anything brought over from Paris? Le Fléau replied haughtily that she had no need whatsoever of her services. Marie Dormoy wished her good-bye. Le Fléau said nothing and, with jealous eyes, saw her go.

Although Marie Dormoy had failed to buy his *Journal litléraire* for her library she remained convinced of its value. So did Vallette. Towards the end of his life he read memoirs written by old friends and never ceased to be annoyed by the mistakes of fact they contained. 'I've more confidence in your *Journal*,' he told Léautaud, 'with things noted down every day.' He was anxious to publish it. Knowing Léautaud's dilatory habits, however, he thought it wise to take an indirect approach. He suggested putting together a volume of passages about Remy de Gourmont taken from the early years. Léautaud agreed and found the selection easy to make. The only problem was how to get it all typed. A professional typist was out of the question, for his handwriting was often illegible and the cost would be enormous. Marie Dormoy proposed herself. Léautaud stared at her in silent, distrustful surprise. Five days later he came round to the idea. He only wanted one copy made. After many lively arguments he gave permission for two. Unknown to him, and very prudently, she made three copies, reserving the third for herself. So began the exhausting task of transcribing the complete *Journal* that was to occupy her, off and on, for eighteen years and to cover 12,000 typewritten pages.

Now that Léautaud was in the mood for action he talked to Vallette about the problems of full-length publication. The *Journal* contained a great deal of material likely to offend people still alive. Vallette was then in his mid-seventies, and who, after he had gone, would be bold enough to take on the responsibility of publishing it? Wouldn't it be best to prepare a contract? 'Draw it up,' he said, 'and I'll sign it.' Next day Léautaud brought in a contract and Vallette immediately signed it on behalf of the *Mercure*.

In old age Vallette sometimes showed signs of declining powers. On several occasions he let other publishers take over books whose potential he was too tired or too indifferent to evaluate. He even wavered in his old principles of independence. When Léautaud, in one of his 'Gazettes', made a jeering attack on religion and brought many protests from readers, Vallette's patience gave way. A letter from a group of young writers praising the article failed to change his mind.

'"What do you expect me to do about your 'young writers' ?" he stormed. "Parbleu! I know very well you've an audience of 400 people who follow everything you write, but what counts as far as I'm concerned are my subscribers. Especially at a time like this, you know as well as I do, when magazines exist on a tightrope. Now you can see what the subscribers think of your writing. *I* don't invent their letters."'

In his arguments with Léautaud the normally staid Vallette would lose his temper. His voice grew loud and trembled with anger, his face reddened, and he banged the desk with clenched fist. What was even more annoying for him was Léautaud's icy calm, however emotional the situation became. The more scathing Léautaud's replies the more impassive was his attitude. The inward anger he felt was poured out later into his *Journal*.

Léautaud's time-keeping, or lack of it, and his small salary were further causes of disagreement. Despite their long acquaintanceship, Léautaud complained, Vallette often treated him as if he were a soldier being disciplined by a sergeant-major. Vallette would embarrass him with rebukes for imagined mistakes in front of fellow writers and distinguished visitors to the *Mercure*. There were rarely any apologies for this tactless behaviour.

Frequently Léautaud thought of finding a job elsewhere. His fear of the unknown, the burden of his animals, always deterred him. There were many advantages to working at the *Mercure*: the income he derived from selling copies of books sent for review, free postage for his letters, a constant supply of ink and paper and envelopes that cost him nothing, and, of course, a superb opportunity for observing literary life.

No doubt his employer was fully aware of this. Moreover,

though Vallette's conduct during the last years may have verged on the insensitive, Léautaud was by no means an ideal employee. Granted his literary reputation was an asset to the *Mercure*, the fact remained that as an office worker he left much to be desired. Vallette, who was at his desk by five o'clock each morning, was naturally irritated to see Léautaud strolling in at ten and taking lunch hours that extended deep into the afternoon. Yet in spite of their many differences over practical matters, he did not forget that Léautaud's position on the magazine was of a rather special kind. He realised that Léautaud was not an 'employé ordinaire'.

However much Léautaud complained about Vallette's meanness and raged at his cavalier attitude, he never denied the basic debt he owed him. This was shown in an amusing and unusual way by Léautaud's attempt to obtain for him the award of Officier in the Légion d'Honneur. Léautaud, who regarded decorations as the toys of fools, who detested asking favours of anyone and who was the reverse of a diplomatist, now set himself seriously to achieve an aim he would normally have ridiculed. He wrote letters and paid calls. The rosette, after some delay, was awarded and Léautaud had the satisfaction of knowing that his activity had not been in vain. A few weeks later Vallette was again irritably drawing attention to his late arrival in the office.

This uncharacteristic episode shows how Léautaud was able to swallow one of his most deep-set prejudices in the attempt to honour a man whom in the same breath he accused of avarice and injustice. Throughout the ups and downs of his curious relationship with Vallette – and there were times when they were furiously opposed to each other – a feeling of gratitude persisted. He knew that but for Vallette he would have had no regular platform from which to express opinions which in those days caused serious offence. To some extent Vallette was the father whom Léautaud had never had: a paternal figure who, while appreciating his work and encouraging him, was also a stern realist whom Léautaud railed at but whom, in the end, he respected.

Vallette remained an efficient administrator until the very end in 1935. He could remember the smallest details of printers' contracts drawn up forty years previously. Nothing escaped his notice in matters of binding, warehousing and dispatch. His mind stayed alert and sharp. Four days before his death in his seventy-seventh year he was driving his car with his usual assurance.

Sometimes he regretted the lifetime he had given to the *Mercure de France*. Once, when Léautaud spoke of what little time he had for writing, Vallette riposted: 'Not a bit of it! In spite of it all you've been able to read, improve your mind, get out and about, see things, write! Whereas, apart from the *Mercure*, I've read nothing, seen nothing, learned nothing, known nothing. The *Mercure*'s swallowed me up completely.'

Indifferent to death as to so many other things, Vallette could not be bothered to follow the diet or take the medicines his doctor prescribed. Forced, most reluctantly, to his bed, he asked for his usual pen to be brought from the office next door so that Rachilde, to whom he was addressing a letter, should not suspect anything from his changed handwriting. He did not want her to come rushing over from their country house. 'Now I'm ill I'll feel more at ease without her being here. You don't know how difficult she is to live with.'

Léautaud spent the last morning with him. From time to time Vallette opened his eyes and looked about him. He took a glass of water with a firm hand and drank it. In a gentle voice he stammered unintelligibly, like a baby trying to talk for the first time. Then he died, quietly and easily. Léautaud went to the funeral wearing a pair of second-hand dancing pumps and a postman's tunic he had picked up cheaply somewhere. He wept. He would never get used to the disappearance of the man he had been accustomed to see and argue with every working day for forty years.

Vallette was irreplaceable. The man chosen to succeed him was Georges Duhamel, one of the *Mercure*'s bestselling novelists. He had been a doctor and then a poet. His early books *La Vie des martyrs* and *Civilisation* contain some of his best writing and were inspired by his experience in the medical service during the 1914-18 war. From the nineteen-twenties onward he kept up a prolific output of novels, often in cycles (one narrated the life of a worthy character called Salavin, another recounted the history of the Pasquier family), which appealed to a vast audience of readers. The strain of sentimentality, of compassion, of unfailing kindness to all, struck a chord at the time. Vallette did not think highly of Duhamel's books, though naturally he was delighted that they sold in such quantities.

Duhamel tended to speak like a character in one of his novels. He was a big man, jovial and full of warmth. Something of a *faux-bonhomme*, thought cynics, who were made uneasy by his booming geniality and his lay preacher manner. His industry was enormous. He went on lecture tours at home and abroad. He revelled in answering the many fan letters sent him by readers who asked his advice on their intimate problems. The Académie Française was his obvious destination and he loved it there, posing with much satisfaction in his ceremonial robes, rehearsing aloud his *discours de réception* with actorly flourishes, and engaging eagerly in the social life that went with it.

Léautaud mockingly described him as 'un écrivain pour familles nombreuses'. Duhamel's effusive protestations of love for humanity and his obvious wish to be on good terms with everyone suggested hypocrisy. He was a careerist, thought Léautaud, and too preoccupied with the impression he made on others. It was amusing that Duhamel – though he denied intent – should have used Léautaud as the basis for a character who keeps a diary in his novel *Le Notaire du Havre*. 'Me, turned into a character in a novel, and a novel by Georges Duhamel?' Léautaud wrote. 'Now I'm famous, in disguise, for a short while, the length of time Duhamel's novels will last.'

Yet Duhamel was a sensitive man who lacked the hardness of the true careerist. Although he was one of the most successful novelists of his time and earned nearly half a million francs a year, he could be deeply wounded and cast into despair by a single bad review, however unimportant the paper in which it appeared. He put himself out to be pleasant to Léautaud, helped him in many ways, and bore patiently the jeers he received in return.

Duhamel's reign at the *Mercure* began with unheard-of innovations. He installed telephones which, until 1935, had been unknown there. Typewriters were brought in – up to then all letters were written by hand – and a strange animal known as a typist walked the corridor. The place was wired for electricity. To his great disgust Léautaud was issued with a reading lamp to put on his cluttered desk: 'I shall look like a bank clerk,' he grunted. His peace was disturbed by workmen washing down walls and clearing out cupboards untouched for many many years.

Duhamel's new broom extended to the contents of the *Mercure de France* as well. He proposed to run film reviews, a type of journalism Vallette always avoided because it was notorious that such reviews were paid for by interested parties. Once the *Mercure* started featuring film notices it would become as suspect as less scrupulous publications. Duhamel went ahead none the less.

The director of the *Mercure* found himself besieged by hopeful authors and would-be contributors. Once Vallette had gone it was as if the flood-gates were opened and every writer in Paris rushed to press his claim. Duhamel began to realise that he had taken on more than he expected. There were manuscripts to read, people to see, letters to write, issues of the magazine to be compiled, books to publish, over and above the routine administration. It was obvious that Vallette had been wise to leave editorial decisions to an expert committee and to avoid involvement in making choices. Duhamel was too kind-hearted, too much of a writer himself, to hurt fellow writers by rejecting their manuscripts.

Early in 1938 Duhamel found that the *Mercure* was too much even for a man of his energy. He could not continue both as novelist and as director of the magazine, so he decided to withdraw. During his brief overlordship he had exhausted himself to no purpose and made many enemies. He handed over with relief to the production manager, Jacques Bernard, who now took his place.

Léautaud was apprehensive. He had not been entirely happy with Duhamel and there had been arguments. However, Duhamel was an educated man, a writer, who in spite of disagreements on matters of principle at least shared common ground with him. Jacques Bernard was not a literary man. He knew everything there was to know about the physical production of the magazine, but his intellectual background was limited. A keen motorcyclist, he had met with a road accident a few years previously and received head injuries that sometimes affected his powers of judgement. As a result his actions were on occasion alarmingly capricious. Having made a decision he would, in a very short space of time, contradict himself and do the opposite of what he originally planned. His attitude, if not hostile, was decidedly ambiguous towards Léautaud, who viewed the future with foreboding.

Change was everywhere apparent in that last uneasy year before the war. At the *Mercure* there were upheavals and uncertainty. In Léautaud's private life there occurred an event which, had it happened ten years earlier, would have shattered him. As it was, he remained quite composed about it. This was nothing less than what turned out to be his final break with Le Fléau. For several years, indeed, they had been at daggers drawn, but as usual, in the intervals, they made love and patched up a frail peace. Now, at last, he could take no more.

She was seventy years old. Age had done nothing to mellow her. The taunts she threw at him were barbed with all her old skill, and her jealous surveillance of him had lost none of its effectiveness. Yet there was a shrillness, a note of desperation in her invective that gave the game away. She was on the losing side and she knew it. For, worried by the approach of war and old age, she asked him to marry her. It was not the first time she had done this. He refused. They met in her flat, ostensibly to discuss a loan she had made him, and there followed a noisy scene. He listened, unmoved, a cigarette drooping from his lips, as she stormed and raged and whipped herself into a mood of shrieking hysteria. Then he picked up his hat and left.

He regretted her as a mistress. There was no doubt that she was a brilliantly accomplished lover. He would always be grateful to her for initiating him into sexual pleasure. With a nostalgic smile he thought of his trips to Pornic, of her little habit of marking the calendar with the dates of their 'séances', of her superb performance in bed. Then he thought of her atrocious character and the smile faded.

He still heard through mutual friends about her activities. They even corresponded. Her letters were sarcastic and abusive. She reminded him of loans unpaid and of ancient discourtesies. Where did he go for love now? she mocked, and advised him to use the services of prostitutes. He was a liar and a thief whom no honest woman would care to know. Yet she went on writing to him. When he did not receive one of these unsympathetic letters for some time he began to get worried. They became something of a ritual to which he had grown accustomed. After a long silence on her part he would see the familiar handwriting on an envelope with something like relief.

Marie Dormoy once analysed his relationship with Le Fléau. 'You desired each other; you didn't love each other,' she said. He agreed. People who glimpsed him in the street would not have thought him capable of sexual passion. They saw a quaint little old figure carrying a dirty bag of animal food, a 'petit vieux' looking like a character out of Dickens. ('From *Nicholas Nickleby*,' said one passerby whom he overheard.) His fellow travellers on the Ligne de Sceaux chuckled as they watched him peel his potatoes in the train on the way home. He did not care. At the end of the journey, he knew, there awaited him all the warmth and affection that Le Fléau had never given him: his cats, his dogs, his monkey and his goose would scramble with noisy delight to the garden gate and welcome him in a flurry of loving excitement.

⟨XIII⟩

THE RADIO STAR

'My choice is made and I will sum it up here: I would rather have been Chamfort than Baudelaire.'

Paul Léautaud

On New Year's Day 1939, 'Maurice Boissard' raised his voice again, and for a second time his drama criticism began to appear in the *Nouvelle Revue Française*. It was eighteen years since, at Gide's invitation, he had featured there, and now Jean Paulhan asked him to write for the magazine. Within a few months history repeated itself. Certain of his observations brought strong protests from readers. Without regret, he gave up his contract.

Jean Paulhan was still keen to publish his writing. Later that year the *Nouvelle Revue Française* featured one of his articles. It caught the attention of Georgette Crozier, his old love whom he had last seen when they parted more than thirty years ago. She wrote to him. He had often thought of her since, and her letter sent him back to the early years of his *Journal* where he had recorded the history of their affair. What he read there moved him strangely. When she left him she went to work in England and spent a long time across the Channel. Now, with the international situation worsening, she decided to come back to France.

Georgette had been one of his more sympathetic loves. In the forty years that elapsed since their affair she had not forgotten him. They met again. He found her 'une petite bourgeoise' with a touch of the schoolmistress in her manner. At first they were hesitant together, but soon they established an easy relationship. She came over to Fontenay and sat in the garden. His life aroused her curiosity and she wanted to find out what he had been doing in the long interval since their last meeting. Who was Marie Dormoy? What was he writing about?

Her hair was white, though her complexion remained smooth and soft. Her features were aquiline still and shapely. Something of her old feeling for him reawakened. They probably slept together. She confessed to him that she had been stupid at the time of their love-affair and regretted leaving him. If they had married then how different life would have been! Her daydreams left him cold. She saw that her manner grated on him and that solitude was what he preferred above all else. Though she said she still loved him, she tried to be tactful and only made him promise to write to her from time to time and let her know how he was. He noted, tongue in cheek: 'J'ai perdu mon Eurydice.'

Hitler's invasion of Poland and the months of the 'drôle de guerre' that succeeded it found Léautaud in a mood of excitement. His own life was so dull, so uneventful, that public emergencies induced a state of exhilaration in him. It had been the same in 1934 when strikes and riots filled the streets with armed policemen, and government ministers fell or hastily resigned one after another. So it was in 1940. A wave of burglaries and robberies with violence inspired him to buy an old revolver and a whistle to summon help in case of attack. Having no one but himself to worry about, he could now, once his precautions were made, concentrate on the novel spectacle that he saw being played around him.

In June 1940, he heard confused reports that France had collapsed. He went out into the streets of Paris to see what was going on. Many shops were shut. There were no newspapers or postal deliveries, and railway stations were closed. In the Boulevard Saint-Germain he saw an uninterrupted stream of people leaving the capital, some in cars packed with luggage, others in lorries, and others still on bicycles or pushing hand carts loaded with their belongings. Among the clogged traffic were farm carts with cows attached to the back. A workman passed by on his bicycle, cases tied at the rear and, in front on the handlebars, a sheepdog ensconced in a little hood. Léautaud congratulated him on remembering to take the dog.

Soon Paris was deserted. He stood in the Place de l'Opéra

and looked in turn along the wide thoroughfares that radiated from it. They were all empty. Shops were boarded up and houses shuttered. As far as his eye could take in there was not a soul to be seen. The silence was complete. The great boulevards of Paris were like the main street of some country town, dead and eerily quiet. It was charming! He remembered how his father, sixty years ago, could walk safely in the street while reading his paper without worrying about the traffic. Now he could do the same. There was no one to jostle him on the pavement. The city had come to a complete standstill. Paris in its new aspect had an endless charm for him. As often as possible he wandered the streets and indulged in his love of 'flânerie' to the full. The place belonged to him. It did not matter that the country was occupied and the future dark. The turn of events had brought with it a privilege that he was doubtless one of the very few Frenchmen to appreciate.

Gradually the realities of enemy occupation became apparent. Next month he happened to see in the Place de l'Odéon that a bookshop he knew well had been deserted for several weeks. He went in and asked the concierge why the door was still open and the shop untenanted. The concierge told him to leave. 'I've known Monsieur Lipschutz for twenty years,' he protested. 'If he were here he'd have been glad to see me.' The concierge replied meaningly: 'Monsieur Lipschutz isn't here. He's a long way away.' Léautaud understood. The bookseller was Jewish.

Soon the black market was flourishing. In Fontenay the local queen of the trade was 'la mère Maillette'. Her shop was a dirty little hole with potato peelings scattered on the floor. It connected with her kitchen which was dirtier still and looked on to a muddy courtyard. She had six or seven beautiful daughters, two sons and a swarm of grandchildren. Her stock contained nearly everything that was scarce elsewhere – real coffee, meat, butter, chicken, tobacco, chocolate, cigarettes, wine, sugar, cocoa, women's underclothes. 'La mère Maillette' wrote down orders with a bit of chalk on the wall or counter, promising delivery for tomorrow if her 'suppliers' didn't let her down. She

gave change out of a frayed bag that dangled from her waist
and bulged with greasy notes.

She was an amiable woman, always anxious to please and
to be of service. Her dress hung in tatters, her hair was un-
combed, and her apron was an old sack. In the crowded confusion of her tiny shop people often helped themselves to the
stock or deftly abstracted a note or two from her dropsical
money bag when she was looking elsewhere. Sometimes
German soldiers were entertained in the back room by her
lovely daughters and she sold them quantities of coloured water
as champagne. She always denied that she made a lot of money.
It was her 'suppliers' who took the real profits. 'If we made any
money would we be dressed as we are, like beggar-women?'
she demanded. 'There's only one thing: we do manage to eat
pretty well.'

It was not often that Léautaud could afford to buy anything
from 'la mère Maillette'. At the beginning of the war his salary
was cut by half as an economy measure. By way of compensation Jacques Bernard offered to start publishing the *Journal
littéraire* in the magazine. The complete manuscript, thanks to
Marie Dormoy, was evacuated with archives from the Bibliothèque Littéraire Jacques Doucet to the safety of the countryside. Now that the great problem of security for his life's work
had been taken from his mind, Léautaud settled down and
adapted himself to the new way of existence that he and his
compatriots had to face. Each day he went to Paris and enjoyed
its deserted aspect. He put up cheerfully with the many short-
ages that had to be endured and worried only for the sake of his
animals. He was used to privations and did not miss the wine he
rarely drank or the rich food he never knew. Lack of firewood
was his chief problem, and with few regrets he chopped up
several pieces of his furniture to put into the stove.

In the spring of 1941 he enjoyed an experience that very few
authors are privileged to know. Following the Armistice which
Marshal Pétain signed with the German victors, France was
divided into two zones. Communications between them were
poor, and among the rumours flourishing in the so-called

'unoccupied' zone in the south, far from Paris, was one that Léautaud had died. Obituaries appeared in various newspapers. They were unusually flattering. A Clermont-Ferrand paper saluted Léautaud as the heir of Chamfort. He was classed with La Bruyère, La Rochefoucauld and Jules Renard. His style was praised for its sobriety and ease.

In Lyon, where he had gone with the staff of *Le Figaro*, André Billy wrote a moving tribute. He recalled a friendship that dated from 1908 and spoke of his sorrow that he would no longer have the pleasure of climbing the stairs of the 'cher vieux *Mercure*' to find Léautaud sitting in his little room, quill pen in hand, a sardonic greeting on his lips. 'I love in him a re-doubtable friend but a true one, whose death causes me great sorrow. Literature has lost one of its original personalities and one most worthy of remembrance.' As a memorialist he would prove, Billy concluded, the equal of Renard and Goncourt.

The opportunity of seeing what his colleagues really thought about him was one that most authors would envy Léautaud, especially as the articles were without exception favourable. The episode amused and delighted him. He was also touched. Rouveyre, then living in Nice, wrote with great distress to a mutual friend on hearing the news. Léautaud was able to tell him that, as had been the case with Mark Twain, the news of his death was greatly exaggerated. Rouveyre the heartless, the cynic, had been very upset. When he learned that the report was false he expressed his relief in the shape of food parcels, clothes, tobacco and money. Once, with thoughtful humour, he sent Léautaud a cow-bell he had found somewhere which would come in handy for summoning the animals.

In contrast, the atmosphere at the *Mercure* was becoming more and more unhappy. Jacques Bernard's management of the firm proved to be erratic and unprofitable. He was a tech-nician, a printer's man, who lacked Vallette's business sense and Duhamel's literary taste. His conduct, always a little un-balanced, was now positively eccentric, and he showed signs of megalomania. The slightest contradiction of his opinions threw him into violent moods of anger. He was a convinced

30. A character out of Molière

31. 'My favourite company'

32. Towards the end – still keeping up his diary

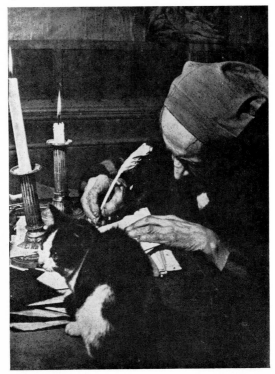

admirer of Hitler and an enthusiastic supporter of the Nazi cause. The German conquest of France gave him deep satisfaction and he looked forward to the time when Nazi domination of the world was complete. He collaborated gladly with the occupying authorities whenever the chance arose.

It was inevitable that one day he and Léautaud should clash. Léautaud's independent views annoyed him, and his refusal to lose his temper in the face of provocation only made Bernard angrier still. Gradually he cut down on the amount of work Léautaud was given to do. He let it be known that should staff reductions be necessary, Léautaud would be the first to go.

On 24 September 1941, Bernard made up his mind.

'Léautaud,' he said, 'I've decided to part with you for the pleasure of not seeing you any more. And, if I have to dip my hand in my own pocket, then I will.'

Léautaud, unable to resist a witticism even at this juncture, coolly replied: 'When you treat yourself to such a pleasure it's certainly worth making a sacrifice for it.'

He went back to his room and collected his belongings. Down from the wall came Marie Laurencin's portrait of him, the Rouveyre drawing and the photograph of Gourmont which had hung there so long. He cleared out his papers and gathered up his stock of quill pens. After forty-six years as a contributor to the *Mercure* and thirty-three as a member of staff, he was brutally thrown onto the street. Outwardly he appeared calm and indifferent. In reality he was shocked, hurt, confused. To be sacked at the age of sixty-nine, without proper notice and in so harsh a manner, afflicted him more deeply than he cared to admit. He could not even write about the incident clearly, for his entries in the *Journal* at this date are vague and disconnected.

He resigned himself to a life of retirement at Fontenay-aux-Roses. There were compensations. He no longer had to rush off in the mornings and leave his pets on their own. Now he could be with them all day and give them his whole attention. The household was easier to run without the need for him to commute back and forth to the office. In some ways Bernard's spiteful action had been to Léautaud's advantage. As soon as the news spread throughout Paris editors and publishers asked him to write articles for them. But for Bernard he would never have had so many freelance opportunities. In addition, the Ministère de l'Education Nationale allowed him a small pension which continued until the end of his days. There was also a grant of 5,000 francs from the Institut which Valéry and Duhamel obtained for him.

He was not very interested in the course of the war. At first he was against an Allied victory, fearing that such an event would only restore to power the shabby gang of politicians who disgraced France before the war and dragged her down with their incompetence. At least, he argued, under the Germans the country was preserved from any further Blums or Daladiers.

As the war continued, however, his interest in England and the English grew. He had always been attracted to what was, for him, that mysterious land across the Channel. It was the only country he had ever wanted to visit. This attraction dated back to the nineteen-hundreds and earlier, when he met Edmund Gosse and Arthur Symons on their visits to the *Mercure* office. They both admired his early writings in the magazine and complimented him on them.

Another English acquaintance had been Gerald Kelly, then a young and promising artist whom Marcel Schwob commissioned to paint his wife Marguerite Moreno. To help Kelly improve his French, Schwob suggested he dine regularly with Léautaud. Léautaud, Kelly found, was

'. . . a most fascinating creature, who recited or read verses as beautifully as anyone I have ever heard: as well as Marguerite Moreno, as well as Madame Sarah. . . . I was very fond of Léautaud, and I never knew why. I thought him a great man. He was a wonderful talker, and I don't think what he wrote down gave us a fair sight of him.'

Sir Gerald, as he later became, painted a portrait of Léautaud. In 1970 it was still in his studio and showed a bearded figure,

vintage 1906, strikingly posed and conveying a vivid like-
ness.

George Moore had also frequented the *Mercure* office during
the nineteen-hundreds. He showed that he was, in spirit, a
sympathiser with the magazine's ideals when he remarked: 'I'm
not a writer for the general public. I prefer to publish my books
in editions of 500 copies, and expensive, rather than many
copies cheaply that wouldn't sell.' Later, Moore was to regret
Léautaud's admiration for Baudelaire and to be puzzled by his
praise for Stendhal. The possessor of a rich and melodious style
himself, he disagreed with Léautaud's rejection of 'music' in
prose and the use of image. 'We don't seem to have the same
tastes,' commented Léautaud after receiving Moore's reply
acknowledging a copy of one of his books he had sent him.

The most Francophile of the English authors Léautaud had
known was Arnold Bennett. They met round about 1903.
Bennett found him 'un être baroque et délicieux', and described
Le Petit Ami as an 'étrange et séduisant roman autobio-
graphique'. They exchanged copies of their books and wrote
to each other. When 'Maurice Boissard' parted company with
the *Nouvelle Revue Française*, Bennett condoled with Léautaud
and wrote at the same time to Gide: 'I have read no good
French novel for a long time, and la NRF *devient de plus en plus
scie*. Especially since Boissard departed. Boissard was really
good.' In his own journalistic writing Bennett held up Léautaud
as an example to all British drama critics.

At the same time, Léautaud emerges somewhat surprisingly
as an influence on a major British writer. In 1908 Bennett
observed in his diary:

'Easily influenced! In reading Léautaud's preface to the *Plus
Belles pages* of Stendhal, I found him defending Stendhal's
hastiness of style; never going back, etc., "getting the stuff
down" (as I say) without affectations or pose; reading a few
pages of the Code to get himself into the "tone" of plain
straightforward writing. Now I quite see the weakness of the
argument, and I knew the clumsiness of Paul Léautaud's style.

Yet so influenced by what he says that I at once began to do my novel more *currente calamo*! Sentences without verbs, etc.'

Another of Léautaud's English correspondents was Lady Alda Hoare. Before her marriage she was Lady Geraldine Mariana, second daughter of Lord Augustus Hervey and sister of the fourth Marquis of Bristol. In 1898 she married Sir Henry Hoare. Her interest in literature was great. Thomas Hardy and his wife were among her other correspondents. For some time she had been a regular subscriber to the *Mercure de France*. Between 1929 and the outbreak of war she often wrote to Léautaud, whose books and publications she bought as soon as they appeared. At one point, knowing his interest in England, she invited him to come and stay with her. Shyness and embarrassment at his poverty prevented him from accepting her invitation.

A writer whom he never met but whose books he enjoyed was Rudyard Kipling, one of the *Mercure*'s 'bestsellers'. Kipling's death moved him to write: 'What a great country England is! How right I am, in my continuing admiration, to set this race above all others. When great writers die they are buried in Westminster Abbey alongside kings. What respect for the mind this shows in people who are contemptuously described as a nation of shopkeepers.'

He also had a Barresian admiration for the personality of Byron and for D. H. Lawrence. Dickens was another author whose eccentricity pleased him. There was a touch of Eugène Sue about *The Old Curiosity Shop* and *Oliver Twist*. (He made the same criticism of Balzac.) Thackeray, he decided, was the better artist. Yet *The Pickwick Papers* delighted him with its quaintness and wealth of 'originaux'. *David Copperfield* was a different matter. The story of David's unhappy childhood reminded him so vividly of his own. He was moved by 'la touchante, l'adorable, l'inoubliable figure du cher petit David'.

An English book of related interest made a deep and lasting impression on him because it went right to the heart of the obsession that haunted him all his life. This, surprisingly enough, was J. M. Barrie's *Margaret Ogilvy*, which the *Mercure* published in a French translation. It is the story of Barrie's relationship with his mother, a Scotswoman of sterling character, ready good humour and immense charity. Her simple faith triumphed over poverty and tragic bereavements. Although her ambition had been to see her gifted son become a minister of religion, when he chose literature as his career instead she put away her disappointment and identified wholeheartedly with him. It was a standing joke between them that she was the inspiration for all the heroines in his books. She would chuckle: '. . . he tries to keep me out, but he canna; it's more than he can do!' When she died Barrie found that she had preserved, in a little box with a photograph of him as a child, the envelopes that contained the first cheques he earned by his writing. They were bound with a ribbon.

If the sentimentality of *Margaret Ogilvy* may not be to the taste of a later age, it is no less genuine. The book is very touching. Its significance for Léautaud is obvious. He envied Barrie his mother. He longed for a Margaret Ogilvy who would have been mentor and friend, who would have encouraged him with a selfless love. Many times he read the book and on each occasion it affected him as sharply as before, even in his seventies. 'One always loves what one doesn't possess,' he explained to Marie Dormoy. The contrast between Margaret Ogilvy and Jeanne Forestier was poignant.

Now that his abrupt severance from the *Mercure* gave him more time to read, he deepened his explorations of English literature. Pepys was a welcome discovery. Addison intrigued him and he was disappointed not to find a French translation of *The Spectator*, for he believed Addison to be as interesting a man as he was a writer. Boswell, it is odd to note, he did not enjoy, though he seems to have based his judgement on reading the intimate papers and not the biography of Johnson.

Like Voltaire before him, Léautaud was impressed by the English ideals of liberty of religion and expression. 'C'est ma patrie civique,' he said of England. He admired the free expression England allowed, even in time of war, and praised the general acceptance of austerity there and willingness to sacrifice for the common good – reactions that, he gloomily surmised, would not be found among French workers. 'The only great nation in the world,' he concluded, 'is England. She often double-crosses others. That's their own look-out. From the point of view of citizenship, society, civil legislation, if there is still a country in the world where a degree of civilisation exists, it is England.'

As the war entered its final stages life became increasingly difficult. Léautaud often went hungry, and the rationing system caused him much anguish on behalf of his animals. That he did not sink below starvation level was due to the kindness of Madame Florence Gould. This wealthy patroness of literature was born Florence Lacaze in America. Her parents were French and she settled in their native country at the age of six. Though possessing American citizenship, she is wholly French by inclination. Her second marriage brought her into the family of Jay Gould, the nineteenth-century American multimillionaire railway magnate. (A French link had already been established in 1895 when his daughter Anna made a famous marriage to Boni de Castellane.) Among her benefactions to literature is the Prix Roger Nimier, which is worth 15,000 francs.

At her palatial home in the Avenue Malakoff she made a habit of entertaining writers to lunch. The food was lavish and often too rich for Léautaud, whose stomach had been conditioned by a lifetime's privation to the simplest of fare. He was further unnerved by the high society manner of the hostess and the obsequious attention of domestics hovering at his elbow. Rather like the Abbé Mugnier at La Vallée-aux-Loups, he was a guest of honour cherished for his entertainment value and admired for his wit.

In Madame Gould's home he looked forward to the conversation of Marcel Jouhandeau, another regular guest. Jouhandeau was one of the few contemporary authors whom he enjoyed. He relished, above all, the malice with which, in numerous volumes, Jouhandeau recounted the epic of life with his impossible spouse Élise. As something of a connoisseur in the matter, Léautaud appreciated his diatribes against the monstrous regiment of women as embodied in this redoubtable female. Other persons he encountered there were Jean Paulhan, whom he knew already, the composer Reynaldo Hahn, and the Comte Étienne de Beaumont, now an elderly shadow trailing past glories of the music and ballet he had sponsored in the golden days of the nineteen-twenties and thirties.

Throughout these luncheons the hermit of Fontenay slumped in his chair firing off cynical gallantries at the women and peppering the company in general with choice sarcasms. When the meal ended and the guests dispersed, it was the custom for the butler discreetly to hand him a parcel. This contained luxuries such as chicken, butter and tobacco. He would open it at home and give to his cats the delicacies that were too exotic for his plain tastes. Others he sold or bartered. Sometimes Madame Gould sent him presents of fruit and firewood. Although he realised that she wished to be kind, he accepted her generosity with his usual lack of grace. He complained when she gave him something he disliked. He did not care either for the effusive manners of café society, the embraces and kisses freely exchanged, the use of Christian names and the easy familiarities. His hostess was always 'Madame' to him, and he preserved a formal eighteenth-century air in his mode of address.

He was indifferent to the liberation of Paris when it came. On 24 August 1944, General Leclerc's army paraded victoriously through the street a few yards from his house. To demonstrate his pacifism he stayed resolutely indoors. With the end of the Occupation he saw a new 'Terreur' sweeping Paris. He was sickened by the acts of private vengeance, the denunciations, the personal vendettas and the odious opportunism which the new regime unleashed. Mediocre writers sought a temporary glory in acts of 'retribution' against 'collaborators' – a glory their own books would never have earned them. Jealous failures tried to incriminate their more successful colleagues. Frustrated playwrights and novelists settled old scores by denouncing those who had in the past rejected their second-rate work. To be chairman of a 'purification' committee was easier, and brought more publicity, than writing good books. 'We already have the P.J. (Police Judiciaire),' wrote Léautaud ironically. 'I suggest we create the P.L. (Police Littéraire).'

Soon he was given a chance to prove the sincerity of his views. Jacques Bernard, the man who had so unjustly sacked him from the *Mercure*, was arrested on charges of collaboration. His open support for the German cause was not so repellent as the fact that he had denounced compatriots to the Nazis and been responsible for deportations. Together with Duhamel and the literary lawyer Maurice Garçon, Léautaud was summoned to give evidence for the prosecution at Bernard's trial. He saw, in the court, what looked like an old man, crumpled, shrunken, pallid. In seven months Bernard had deteriorated into a wreck scarcely able to stand without the support of his gaolers at each side.

'What have you to say about Jacques Bernard's behaviour?' the judge asked Léautaud.

'Nothing,' he replied meekly. 'I didn't concern myself with it.'

Judge and jury paused in surprise. Didn't Léautaud know that Germans visited the *Mercure* offices? Hadn't he seen and heard what went on there.

'No, I never bother myself about anyone or anything.'

After a few more questions the judge dismissed him. Obviously the witness had been an odd-job man who emptied the waste-paper baskets and swept the floors. He was probably illiterate too, for had he not admitted that he never read the *Mercure*?

Outside the court Léautaud was jubilant. His little act pleased him. 'I'm very satisfied,' he observed to Marie Dormoy. 'I've said nothing, Bernard is a rascal, but it's not my job to accuse him.' The thought of the wretched Bernard in the accused's box came back to him and the mischief faded from his eyes. He forgot the evil Bernard had done him. 'Le malheureux! le malheureux!' he sighed.

A year earlier Valéry had died. The ambiguity of Léautaud's

relationship with Valéry prevented him from going to see the invalid during his last illness. In any case, Valéry was too weak to receive callers. Léautaud paid his last respects to the corpse. He emerged from the room with eyes full of tears. Not long before, Valéry had made a significant remark to Marie Dormoy: 'Jadis, pour moi, il n'y avait que Mallarmé. Maintenant je me dis: Il y a aussi Verlaine.' Marie Dormoy reported the comment to Léautaud. When, furthermore, he heard that Valéry's death-bed reading had been Voltaire's correspondence, he felt that the lost sheep had at last returned to the fold. He attended the funeral, sad and downcast, nibbling from time to time a piece of stale bread he carried in his pocket.

The judge at Bernard's trial was not alone in his ignorance of Léautaud's work as a writer. It was nearly fifty years since *Le Petit Ami* and *In Memoriam* had made their little sensation, and Léautaud remained, in Vallette's words, the chosen author of 400 readers – or, as someone else put it, 'the Chamfort of the 6th *arrondissement*'. This was a state of affairs his old friend André Rouveyre decided to change. He proposed to issue an anthology of Léautaud's writing. His subject gave him no help at all. The idea embarrassed and irritated Léautaud. Anthologies were for great authors. For someone of his achievement, the project was ridiculous and pretentious. Since Rouveyre was so keen on going ahead Léautaud could not stop him, but he would certainly not give him any assistance.

The *Choix de pages* came out in 1946. It is an excellent survey and presents a balanced picture of Léautaud as autobiographer, diarist, drama critic, essayist and moralist. Léautaud remained aloof during its preparation and only saw the contents for the first time when he arrived at the publisher's office to sign copies sent out for review. Rouveyre being Rouveyre, malice was not absent from the selection. He had included a private letter Léautaud wrote him about Gide. Léautaud, while expressing admiration for certain of Gide's books, had spoken of Gide's hypocrisy, his duplicity, his weakness for compliments and his preciosity.

When Léautaud's eye fell on this letter staring up at him in bold print, he was furious. 'Vous êtes un coquin!' he shouted at Rouveyre, using what was, for him, a term of violent abuse. He ripped the book and threw the pieces to the ground, adding for good measure the ink-pot. As the ink soaked into the tattered shreds he stamped out of the room slamming the door behind him. The letter he wrote to Rouveyre after this incident remains unknown, since under the terms of the latter's will it cannot be made available until the year 2006. What is certain is that his friendship with Rouveyre came to an abrupt close. 'What perverse pleasure did it give you to try to make me quarrel with dear Léautaud?' Gide wrote to Rouveyre. He was determined not to let Rouveyre's mischief-making come between him and Léautaud. He told a friend: 'I'll always take anything from Léautaud. As for Rouveyre, I don't even want to see him again.' All the same, he was perplexed by Léautaud's harsh remarks. Did Léautaud, Gide wondered, construe his friendliness as an unworthy desire to curry favour? Gide knew that something tortuous in Léautaud's character made him distrust compliments. He was right.

Another friendship nearly collapsed about this time. The incident involved Marie Dormoy, Matisse and a picture of Léautaud which the artist drew. Marie Dormoy was a friend of Matisse and thought a sketch by him would make an interesting frontispiece to one of Léautaud's books. At first Léautaud was conquered by the charm of Matisse and sittings went well. More than twenty sketches were drawn and Matisse, as a gesture, wished to give one to Léautaud. There was a little ceremony in the artist's studio at the handing over. The sketch was duly unveiled in Léautaud's presence. He sat stiffly in his chair. For a few moments he looked at the picture. Then he turned away and shut his eyes. While Marie Dormoy hastened to congratulate Matisse in a rush of nervous compliments, Léautaud remained stubbornly dumb.

Some time later he asked Marie Dormoy if he might borrow the sketch on some pretext or other. Days passed, weeks and then months. Marie Dormoy at last asked him what had happened to the picture, which, of course, belonged to her.

'I've sold it,' he chuckled, adding that had he been unable to find a buyer he would have thrown 'the stupid thing' into the dustbin. Worse still, he had sold it to Rouveyre, who was only too happy to tell Matisse about the transaction. Marie Dormoy's embarrassment and humiliation were intense. On this occasion she came close to deserting him for ever. In the end, as always, she forgave him – though she did not forget.

The *Mercure de France* was by now appearing regularly again after being closed for a period. The new management invited Léautaud to rejoin the staff. He preferred his freedom. In any case, he did not approve of the organisation. In the old days the editorial staff had consisted of Vallette, who alone supervised publishing matters, and two others. Now there were six employees to do this. It had been Vallette who, single-handed, drew up each year's balance-sheet and presented it at the annual shareholders' meeting. These days the management employed a chartered accountant and his assistant for the purpose.

Léautaud did not, though, withdraw entirely from the *Mercure*. He was the magazine's oldest contributor and its most celebrated personality. Extracts from his *Journal* were featured in several issues. They recalled a period that had gone for ever, an age that the war had abruptly cut off. The most colourful personality in it was Le Fléau, though now she was but a wraith compared with the rampant creature she had been in her maturity. She spent the war at her house in Pornic. After Paris had been liberated she returned to the flat in the Rue Dauphine. One Saturday afternoon at the beginning of 1946, as she walked along the pavement, a boy on skates hurtled from nowhere and knocked her down. In the fall she broke her leg badly and had to be taken to hospital. She was about seventy-seven years old. The accident was the beginning of the end. From then onwards she was confined to bed.

Léautaud went, against his inclination, to visit her. He was shocked and depressed by what he saw. She lolled in her bed, ragged, grimy, unkempt. The smell was revolting. Sometimes she would write letters scrawled in an unreadable hand, letters that wandered and did not make sense. Her great preoccupation was her will. Constantly she changed it, and the heirs who could expect her bounty varied from day to day. She rambled, barely coherent, and lost the thread of what she wanted to say in disjointed mutterings. Léautaud could scarcely believe his eyes: was this stinking wreck the same woman who once had been so desirable, so amorous, so skilled in the ways of love? He shuddered.

Towards the end she settled for good in Pornic. She could not get up or dress or even eat without help. A friend came to look after her. In the morning of 15 April 1950, she died at the age of eighty-one.

When Léautaud heard the news he was overcome with melancholy. He thought of her in her prime, singing the popular song 'Indiana' (a hit number of the day that was even a favourite with Proust), and putting into her voice all the seduction of which she was a past-mistress. She appeared in his mind's eye, a Rubens-like beauty, the perfection of plumpness, as he had always liked his women. Another vision came before him: the crumbling body in its wooden box under six feet of earth, the charms rotted away, and the flesh, that flesh he had loved, condemned to a remorseless decay until there should be nothing left of it. In the stress of despair he made a bonfire in the garden and burned a huge pile of letters, manuscripts and notes that included a new version of *In Memoriam*. He felt oddly alone and deprived now that Le Fléau was no longer there to scream invective at him and scratch his face.

Just at this point there came an intervention that helped to rescue Léautaud from the low spirits into which he had fallen. During the war he had made the acquaintance of a young writer, poet and scholar called Robert Mallet. They met in the Bibliothèque Jacques Doucet, where Mallet was researching his doctoral thesis on Francis Jammes. The young man began his career teaching French literature in Tananarive and later became Recteur of the Académie d'Amiens. He is now Recteur of the Académie de Paris. At their first meeting he was intrigued by Léautaud's conversation and his fine, deep, almost theatrical voice.

After the war Monsieur Mallet produced numerous literary programmes for the French radio. He remembered his meeting with Léautaud and thought of him as a subject for a broadcast. Here was a man who had known many leading writers of the past half-century and who, moreover, could talk about them in an interesting and amusing way. Léautaud refused immediately. He loathed the radio because it spread inanity and, thanks to neighbours who listened to it in their garden, ruined his peace and quiet. Mallet pointed out that he would be paid for his services. 'Paid?' said Léautaud. 'Paid for it? I'm not a hireling! I'm not a clown, a variety turn.'

The combined diplomacy of Mallet and Marie Dormoy eventually persuaded him to approach the microphone. He was interviewed in a series of ten broadcasts and reminisced about his early life, the writers he had known, his ideas on literature and his love of animals. The questions put to him by Robert Mallet were cleverly framed to reveal his character and elucidate the contradictions that made up his personality. He responded with vivacity. His voice rang out buoyantly – 'Ouais! Ouais! . . . Hohohoho! . . . Hihihihi!' – or sank to a hushed eloquence when he recited, from memory, some verses by Francis Jammes. Although he was now eighty years old his youthful tones, for many listeners, seemed those of a man half his age. On evenings when he was due to be heard engagements were put off and dinner was postponed throughout the country. If people were shocked by his comments on his mother and father, his views on the treachery of women and his sallies against patriotism, they were diverted by his wit. The ten programmes that were originally planned were in the end expanded to forty-three.

Almost overnight Léautaud became a national celebrity. His postbag reached the proportions of a film star's. Women wrote to him by the score. His cynical tirades against their sex had a queer fascination for them. They were touched by the account of his unhappy childhood. Some of them actually presented themselves at his door and intimated that they would not be unwilling to offer him their charms. They only confirmed his pessimistic view of womanhood. And anyway, he was too old. He could just manage to appreciate a naked pair of handsome breasts, but that was as far as he went.

After a lifetime of poverty he was now enjoying a fame he had never dreamed of, a fame his writings alone would never have brought him, and one that he owed entirely to his personality. The transcripts of his *Entretiens avec Robert Mallet* were published, and sold in a few days more copies than *Le Petit Ami* had done in twenty years. Reprints of his books were rushed off the press and found eager buyers. At long last the first volume of his *Journal littéraire*, which covered the years from 1893 to 1906, was brought out. Within six weeks the entire edition of 6,000 copies was snapped up and a similar quantity had to be hurriedly reprinted to satisfy the demand.

The proceeds from his broadcasts represented wealth that he had never dared to conceive of before. With this money so easily earned he went on a spending spree. His first purchases included six pairs of shoes, six hats, two overcoats, an electric coffee grinder and luxury foods for his animals. The ramshackle house at Fontenay became a place of pilgrimage for sightseers, journalists and photographers. He was a character as famous as Maurice Chevalier, as Fernandel, as Bourvil. His fame received the inevitable consecration: a long article with many colour photographs in *Paris-Match*.

━⊃XIV⊂━

LAST THINGS

Boswell: *But is not the fear of death natural to man?*
Johnson: *So much so, Sir, that the whole of life is but keeping away the thoughts of it.*

It had all come too late. Of course, he enjoyed having more money than he'd ever had in his life before. It was flattering to be sought after and interviewed by newspapers and magazines. Few writers had known his luck in finding such a large audience for his views. Yet 'success' had an empty ring. He had always lived simply, and once he bought himself and the animals presents there was nothing much else to spend the money on. As for the women who chased him, they were bores. There was, it is true, a mystery woman at the end. He never wrote about her. All that is known of her is a nude photograph in which the face is modestly hidden by hair. It was found in his pocket when he died. Stuck to the back was a piece of paper on which he had written: 'S'il m'arrivait de partir, ne parle jamais de moi. Que personne ne sache, ne se doute seulement combien je t'ai aimée. Garde ce souvenir en toi, comme un secret.'

His eyesight now was so bad that he could barely deal with correspondence. He would ask Marie Dormoy to read aloud the letters he received. Fits of giddiness made it difficult for him to get about, though in the house he could guide himself by holding on to walls and chairs. He was haunted by thoughts of mortality. The death of André Gide increased his gloom. The article he wrote to commemorate their ambivalent friendship was called 'Une Certaine Grandeur', a title which, in its careful choice of epithet, expressed what he felt about Gide. While admitting that he lacked enthusiasm for Gide's writing, Léautaud remarked that he could not help feeling sympathy and respect for him. He admired his self-effacement, his courage in publishing *Corydon*, his lack of interest in official honours. Gide's

refusal at the Liberation to join in the public orgy of denuncia-
tion also impressed him. Most of all, he admired Gide's stoic
attitude to death, his submission, his acceptance of the phenomenon with serenity, courage and understanding. 'I saw him
again on his deathbed with that rather Chinese face of his. At
that moment I found I was using a rather pompous expression.
I tried it out on other people in conversation. They used it, too:
"A certain greatness."'

With Robert Mallet Léautaud visited Gide's grave at Cuver-
ville several months after the funeral. He spoke of Gide's courage at his last moment. That was the important thing: not to
be diminished by death. He wondered what Le Fléau must be
looking like now in her grave. Gide, thin as he was, had probably not decomposed much. The coffin had been made of stout
wood and must still be intact.

'Death revolts me!' he told Mallet. 'And yet I ought to start
getting used to the idea that I shall die soon. Well, I can't, no,
I can't. When they say that old people get used to it, don't you
believe them. I cling on to life, I cling to it as I did when I was
twenty. I even think I cling to it more than I did then. Which
doesn't prevent me from finding it unbearable. . . . You like
life, but you'd prefer not to have come into the world because
you have to leave it! You've asked for nothing. You're here.
And you'll leave without having any say in it. Really, it's stupid!'

For some time they argued beside the grave. Then Léautaud
said: 'The true life, you know, is the monk's.'

'I think there's something of the monk in you,' replied Mallet.

'Yes, it could be. I like solitude, an ordered life and meditation.'

Evening came on and it turned cold. They visited the church
before leaving. Léautaud inspected the surroundings. 'It's even
colder in here than outside! We must go. I don't want to catch
my death in a church!' His screeching laugh rang out. It echoed
through the vaults and he fell silent.

It was becoming more and more difficult for him to look
after his animals. When one of them died he did not replace it,

and the number of his pets shrank considerably. He was left with five cats and the monkey Guénette. For over twenty years he had pampered her and borne with her virulent fits of bad temper, her destructive manias and filthy habits. Now that she too was old she could sleep very little. She deliberately kept him awake at nights. He reached the terrible decision: she must be put down. The thought of taking her to a veterinary surgeon was too much for him. One day he borrowed a wash-tub and enlisted the aid of a local gardener. Drowning, he decided, would be the quickest, most merciful way.

They filled the tub with water and Léautaud picked up Guénette. She struggled, scratched his hand and bit his fingers. He nearly fell over. Once she was on the point of escaping. The burly gardener thrust her down under the water. She looked up, despair in her eyes, and stared at Léautaud. He could bear it no longer and went away, leaving the gardener to finish the job. 'Je n'en pouvais plus!' he quavered to Marie Dormoy when he told her the story. 'Mais je n'en pouvais plus!' He could not forget the look in Guénette's eyes.

Soon he was left with only two cats, his favourites Loulou and Jaunet. They picked their way through the empty, silent house, and wandered in the garden where hundreds of their predecessors lay buried. Sometimes they would curl up on the cracked doorstep, or scratch at the few sticks of furniture that remained, already splintered and shredded by generations of cats and dogs before them. Cobwebs trembled everywhere in the breeze that came in through broken, ill-fitting doors. Shelves sagged dismally under the weight of books and papers begrimed with dirt. Candle-grease spotted tables and floors, for Léautaud disapproved of electricity – only for reasons of emergency had he agreed to Marie Dormoy's suggestion of a telephone – and he still preferred to write his *Journal* in an eighteenth-century atmosphere of flickering candle-light. Dust and filth lay in neglected corners. The windows were cracked and obscured with mud thrown up by years of rain and storms.

The disorder in which he existed was the price he willingly paid for living on his own. In blessed solitude he ate a dinner that usually consisted of a few boiled potatoes, a bit of cheese and a glass of water, though more often than not he gave it to the cats before he was halfway through. He looked in his mirror, fogged with stains and discolorations, and laughed wryly at the old bachelor he saw there: a skinny old gentleman wearing a cotton bonnet, glasses that slipped down to the end of his nose, a torn jacket, holed trousers and worn slippers.

He had made a deliberate choice to live in this way. He did not want pity. A happy family life, the consolations of love and the pleasures of friendship were not for him. Religion he rejected completely and did not seek to put anything in its place. This emphatic negation could not have been possible without a total denial of much that the world has to offer. It drew its strength from Léautaud's consistent refusal of opportunities for gaining reputation and advancement. His example embodies the highest of literary ideals as enunciated by Boileau in those famous lines:

> 'Travaillez pour la gloire, et qu'un sordide gain
> Ne soit jamais l'objet d'un illustre Écrivain.'

Léautaud and Boileau! The combination is bizarre. It is doubtful if Léautaud had ever read a line of *L'Art poétique*. Yet if for 'la gloire' in Boileau's verse we substitute 'soi', we would find a striking declaration of Léautaud's beliefs. For him, too, the art of writing was an 'art divin'. Upon his tombstone he wished the proud legend to be engraved: 'Paul Léautaud, écrivain français. . . .'

This quality of independence was his most valuable asset as a critic. It is one of the rarest things in criticism. Sainte-Beuve did not always display it and neither do his successors. His reticence on certain subjects and his evasiveness on others sprang from self-interest. Léautaud never allowed such considerations to inhibit him. The claims of friendship did not prevent him from savaging Valéry's *La Jeune Parque*. The threat of losing a well-paid post as drama critic did not deter him from attacking Jules Romains's play. He was adamant that his articles be printed without excisions dictated by interest or prudence. For the pleasure of saying honestly what he thought, he was ready to sacrifice everything. This is no small achievement amid the jealousies and importunities of the theatrical and publishing worlds.

Independence, again, is the leading characteristic of his position as a writer. He believed that he had failed if what he had written could have come from anyone else. The greatest compliment that could be paid him was to say that his writing was like his conversation, unique and individual. Saint-Simon, Balzac and Stendhal were often reproached for writing badly, he observed. That was because they were too big, too full of character, to waste time trying to write in the flat, careful style that suited everyone.

He had a Stendhalian belief that the individual pursuit of happiness was more important than duty or patriotism or society. Writing represented happiness. Therefore writing must come before everything else. It follows that the prime consideration of writing must be to give the author pleasure. There was the sensual pleasure that came from the noise of pen on paper. There was that 'moment du plaisir' when the mind is in a state of excitement and ideas bubble up so fast that the pen races to keep up with them.

The author has only himself to please. If he strikes off a phrase that happens to delight a reader, that is no business of his. He writes for himself alone and not for readers, critics or posterity. Material rewards and public recognition do not concern him. He should concentrate solely on expressing himself with truth and spontaneity. There is no need to strive after 'ronds de jambe'. If what he has to say is worth hearing, he does not need to rely on beautiful ornament and rare epithets. The idea that cannot be expressed in the everyday language of intelligent men is not worth expressing. It does not matter that the same word may be used two or even three times in a sentence. To tamper with it would damage the precious thread of spontaneity.

The doctrine has its limitations. Léautaud failed to realise that certain ideas do not lend themselves to simple language. As a confirmed materialist he could not see that there are concepts that, by their very abstruseness, cannot be formulated in easy phrases that trip from the pen in 'les moments du plaisir'. Nor did he appreciate that his insistence on clarity and brevity ignores the powerful effect that can be created by imprecision when used as a conscious stylistic device. If his views were to be fully accepted, many of the greatest pages in French literature would be condemned.

Léautaud serves as an antidote. He is there as a corrective to lyrical transports. His virtues are those of sobriety, economy and good sense. Say what you have to say as clearly as possible, he advises, and if you have genius it will arise naturally from your writing. Rather than aim deliberately at picturesqueness or beauty or wit, let them come in the course of writing. Do not woo them. If they are there, they will present themselves unbidden. If not, you will in the meantime have at least made yourself clear and readable.

Every writer has to work out his own salvation. Léautaud certainly found his. The style he created was ideal for his own purpose. No one else could have written what he wrote. He insisted on complete liberty, for it was not the job of the writer to be committed to social or political or religious ideas. The Communist writer had lost his freedom just as surely as the right-wing author and the Christian apologist.

In La Bruyère's famous words, 'tout a été dit'. The writer can only repeat what has long ago been said by earlier ages and add to it his tone of voice. What counts is the manner in which he says it. Léautaud is a constant reminder that the only lasting reward is the pleasure a writer derives from his work; that fulfilment can only come from being true to oneself; that freedom is the essential requisite of creation; and that literature and things of the mind can only properly be cultivated for their own sake.

As an autobiographer Léautaud is again unique. His self-disclosures are not confined to the *Journal littéraire*. The whole of his work is an exercise in unabashed self-revelation. Whether he is writing about the streets of Paris or about the death of a cat, every sentence is indelibly stamped with the mark of his personality and attitudes. The sum of his writing gives a portrait which is unrivalled for the degree of ruthlessness it achieves. His experience of life produced in him a bitterness akin to La Rochefoucauld's, though he did not, like that moralist he so admired, externalise it in shapely epigrams. He could not stand back from his feelings. Sadness he found more beautiful than happiness, and evening lovelier than morning. He preferred autumn to summer, solitude to family life and society, death to birth, and melancholy to gaiety. He liked better a great talent ignored than a millionaire bestseller, an old lover alone with his memories than a happy grandfather surrounded by his grandchildren.

For Léautaud, the proper study of mankind is man – man, that is, in the physical sense. Since the only man he knew at all well was the person called Léautaud, his writing became a lifelong exploration of himself. This he carried out with a thoroughness and frankness that can have few equals in literature. He reveals things about himself that common decency would urge others to hide. Often with unconscious naivety he pictures himself in situations that show him in a grotesque light from which a sense of humour would have saved him. He indulges in displays of rancour and waspishness that many people would be ashamed to acknowledge. The most important justification of the *Journal littéraire* is his urge for truth.

This obsessive drive to find out the truth about himself is his strength as an autobiographer. Not many people tell the whole truth about themselves. There are things we are not prepared to admit even to ourselves. Léautaud is ready, indeed eager, to tell all. In the course of more than sixty years of determined confession, he permits nothing to hamper him in his quest for the truth.

The fleshly envelope of life was all he knew about. He denied everything that he did not experience through the senses. When a friend remarked, on the death of François Coppée, that the poet had perhaps now gone on to discover the mystery that lies behind mortality, Léautaud retorted:

'Birth is a physical phenomenon, life is another, and death yet another again. Do you think I feel myself diminished at the idea that I was born of a coupling like that of animals and that I shall die like an animal? No, I find it quite as impressive, to say no more, as all your bigoted talk. It's rhetoric, all of it, the rhetoric of existence, of people who have a mania for dressing everything up in big words.'

He lived all his life in poverty and the contemplation of death. As François Mauriac has pointed out, the spirit of poverty and the thought of death are two paths that lead to God. Once again Léautaud appears as a monk – but a monk who violently denies that there can be a God. Yet the dead fascinated him. He stared with a burning curiosity, with an insatiable desire for the answer, at the faces of those he had known in life. They none of them told him what he wanted to know.

However near the prospect of death, as an old man he still could not forget the passions of his youth. The notoriety of his broadcasts spread to Geneva, the town where his mother had settled. A friend of her family there wrote and told him many new details about her that he had not heard of before. The old wound opened again. The octogenarian found himself longing for Jeanne Forestier with all the ardour of a young man – and hating her, at the same time, for her inaccessibility.

In November 1955 he made a last excursion to Paris. The publishing firm of Plon had lost one of his manuscripts and he brought an action against them. He went into the courtroom to hear his counsel Maurice Garçon argue the case with his usual dexterity. When he came out he was surrounded by photographers and journalists. They took pictures of the shrunken little old man. He wore a fur hat and carried a decrepit shopping bag on his arm. As the flashlights popped he grumbled and protested. Secretly he was delighted.

On 2 January 1956, he wrote in his *Journal*: 'I am in an awful state of mind, I have the feeling that I am going to die, that I'm at the end of it all. To such an extent that when replying to New Year greetings I've received, I couldn't help writing a few words about my detachment from everything, my indifference to death.' On the 18th he reached his eighty-fourth birthday. Throughout the next few weeks he noted the details of his failing physique as coldly as if he were writing about somebody other than himself. His place awaited him in the cemetery at Chatenay, a site he had chosen with care in a quiet corner where, he hoped, his remains would lie in the solitude he had always craved while alive. A brutal irony has since decreed that the road that runs beside his grave should turn, with the increased traffic, into a source of cacophonous hell.

Towards the end of the month he was so weak that he could not look after himself. Marie Dormoy persuaded him to enter Dr Le Savoureux's clinic at La Vallée-aux-Loups. She arrived with her car to take him there. He was grey-faced and tired. The two remaining cats had been given away to friends. 'I don't feel I shall ever come back here,' he said, looking around him at the tumble-down place. His luggage comprised writing paper, a few quill pens, a packet of handkerchiefs and some woollen hats. In his pocket he carried a copy of Diderot's *Le Neveu de Rameau*. As they left he locked the front door for the first time in all the forty-six years he had lived there.

After a few days at La Vallée-aux-Loups he began to feel better. He was even gracious to Marie Dormoy, and for a change he spoke gently with her. Long afterwards, on looking through his papers, she came across an account of a dream he'd had. He was walking up a hill and thought he saw Valéry at the top. When he went towards him the figure vanished. A funeral hearse appeared. 'There were two men there. I asked them who was in the coffin. They answered: "Marie Dormoy." I sobbed.' When she read this Marie Dormoy forgot about all the insults and the unkindnesses she had had to put up with during their long association.

At La Vallée-aux-Loups he looked with curiosity at the Chateaubriand relics Dr Le Savoureux had collected there. He had seen them all before, as a dinner guest with Valéry and the Abbé Mugnier. Now he inspected them more closely. If he admired Chateaubriand as a man, his florid writing had always aroused his dislike. Yet he spoke with an unusually mellow tone about him. Something, thought Marie Dormoy, must have happened to make him change his literary opinions so sharply.

On Wednesday, 22 February, he was in good spirits. At two o'clock a nurse brought him a drink. He handed back the cup and snapped, with a return to his old manner: 'Et maintenant, foutez-moi le camp.'

Later that afternoon Marie Dormoy called to see him. She entered the room and saw him lying on the bed fully dressed in the blue dungarees, old sweater and rabbit-fur cap. He was perfectly still. His eyes were closed. His hands turned back, palms upward. The expression on his face was calm, relaxed, happy. The secret he had always wanted to know was his at last.

LÉAUTAUD'S WORKS

A full list of Léautaud's contributions to newspapers and magazines will be found in Marie Dormoy, *Léautaud* (*Bibliothèque Idéale*, Gallimard, 1958), pp. 259–67. This also gives details, pp. 253–7, of the various editions and printings of his work.

Le Petit Ami (Mercure de France, 1903)

Henri de Régnier, in *Les Célébrités d'aujourd'hui* (series) (Sansot, 1904)

Stendhal: Les Plus Belles Pages (anthology with introduction) (Mercure de France, 1908)

Chronique dramatique: Ma pièce préférée, par Maurice Boissard, Les Amis d'Édouard no. 46 (Champion, 1923)

Chronique dramatique: Madame Cantili, suivi de Mots, Propos et Anecdotes par Maurice Boissard (La Centaine, 1925)

Chroniques: L'Alphabet des lettres (A la Cité des Livres, 1925)

Villégiature, suivi de Un Livre sur Paris, par Maurice Boissard (Éditions de la Belle Page, 1926)

Journal littéraire, fragments sur Remy de Gourmont, 1897–1905 (Champion, 1926)

Le Théâtre de Maurice Boissard, 1907–23 (NRF, 1926)

Adolphe van Bever, Les Amis d'Édouard no. 114 (Champion, 1927)

Gazette d'hier et d'aujourd'hui: Petit Supplément à une Gazette scandaleuse (La Centaine, 1928)

Mélange: 'Souvenirs de Basoche', 'Ménagerie intime', 'Amour', 'Femmes', etc. (Éditions de la Belle Page, 1928)

Dialogue (offprint from *La Nouvelle Revue Française* (1 Dec. 1928)

Lettres, 1902–18 (Éditions Mornay, 1929)

Passe-temps: 'Madame Cantili', 'Souvenirs de Basoche', 'La Mort de Charles-Louis Philippe', 'Un Salon littéraire', 'Ménagerie intime', 'Villégiature', 'Notes et Souvenirs sur Remy de Gourmont', 'Mademoiselle Barbette', 'Admiration amoureuse', 'Adolphe van Bever', 'Mots, Propos et Anecdotes' (Mercure de France, 1929)

Fagus (offprint from NRF, 1 Dec. 1933)

Amour (Éditions Spirale, 1934)

Le Chat (offprint from *Mieux Vivre*, Aug. 1937)

Notes retrouvées (J. Haumont, 1942)

Georgette, 'Journal littéraire 1903', suivi de 'Petites Notes sur Alfred Vallette' et de 'Fagus' (Éditions de la Nouvelle Revue de Belgique, 1942)

Le Théâtre de Maurice Boissard, vol. ii (NRF, 1943)

Marly-le-Roy et environs (Éditions du Bélier, 1945)

Choix de Pages, par André Rouveyre (Éditions du Bélier, 1946)

Propos d'un jour: 'Amour', 'Notes retrouvées', 'Marly-le-Roy et environs', 'Gazette d'hier et d'aujourd'hui' (Mercure de France, 1947)

Petit Débat littéraire: M. Georges Duhamel, de l'Académie Française; Paul Léautaud (Fontenay-aux-Roses, at the author's expense, 1948)

Journal littéraire, fragment (L'Originale, 1948)

Souvenir de Basoche (L'Originale, 1948)

Entretiens avec Robert Mallet (Gallimard, 1951)

Oeuvres: Le Petit Ami, précedé d'Essais et suivi de In Memoriam et Amours (Mercure de France, 1956)

Lettres à ma mère (Mercure de France, 1956)

Journal littéraire, vol. I, 1893–1906 (Mercure de France, 1956)

Journal littéraire, II, 1907–9 (Mercure de France, 1956)

Journal littéraire, III, 1910–21 (Mercure de France, 1956)

Journal littéraire, IV, 1922–4 (Mercure de France, 1957)

Journal littéraire, V, Jan. 1925–June 1927 (Mercure de France, 1958)

Journal littéraire, VI, July 1927–June 1928 (Mercure de France, 1959)

Journal littéraire, VII, June 1928–July 1929 (Mercure de France, 1959)

Journal littéraire, VIII, Aug. 1929–May 1931 (Mercure de France, 1960)

Journal littéraire, IX, May 1931–Oct. 1932 (Mercure de France, 1960)

Journal littéraire, X, Oct. 1932–Jan. 1935 (Mercure de France, 1961)

Journal littéraire, XI, Jan. 1935–May 1937 (Mercure de France, 1961)

Journal littéraire, XII, May 1937–Feb. 1940 (Mercure de France, 1962)

Journal littéraire, XIII, Feb. 1940–June 1941 (Mercure de France, 1962)

Journal littéraire, XIV, July 1941–Nov. 1942 (Mercure de France, 1963)

Journal littéraire, XV, Nov. 1942–June 1944 (Mercure de France, 1963)

Journal littéraire, XVI, July 1944–Aug. 1946 (Mercure de France, 1964)

Journal littéraire, XVII, Aug. 1946–Aug. 1949 (Mercure de France, 1964)

Journal littéraire, XVIII, Aug. 1949–Feb. 1956 (Mercure de France, 1964)

Journal littéraire, XIX, 'Histoire du journal', 'Pages retrouvées', 'Index général' (Mercure de France, 1966)

Le Théâtre de Maurice Boissard, vol. i, 1907–14. Foreword by Marie Dormoy (Gallimard, 1958)

Le Théâtre de Maurice Boissard, vol. ii, 1915–41 (Gallimard, 1958)

Journal particulier, vols i and ii. Preface by Pierre Michelot (privately printed, Éditions du CAP, Monaco, 1956)

Bestiaire. Preface by Marie Dormoy (Grasset, 1959)

Poésies. Introduction by Pascal Pia (Le Bélier, 1963)

Passe-temps II: 'Souvenir', 'Marcel Schwob', 'Le Stendhal-Club', 'Le Paris d'un Parisien', 'La Comédie-Française', 'Voyage', 'Propos', 'Fagus', 'Petites notes sur Alfred Vallette', 'Le Grand Match', 'Actualités amoureuses', 'Occasions pour films', 'Amants', 'Le Mépris de l'amour', 'Le Lion amoureux', 'Vacances', 'Mondanités', 'Comédiens', 'Pensées de guerre', 'Guillaume Apollinaire', 'Une Réception académique et qualques propos', 'Une Certaine Grandeur' (Mercure de France, 1964)

Le Petit Ouvrage inachevé. Introduction by Marie Dormoy (Le Bélier, 1964)

Lettres à Marie Dormoy (Albin Michel, 1966)

Journal littéraire. Choix par Pascal Pia et Maurice Guyot (Mercure de France, 1968)

Paul Léautaud, André Billy. Correspondance, 1912–55 (Le Bélier, 1968)

Paul Léautaud en verve. Mots, propos, aphorismes, Choix et présentation de Hubert Juin (Pierre Horay, 1970)

Correspondance générale, 1878–1956, Recueillie par Marie Dormoy (Flammarion, 1972)

PREFACES

Aimienne (Jean de Tinan) (Mercure de France, 1899)

Lettres de Fagus à Paul Léautaud. Foreword and Notes by Léautaud (La Connaissance, 1928)

Picasso et ses amis (Fernande Olivier) (Stock, 1933)

Chats (Ylla) (OET, 1935)

Catalogue de l'Exposition Paul Verlaine (Bibliothèque Littéraire Jacques Doucet, 1946)

Il y a (Guillaume Apollinaire) (Éditions du Salon Carré, 1947)

Le Chat Miton (Marie Dormoy) (Éditions Spirale, 1951)

CONTRIBUTIONS TO COLLECTIVE WORKS

Glossary–index in *Parnasse satyrique du XVe siècle* (Marcel Schwob) (H. Welter, 1905)

'Ménagerie intime' in *Les Plus Jolies Histoires de bêtes* (Marcel Berger) (Émile-Paul, 1937)

'Le Petit Ami (fragment, nouvelle version)', in *Almanach des Lettres et des Arts* (Éditions du Pavois, 1945)

Portrait de Paul Léautaud par André Suarès, suivi d'une lettre de Paul Léautaud, avec une préface de Robert Mallet (Éditions de la Librairie Universelle, 1951)

IN COLLABORATION

Ad. van Bever and Paul Léautaud. *Poètes d'aujourd'hui, 1880–1900: Morceaux Choisis, accompagnés de Notices biographiques et d'un Essai de Bibliographie* (1 vol., Mercure de France, 1900)

Poètes d'aujourd'hui (2 vols, Mercure de France, 1908)

Poètes d'aujourd'hui (3 vols, Mercure de France, 1929)

GRAMOPHONE RECORDINGS

Details of recordings of Léautaud held in the ORTF archives are given in Dormoy, *Léautaud* (Gallimard, 1958), pp. 279–80. The following are items which are, or have been, available commercially.

Propos d'un jour. Avec un texte de Robert Mallet (Phillips no. 432 105 NE)
Maximes et textes (Phillips no. 76 711 25–A)
Entretiens de Robert Mallet et Paul Léautaud:
  1. 'L'Enfance' (Adès 13.101, 1967)
  2. 'Les Années d'apprentissage littéraire' (Adès 13.102, 1967)
  3. 'Les Poètes d'aujourd'hui' (Adès 13.103, 1967)
  4. 'Le Petit Ami' (Adès 13.104, 1967)
  5. 'La Mort' (Adès 13.105, 1967)
  6. 'Les bêtes' (Adès 13.106, 1967)

BIBLIOGRAPHY

PART I

(List of works wholly devoted to Léautaud or containing useful mentions of him.)

Arland, Marcel, *Essais et nouveaux essais critiques* (Gallimard, 1952), pp. 102–5

Auriant (Alexandre Hadjivassiliou), *Une Vipère lubrique: Paul Léautaud* (Ambassade du Livre, Bruxelles, 1966)

Baes, Rachel, *Trois entretiens avec Paul Léautaud (hors commerce,* 1949)

Barney, Natalie, *Traits et portraits* (Mercure de France, 1963), pp. 115–24

Bennett, Arnold, *The Savour of Life* (Cassell, 1928), p. 87; *Journals*, vol. I (Cassell, 1932), p. 285; *Correspondance André Gide–Arnold Bennett. Vingt ans d'amitié littéraire (1911–31).* Introduction and Notes by Linette F. Brugmans (Geneva, Librairie Droz, 1964), p. 22; *Letters of Arnold Bennett*, vol. III, 1916–31, ed. James Hepburn (Oxford University Press, 1970), pp. 196–7

Billy, André, *La Littérature française contemporaine* (Armand Colin, 1928), pp. 147–8; *Intimités littéraires* (Flammarion, 1932), pp. 7–27; *Le Pont des Saints-Pères* (Fayard, 1947), pp. 31–67; *L'Époque contemporaine* (Tallandier, 1956), p. 117; *Paul Léautaud, André Billy. Correspondance 1912– 55* (Le Bélier, 1968); *Les Propos du samedi* (Mercure de France, 1969), pp. 82, 120, 146, 158, 211

Boisdeffre, Pierre de, *Une Histoire vivante de la littérature d'aujourd'hui* (Librairie Académique Perrin, 1961), pp. 207–8, 621; *Une Anthologie vivante de la littérature d'aujourd'hui* (Librairie Académique Perrin, 1965), pp. 84–9

Buthaud, Étienne, *Paul Léautaud, Basoche et Littérature* (Cour d'Appel de Poitiers, Poitiers, 1958)

Cabanis, José, *Plaisir et lectures* (Gallimard, 1964), pp. 176–8

Cent Écrivains Français répondent au 'Questionnaire Marcel Proust'. Preface by Léonce Paillard (Albin Michel, 1969), pp. 188–90

Charavay, *Bulletin d'autographes* (Dec. 1969)

Charensol, G., *Comment ils écrivent.* Preface by Fernand Vanderem (Éditions Montaigne, 1932), pp. 129–31

Clouard, Henri, *Histoire de la littérature française. Du Symbolisme à nos jours*, vol. II, 1915–40 (Albin Michel, 1949), pp. 142–4, 155, 598, 649

Connolly, Cyril, *Previous Convictions* (Hamish Hamilton, 1963), pp. 209–12

Derennes, Charles, *Le Bestiaire sentimental: Émile et les autres* (Albin Michel, 1924), pp. 83–93

Dormoy, Marie, 'La Nuit de Noel chez Paul Léautaud' (offprint from *La Revue vivante*, 1949); *Léautaud* (Bibliothèque Idéale, Gallimard, 1958); *Souvenirs et portraits d'amis* (Mercure de France, 1963), pp. 256–300;

Paul Léautaud. Images et textes réunis par Marie Dormoy (Mercure de France, 1969); *La Vie secrète de Paul Léautaud* (Flammarion, 1972)

Duhamel, Georges, *Le Temps de la recherche* (Paul Hartmann, 1947), pp. 191-5, 200

Dutourd, Jean, *Petit journal, 1965-6* (Julliard, 1969), pp. 19-20, 198-9

Ernest-Charles, J., *Les Samedis littéraires*, 2nd series (Perrin, 1904), pp. 143-5

Fagus, *Pas perdus* (Le Divan, 1926), p. 98; *Lettres à Paul Léautaud* (Éditions de la Connaissance, 1928)

Gandon, Yves, *Mascarades littéraires* (Aux Éditions M.-P. Trémois, 1930), pp. 55-67

Ganne, Gilbert, *Interviews impubliables. Nouvelle Édition revue et augmentée* (Plon, 1965) (1st edn, André-Bonne, 1952), pp. 35-44

Gide, André, *Feuillets d'automne* (Mercure de France, 1949), pp. 137-8; *Journal 1889-1939* (Pléiade, Gallimard, 1951), pp. 281-2, 438, 1313-14; *Journal 1939-49* (Pléiade, Gallimard, 1954), pp. 298-9; 'Ainsi soit-il', ibid., p. 1191; *Correspondance avec Paul Valéry, 1890-1942*, ed. R. Mallet (Gallimard, 1955), pp. 341, 396, 455; *Correspondance avec André Rouveyre*, ed. Claude Martin (Mercure de France, 1967), pp. 162-3, 174-6, 254, 257; *Correspondance avec Roger Martin du Gard*, vol. i (Gallimard, 1968), pp. 215, 312-13

Gillois, André, *Qui êtes-vous?* (Gallimard, 1953), pp. 13-24

Gourmont, Remy de, *Le Problème du style* (Mercure de France, 1902), pp. 157-68

Guth, Paul, *Quarante contre un* (Corréa, 1947), pp. 183-8

Jouhandeau, Marcel, *Nouveau Bestiaire* (Grasset, 1952), p. 14; *Carnets de l'écrivain* (Gallimard, 1957), pp. 331-43; *Confrontation avec la poussière* (Gallimard, 1970), pp. 31-2

Le Cardonnel, L. and Vellay, C., *La Littérature contemporaine (1905)* (Mercure de France, 1905), pp. 78-84, 115

Le Révérend, Gaston, *Le Haut-parleur* (Aux Éditions de la Fenêtre Ouverte, 1927), pp. 121-75; *Irrévérences* (Éditions de la Belle Page, 1927), pp. 20-2

Loliée, Marc, *Bulletin LV (Autographes)* (Jan., 1970)

Mahieu, Raymond. Paul Léautaud. La Jeunesse et les débuts de la maturité (1872-1914) (doctoral thesis, University of Louvain, 1970); *Stendhal, tentation de Léautaud* (Stendhal Club, n.d.)

Mallet, Robert, *Une Mort ambiguë* (Gallimard, 1955), pp. 74-84, 86-93, 128-31, 140-4, 156-65, 201-4

Martin du Gard, Maurice, *Impertinences: Portraits contemporains* (Camille Bloch, 1924), pp. 17-23; *Carte Rouge. Le Théâtre et la vie, 1929-30* (Flammarion, 1930), pp. 247-51; *Les Mémorables*, vol. i (Flammarion, 1957), pp. 99-104; *Les Mémorables*, vol. ii (Flammarion, 1960), pp. 49-52

Masson, G.-A., *Le Parfait Plagiaire. Pastiches* (Éditions du Siècle, 1924), pp. 241-7

Maugham, Somerset, *Points of View* (Heinemann, 1958), pp. 189, 193, 228–35

Mauriac, François, *Bloc-notes* (Flammarion, 1958) pp. 139–40, 232–3; *Mémoires intérieurs* (Flammarion, 1959), pp. 224–8

Mercure de France, 'Pour les quatre-vingts ans de Léautaud' (issue dated 1 Feb. 1952); 'Hommage à Paul Léautaud' (issue dated May 1957)

Paupe, Adolphe, *La Vie littéraire de Stendhal* (Librairie Ancienne Honoré Champion, 1914), pp. vii, 26, 183, 184

Perret, Pierre, *Adieu, Monsieur Léautaud* (Julliard, 1972)

Perrin, Michel, *Monnaie de singe* (Calmann-Lévy, 1952)

Rachilde, *Portraits d'hommes* (Mercure de France, 1930), pp. 199–210

Rees, Garnet, *Remy de Gourmont. Essai de biographie intellectuelle* (Boivin, 1940), pp. v, viii, 61, 62, 125, 126, 138, 139, 185, 235, 243, 268, 279

Rousseaux, André, *Littérature du vingtième siècle*, vol. vi (Albin Miçel, 1958), pp. 67–75

Salle Drouot. Catalogue de la vente du 19 avril 1970. (Autographes)

Talvart, H. and Place, J., *Bibliographie des auteurs modernes de langue française (1801–1956)* (Éditions de la Chronique des Lettres Françaises, vol. xii, 1928–65), pp. 7–21

The Times Literary Supplement, 'Diary of a Solitary' (middle page article in issue dated 30 Aug. 1957); 'The Wisdom of Age' (14 Mar. 1952), p. 188

Valcault, Véronique, *Le Monologue passionné* (novel) (Julliard, 1961)

Valéry, Paul, *Lettres à quelques-uns* (Gallimard, 1952), pp. 64–5, 66–7

PART 2

(List of works containing short but interesting references to Léautaud.)

Aegerter, E. and Labracherie, P., *Au temps de Guillaume Apollinaire* (Julliard, 1945), p. 57

Albalat, Antoine, *Trente ans de Quartier Latin* (Société Française d'Éditions Littéraires et Techniques, 1930), pp. 116–17, 155–6

Casella, G. and Gaubert, E., *La Nouvelle Littérature, 1895–1905*, 2nd edn (Sansot, 1906), pp. 196, 286

Champion, Pierre, *Marcel Schwob et son temps* (Grasset, 1927), pp. 215, 237

Humbourg, P., *Fantômes sur papier blanc* (Éditions Bellenand, 1951), pp. 92, 169, 240

Lalou, René, *Histoire de la littérature française contemporaine* (2 vols, Presses Universitaires Françaises, 1947), pp. 114 (note), 874, 884

Mélia, Jean, *Stendhal et ses commentateurs* (Mercure de France, 1911), p. 400

Montfort, Eugène de, *Vingt-cinq ans de littérature française* (Librairie de France, 1922), p. 306

Renard, Jules, *Journal, 1887–1910* (Pléiade, Gallimard, 1960), p. 1254

Romains, Jules, *Amitiés et rencontres* (Flammarion, 1970), pp. 39–41

Salmon, André, *Souvenirs sans fin, 1ère époque, 1903–8* (Gallimard, 1955), pp. 251–9 (the *Mercure* circle in general); *Souvenirs sans fin, 2ᵉ époque, 1908–20* (Gallimard, 1956), pp. 32, 83, 101, 102, 108

Séché, Alphonse, *Dans la mêlée littéraire* (Société Française d'Éditions Littéraires et Techniques, 1935), pp. 54–6, 213

Treich, Léon, *Almanach des lettres françaises et étrangères* (2 vols, Crès, 1924), I, pp. 121, 350, 361, 363; II, pp. 33, 162, 249

Van Parys, Georges, *Les jours comme ils viennent* (Plon, 1969), pp. 342, 432–3, 436–7, 477–8, 530, 538–9, 555, 570–1, 572–3, 578, 588, 590, 594, 612, 617, 643–4

INDEX